Gospel People?

GOSPEL PEOPLE?

Evangelicals and the Future of Anglicanism

JOHN MARTIN

First published in Great Britain 1997
Society for Promoting Christian Knowledge
Holy Trinity Church
Marylebone Road
London NW1 4DU

British Library Cataloguing-in-Publication Data

A catalogue record of this book is available from
the British Library

ISBN 0–281–04975–0

Typeset by Wilmaset Ltd, Birkenhead, Wirral
Printed in Great Britain by
The Cromwell Press, Melksham, Wiltshire

To my late father, Harry Martin (1917-85),
whose abiding legacy is that he instilled
in me deep reverence and love
for the Bible.

CONTENTS

ACKNOWLEDGEMENTS

Every generation it seems to fall to the Editor of the *Church of England Newspaper* to write or edit a volume aimed at explaining evangelicals to the wider Church. This book reached its final form after I left the paper. I tread warily in the footprints of illustrious predecessors, notably John King. I have to confess that writing this book was not at first one of my burning ambitions, but when Judith Longman of SPCK put the offer I found the temptation irresistible. My editors, Philip Law and Rachel Boulding, have personified the dual virtues of patience and enthusiasm. A lot of people have helped in this book's long gestation. I record my thanks to Jane Williams, Graham Dale and Andrew Carey for their contributions with research. Special thanks to Canon Colin Craston who read almost the entire manuscript and offered many wise suggestions. Most of all thanks to my wife, Deirdre, who shared our first years of married life with this project. When my application flagged she would quietly rope in neighbours, friends, and relatives – even my hairdresser – to tactfully ask, 'Just how is that book coming along?'

INTRODUCTION

When the Crown Appointments Commission chose the little-known Bishop of Bath and Wells, Dr George Carey, as the 102nd Archbishop of Canterbury, it confirmed something that observers of the Church of England had suspected for some time. By jumping a generation and appointing someone whose roots were unmistakably evangelical, it made a clear statement about the future of the Church of England. For the time being anyway, its fortunes lie in the hands of the evangelicals.

Some generations ago, the Bishop of Durham, Hensley Henson, labelled evangelicals 'an army of illiterates generalled by octogenarians'. But times have changed. In our day, David Edwards, former Provost of Southwark and one of the astutest observers of the contemporary scene, once told me that he believed evangelicals 'are the most vigorous movement in the Church of England today'.

There has been an enormous change in evangelical fortunes since the end of World War II. In 1950, statistically they were a 'shadow of a shade', to steal a phrase from Sir Walter Scott about the Scottish Episcopal Church decimated by the effects of the Penal Laws. Now evangelical parishes hold their own amid the spiral of numerical decline that has hit the Church of England in the last three decades. Over half of the ordinands entering the Church's ministry graduate from the evangelical colleges. If the Advisory Board for Ministry left the selection of colleges to market forces and gave ordinands a free choice, the percentage would be even higher.

During the last five years, evangelicals enjoyed their highest-ever representation in the House of Bishops. Thirty years ago, there was hardly an evangelical among the ranks of the country's theological professors and senior academics. By 1994 at least fifteen could be identified.

The focus of this book is the Church of England. It has to be said immediately that the burgeoning of evangelical fortunes is in no way confined either to the Church of England, or the British Isles. In the United States a recent Gallup survey found that 89 per cent of the fastest growing denominations were evangelical. In Latin America, if the current rate of growth is sustained, a continent that was once a Roman Catholic stronghold will be evangelical by the year 2025. The story of evangelical expansion and growth is being repeated all over the world, in Africa, East Asia, Korea, and Australasia.

In many ways the inspiration for this book is Anthony Sampson's *Anatomy of Britain*, though it is not in my nature to be as systematic as that author in the treatment of his subject. It has two kinds of readers in mind. First, it is for people who want to be informed about what evangelicals stand for and what makes them tick. Second, it seeks to address issues the evangelical constituency is currently facing. This is not an academic treatment. I come to the task as a journalist and a layman, and of necessity my brush is broad.

In pursuing this project I have been friendly but not uncritical. Evangelicals tend to be *fissiparous*, to use a term made famous by Archbishop Donald Coggan. It simply means that they are prone to division. In our day there is ample evidence that the rise in evangelical fortunes and numbers has been the cause of a fresh capacity for fissiparousness.

Then there is the evangelical tendency to be anti-intellectual. This recently prompted Mark Noll to write *The Scandal of the Evangelical Mind* (Eerdmans, 1994). Noll's main concern is trends in the USA. But in the last century, Anglican evangelicals, ground down by Darwinism, biblical criticism, and Tractarianism, reacted by pulling up the drawbridge rather than taking on the world of ideas. Today's evangelicals are beset by the temptations of withdrawal syndrome. Occasionally, too, I have discerned an uncomfortable tendency towards sectarianism among some evangelicals. Ironically enough, it is often most manifest in the way evangelicals criticize the beliefs of various sects and other people they disagree with. It is all too easy for evangelicals who are comfortable in their large and 'successful' churches to feel that they are the only ones who have got things right.

A word about where I am 'coming from' as an author. I was born in an isolated Australian farming hamlet called Bogan Gate, of a Brethren mother and a Presbyterian father. We did not get mains electricity until I was six. I did a fair proportion of my early schooling by radio and post. I was third youngest of about twenty grandchildren on my father's side of the family and the first to complete secondary school, let alone go to university. I am grateful, however, that as a youngster my parents helped me to know and love the Bible.

In my teenage years I was sent to an Anglican school in Sydney where I encountered the liturgy of the Church. Later, as President of my university's Evangelical Union, I discovered the high-octane Christianity that is summed by all that the Anglican diocese of Sydney stands for. I found a faith that was self-confident and ready to give an answer for the hope within. Moreover, it was an evangelicalism that found few problems about being Anglican. The Sydney brand, at least, never found it necessary to stay on the margins of church structures and systems, unless it deliberately chose to.

Coming to London in 1979, I spent six years on the staff of the Anglican Communion Office. That put me in touch with other traditions within Anglicanism and, more importantly perhaps, the Church in the two-thirds world. For some years I edited *Home & Family*, magazine of the Mothers' Union, on a part-time basis. For seven and a half years I served as editor of the *Church of England Newspaper* (*CEN*), traditionally the mouthpiece of evangelical Anglicanism. Serving the constituency in that role was stretching and highly rewarding. It gave me a unique vantage point, not only to study the remarkable animal called the Church of England, but to witness at close hand the evangelical contribution to it. Given where I started out I marvel at how privileged I have been.

I am convinced that evangelicalism is by no means a static entity. One only needs to read documents setting out agendas evangelicals followed in the 1920s and 1930s to see the point. Nor can evangelicalism safely stand apart and claim all-sufficiency. On its own, evangelicalism is a bit like an English doughnut without its jam filling. Its solid core is the evangel and it cannot afford to compromise this. But it stands to be much enriched by interacting with other Christian traditions: catholic concern for liturgy and historic continuity; protestant determination to stay in a state of constant reform; and the liberal willingness to face the hard questions that living in a postmodern world entails. At its best, evangelical Anglicanism does that.

I suspect that some will find views expressed in this book surprising. Readers of the *CEN* will see that my tone is not as strident as the paper sometimes appeared to be under my editorship. Over the years there were many times when I was uncomfortable about the necessity to present nuanced church debates in 'tabloidese'. This book was completed in the months following my departure from the *CEN* and this has afforded me greater freedom to be myself and express my views unfettered. I have not felt compelled to take a 'party line' on some issues which are controversial.

In preparing this book, I obtained comments on specific topics from some leading Anglicans. I am grateful to them for those of their thoughts which I have incorporated in the text.

The gestation time of this book has coincided with a period of turbulence and growing disunity among evangelical Anglicans. I seek to trace some of the causes of this turbulence, and humbly offer encouragement to evangelicals seeking a way through.

There is a famous and oft-quoted Chinese curse that says: 'May you live in interesting times.' These are 'interesting' times, not only for evangelicals, but for the Church as a whole. Postmodernism is rapidly changing the spiritual landscape. Several times during their history, evangelicals have found themselves in a position where they could have been the premier influence in the Church of England, only to melt away into insignificance. Present disunity may yet cause history to repeat itself. It is imperative that evangelical unity is recovered, not simply for its own sake, but because the future witness of the Christian faith demands it.

SECTION 1

SETTING THE SCENE

1

WHO ARE THE
EVANGELICALS?

In an age of widespread nihilism, [evangelicals] have a burning and shining sense of mission. In an age of religious famine, they know God through Christ. In an age of the unhappy cult of fun (or to be franker, lust), their lives are given shape by their prayers and the purity and joy of their homes are conspicuous. In an age of brash vulgarity, they are in touch with the life of the spirit, which is the true glory of man.(David Edwards, *Church Times*, April 1967.)

At the Sixth Assembly of the World Council of Churches (WCC) held in Vancouver in the summer of 1983, a small group of men and women laboured long into the night crafting an 'evangelical statement'. It was meant to be a critique of the assembly themes and the direction in which the WCC was heading. As might be expected, it called on the WCC to make the Bible more central to its thinking and for greater commitment to evangelism.

The statement invited delegates of evangelical sympathy to show solidarity by signing it. Accordingly, copies were displayed at strategic places all over the campus of the University of British Colombia. Those who drafted it expected at best a couple of hundred signatures and braced themselves for angry reactions. They were absolutely amazed when assembly delegates signed in their hundreds. One member of the Church of England delegation who cheerfully signed was a woman well known as an out-and-out liberal. When I asked her why, she said she agreed fully with every word in the statement.

This story highlights some important issues that need to be considered when it comes to defining the meaning of 'evangelical', 'evangelicals' and 'evangelicalism'. Evangelicals in Vancouver were well grounded in the main tenets of their tradition. Yet when they put an 'evangelical statement' on paper, they found that many people from other Christian traditions could subscribe to it.

'Evangelical' is a word with a long and honoured history. It derives from the Greek word *euangelion*. Its first known use in English was in 1531 when Sir Thomas More used it in labelling supporters of the Reformation 'evangelicalles'.

According to Dr John Stott, Rector Emeritus of All Souls, Langham

Place, London, 'Originally it was simply the adjective corresponding to the noun "evangel" or "gospel". It then came to be applied in particular to the sixteenth century Reformers, although they were at pains to emphasise that they were renovators, not innovators.'[1]

Bishop John Jewel made a similar point in his famous *Apology* (1562). 'It is not our doctrine; we wrote it not, we found it not out, we were not the inventors of it, we bring you nothing but what the old fathers of the Church, what the apostles, what Christ our Saviour himself hath brought before us.'

John Stott made the same point in an address to the Universities and Colleges Christian Fellowship in 1982.

> At the risk of oversimplification and of the charge of arrogance, I want to argue that the evangelical faith is none other than the historic Christian faith. The evangelical Christian is no deviationist, but a loyalist who seeks by the grace of God to be faithful to the revelation which God has given of himself in Christ and in Scripture. The evangelical faith is not a peculiar or esoteric version of the Christian faith. It is not a recent innovation. The evangelical faith is original, biblical, apostolic Christianity.

So if evangelicals do not claim to represent a distinctive doctrinal stream, what is it that makes them a distinctive force in the life of the Church? Henry Venn, an eighteenth-century evangelical divine, one of the founders of the Clapham Sect, and author of *The Complete Duty of Man* (1763) believed it to be 'not so much in their systematic statement of doctrine, as in the relative importance which they assign to the particular parts of the Christian system, and in the vital operation of Christian doctrines upon the heart and conduct'.

In a debate with David Edwards in *Essentials* (Hodders, 1988), John Stott makes the same point.

> The hallmark of evangelicals is not so much an impeccable set of words as a submissive spirit, namely their *a priori* resolve to believe and obey whatever the Scripture may be shown to teach. They are committed to Scripture in advance, whatever it may be later found to say. They claim no liberty to lay down their own terms for belief and behaviour. They see this humble and obedient stance as an essential implication of Christ's lordship over them.[2]

So, then, while evangelicals would claim they are contributing nothing essentially new, they have their own distinctive emphases and give special weight to certain doctrines and activities.

There are all manner of popular definitions on offer. Clive Calver, Director of the Evangelical Alliance, records a definition from a Welsh preacher: 'An evangelical is a person who has committed his or her life to Jesus Christ, seeking to live under his Lordship and authority, believing and accepting the

Bible for what it says.'[3] Others have variously used the label 'gospel people' or even 'Bible people' in an endeavour to get to the essence of evangelicalism.

All this adds weight to the view that being 'evangelical' is not so much a particular doctrinal position as a matter of style, and a tendency to give special emphasis to certain aspects of Christianity.

Thoughtful people know that, over centuries, 'evangelical', and 'evangelicalism' have been used to identify groups; for instance the Lutherans, who actually stand for quite different emphases from those of their contemporaries who reserve the 'evangelical' label for themselves. Moreover, the popular definitions used above are in fact very elastic, and can embrace people who would not necessarily identify with people who belong to groups who lay a firm claim to being 'evangelicals'.

'Evangelical' is

the best word available to describe a fairly discrete network of Protestant Christian Movements arising from the eighteenth century in Great Britain and its colonies. This historical sense of 'evangelical' is complemented by a parallel use of the term designating a consistent pattern of convictions and attitudes.

They are,

biblicism (a reliance on the Bible as ultimate religious authority), conversion-ism (a stress on the new birth), activism (an energetic, individualistic approach to religious duties and social involvement), and crucicentrism (a focus on Christ's redeeming work as the heart of essential Christianity).[4]

In the remains of this chapter I will comment on these characteristics and apply them to evangelicalism in its Anglican form.[5]

Evangelical Essentials

Where shall my wandering Soul begin?
How shall I All to Heaven Aspire?
A slave redeem'd from Death and Sin,
A Brand plucked from Eternal Fire.[6]

These words, from the pen of Charles Wesley, were written on 23 May 1738, the day before the epoch-making scene in Aldersgate Street in the City of London where the heart of his brother John was 'strangely warmed'. While few today would use such quaint language, Wesley's words take us to the heart of what in practice it means to be an evangelical. Everything else flows from it. Someone once came up to the American evangelist Billy Sunday and asked, 'Mr Sunday, why is it that you are always telling people "ye must be born again"?' 'Simple,' said the evangelist. 'It's because ye must be born again!'

What, then, are the essential marks of evangelicalism today? I will pick up the key characteristics of evangelicalism delineated above.

1. *The Scriptures*

Bishop J. C. Ryle said that the leading principle of evangelicalism was 'the absolute supremacy it assigns to Scripture'. We shall be looking at this issue in more depth later, but it is important to describe the place of the Bible in the day-to-day life of people who may be regarded as evangelicals. John Wesley, who was in fact a highly cultured man, said: 'Let me be *homo unius libri*' (a man of one book). Over the generations, many evangelicals have been like the American television evangelist, Morris Cerullo. In 1992, I went to interview him for a column in the *Church of England Newspaper* which asked about the most influential books in the life of the subject. Much to my frustration he would only talk about the Bible. Most contemporary evangelicals, especially those of the Anglican variety, are likely to be broader than that.

Most evangelicals at least aspire to a rule of life where they read the Bible every day. Still the most popular way of meeting that requirement is to subscribe to daily Bible reading notes, among which the most popular include those produced by Scripture Union, the Bible Reading Fellowship and *Every Day with Jesus* by Selwyn Hughes. Bible study and discussion is the core activity of home groups. Exposition of a passage of Scripture is the characteristic format for sermons by evangelical vicars. Generations of tertiary graduates have been brought up having subscribed to the Inter-Varsity Fellowship's doctrinal basis which declares the 'infallibility of the Scriptures as originally given and their supreme authority for all matters of faith and conduct'. For countless others, the Bible is simply 'the word of God', to be treasured and relied on as a daily companion.

I will seek to deal with the evangelical attitude to Scripture in a later chapter, but it may be helpful to amplify just a little further here. John Stott once more, from *Essentials*:

> Evangelicals regard it as essential to believe not just 'the gospel revealed in the Bible', but the full revelation of the Bible; not just that 'Christ died for us' but that he died 'for our sins', in some sense 'bearing' them objectively in our place, so that in holy love God can forgive penitent believers; not just that we 'receive the Spirit' but that he does his supernatural work in us, variously portrayed in the New Testament as 'regeneration', 'resurrection', and 're-creation'. Here are three aspects of the divine initiative, God revealing himself in Christ and in the total biblical witness to Christ. God redeeming the world through Christ who became sin and a curse for us. And God radically transforming sinners by the inward operation of his Spirit.[7]

10

Evangelicals, then, claim a common commitment to the authority of the Bible. The question, however, is what that means in practice, and how the Bible is to be interpreted and understood. This has become the focus of a major debate within evangelicalism and is a subject to which I will be returning.

2. *Conversion*

One of the mainsprings of evangelicalism is the call to conversion. Robert Bickersteth, Bishop of Ripon (1857-84) once said there was 'no sermon worthy of the name which did not contain the message of the Gospel, urging the sinner to be reconciled to God'. Evangelicals hold this conviction because they believe, with the theologians of the Reformation, that the human race is estranged from God because of an innate sinfulness. This sinfulness leaves no part of the personality untouched and unspoiled. There are no human actions, not even good works, which are capable of winning merit with God. So salvation cannot be earned. It must be received through trust in the work of Christ, in particular his death and resurrection.

Conversion, according to a 'call to conversion' issued in 1988 by the Lausanne Committee for World Evangelization, means 'turning from sin in repentance', moving 'from spiritual death to spiritual life'. It is impossible to exclude the necessity of conversion as an essential part of Christianity.

The evangelical insistence on the necessity of conversion has important implications for involvement in ecumenism as well. In common with the Reformer, Martin Luther, evangelicals hold that the human person is justified by grace through faith – acceptance by God rather than through human merit or good works. For this reason they have always scrutinized the Agreed Statements of the Anglican-Roman Catholic International Commission (ARCIC) with extreme care. Throughout the 1980s they insisted that justification should be on the ARCIC agenda as a matter of urgency. When the Commission finally produced its Agreed Statement, *Salvation and the Church* (1990), many evangelicals were angry at the impression given that the differences between the Reformers and the Catholic Church in the sixteenth century were largely a misunderstanding.

For many evangelicals of the current generation, in particular the laity, these weighty matters appear peripheral. Unlike earlier generations, only a small proportion are likely to be able to expound the doctrine of justification, or explain the difference between propitiation and expiation in understanding the atonement. Even fewer will rate these issues as important. That is a loss. Nevertheless, young evangelicals are still taught to pray for the conversion of their family and friends. They take great pains to be 'ready to give an answer for the hope that is within them'.

11

3. *Activism*

Evangelicals are people who get things done. Walk into the offices of just about any evangelical voluntary society and in every probability it will be in absolute contrast to the normal image of people in church organizations: they will be high-tech, streamlined, efficient and modern. The same is true of church offices in the great majority of evangelical parishes. In the last decade or so, evangelicals have been at the forefront of a wave of church refurbishment. John Wesley's habit of life was to be 'always on the stretch for God'. So too was Lord Shaftesbury whose diary recorded: 'Toil, toil, toil, nor should I lament, could I say fruit, fruit, fruit.' (April 1850).

Many a middle-of-the-road Anglican vicar has found that the arrival of a single evangelical family in the parish will signal change. Very soon that family will have become the core of the Sunday school or youth group, they will have begun to evangelize their neighbours and will soon be agitating for the vicar to agree to family services, guest services, the creation of nurture groups for new believers and home groups, and to enter into genuine partnership with the laity by paying more than lip-service to the idea of 'every member ministry'. More often than not, it is likely to produce tensions as well as rewards.

Throughout his career, Archbishop George Carey has epitomized the classic evangelical impulse to be up and doing. He rises very early. He begins his day with a combination of prayer and physical exercise. His pattern of life is to fill every moment. About a year before he was appointed Archbishop, he told the Anglican Evangelical Assembly: 'Quite early in my career the idea began to be fashionable that clergy should divide the day in three – morning, afternoon and evening – and only work in two of these. For my part I have never done that.'

Hannah More (1745-1833), who pioneered educational work in the mining villages of the Mendips as well as being an important literary figure of her day, once said: 'Action is the life of virtue, and the world is the theatre of action.'[8] There are growing numbers of evangelicals today who are high achievers in theological studies. Their main concern, however, is not so much quarrying new ideas as finding a theology that 'works'. Few devote a high proportion of their time to the study, but if they do it is for two purposes: to resource their preaching and to improve their grasp of management principles. They are more likely than their counterparts from other Anglican traditions to have an eye on the American scene. Many are aware of American studies in church growth. That is one reason why, on the whole, evangelical parishes have larger congregations. Moreover, it has always been an evangelical characteristic to resolve issues by doing rather than by introspection. Hence the advice of the Moravian missionaries to the troubled John Wesley, 'Preach faith until you have it, and because you have it you will preach it.'

Why this impulse for activism? I suspect it grows out of the essentially middle-class nature of evangelicalism. In his day, John Wesley specially appealed to the artisans and people on the move economically. Evangelicalism today has a similar appeal to those in society who want to 'get on' economically and it brings a lot of them together. Evangelicalism must therefore ask itself why it has not always thrived in the inner cities, compared for example with catholics (of both the Anglican and Roman kinds). On the other hand, it can be argued that England should not necessarily be regarded as the centre of gravity for evangelicalism, and that the movement is growing fastest in some of the poorest countries of the world in Africa and Latin America. In due time this is sure to have an impact on the demography of evangelicalism in Britain.

4. The Cross

Perhaps the most significant difference between evangelical Anglicans and other members of the Anglican Communion is that while the latter lay primary emphasis on the incarnation in their theology and preaching, for generations evangelicals have focused on the cross. When the *Church of England Newspaper* conducted a survey to discover what were their favourite hymns in 1992, the paper's mainly evangelical readership put Isaac Watts's 'When I survey the wondrous cross' at the top of the list. In a survey of evangelicals taken in 1896, the *British Weekly* newspaper found that the most-used evangelical preaching text was Galatians 2.20: 'I have been crucified with Christ; it is no longer I who live, but Christ who lives in me; and the life I now live in the flesh I live by faith in the Son of God, who loved me and gave himself for me.' A generation ago, practically every evangelical Anglican minister had James Denney's classic work *The Death of Christ* (1902) on the study bookshelf. Now most would possess one of its more modern successors, such as Leon Morris's *The Cross and the New Testament* (1968) or John Stott's *The Cross of Christ* (1986).

Having said that, a generation has grown up which is not content to merely sit and listen to sermons about the cross. Nor is it fully satisfied with a highly individualistic view of salvation that grows out of a narrow interpretation of teaching about substitutionary atonement, where great stress is placed on the proposition that 'Christ died in my place'. Some of the more conservative critics suggest this is a sure sign that the constituency is going off the rails. Another way of seeing it is that some modern evangelicals have chosen to emphasize that Christian discipleship implies self-denial and 'taking up your cross daily'.

5. The Search for Holiness

The core of the evangelical search for holiness is commitment to regular Bible study, prayer and devotion. Hannah More insisted that no day could be successfully completed unless it began in this manner. 'The hour of prayer or meditation is a consecration of the hours employed . . . In those hours we may lay in a stock of grace, which if faithfully improved, will shed its odour on every portion of the day.'

Often this commitment has meant an austere lifestyle which was Sabbatarian, opposed to drinking beer, wines and spirits, gambling, playing cards, dancing and even the cinema. Less than a generation ago, 'worldliness', which took in all these activities, was often regarded by evangelicals as one of the deadliest of sins. Separation from the world was something to be undertaken with seriousness and vigilance. Bishop J. C. Ryle (1816-1900) once said: 'What heart has ever been softened or brought to repentance by gazing at Titians or Vandykes? . . . What worldly man was ever turned to God by listening to polkas, waltzes or opera music?'[9]

The streak of Puritanism which is at the heart of the evangelical mindset lives on. Some evangelical clergy are wary, for example, of marrying cohabiting couples in church. Evangelicals provided a powerful base of support for the contemporary 'Keep Sunday Special' campaign. But many of these shibboleths have been discarded by evangelicals of the present generation. When the *Church of England Newspaper* ran a series of interviews with well-known evangelicals about their leisure habits, the great majority admitted to enjoying wine. Many are much less strict than their predecessors about Sunday observance. Evangelicalism has been somewhat mellowed by a realization that while it has its Puritan roots, it is also a movement one of whose signature tunes is John Newton's famous hymn, 'Amazing Grace'.

A cursory glance at history will show convincingly that there has always been more to evangelicalism than mere concern with personal salvation. Holiness is not merely a private, personal matter. Of necessity it leads into the public arena with a concern for social justice and uprightness. An oft-quoted verse is Proverbs 14.34, 'Righteousness exalts a nation, but sin is a reproach to any people.' Throughout evangelical history, there are plenty of examples of how this has worked out in practice. One has only to cite the examples of William Wilberforce, the Clapham Sect, the role of the Church Missionary Society in creating Freetown in Sierra Leone as part of the fight against slavery, or the social reform led by Lord Shaftesbury, to show that the evangelicals have always been people who both trusted in the atonement made on the cross, and sometimes at great cost to themselves carried their cross daily.

Recovery of this understanding in this generation saw the creation of TEAR Fund, the transformation of the Mildmay Mission Hospital in East London into an AIDS hospice, and much more. The evangelical social conscience is the subject of a later chapter. But it may also help explain why a great deal of current evangelical social action is involved with issues of 'individual' morality; for example, campaigns against abortion, euthanasia and pornography.

Evangelical Anglicans

As I have already indicated, this book is primarily about evangelicalism in its Anglican form. But it is important to emphasize the strength of evangelicalism is growing in all Churches worldwide. Recent projections indicate that by the year 2000, 42 per cent of world Christianity will be evangelical.

In England, the Evangelical Alliance, the umbrella group bringing together evangelicals in their infinite varieties from all denominations, can justifiably claim to speak for over a million churchgoers. Worldwide, numerical growth is making it possible for evangelicals to mount serious challenges for leadership in mainline protestant Churches where conservative theology was thought to be a relic from the past. Evangelical missionary work is changing the religious face of entire nations.

Over many generations, evangelicals have claimed that the foundations of Anglicanism are evangelical. As Dr J. I. Packer has said, 'Anglicanism is evangelical in its essence.' The donnish former *Times* religious affairs correspondent, Clifford Longley, has said, 'The Church of England has been well described as a Catholic Church of a Protestant nation, and by and large most English people's perception of Christianity, whether they agree with it or not and whether they like the current Church of England or not, is close to traditional evangelicalism.'

Evangelicals lay claim to the entire inheritance of Anglicanism, the Scriptures, the catholic creeds, and the historic formularies of the Church of England as contained in the Thirty-nine Articles and the Book of Common Prayer.

Nevertheless, evangelical fortunes have ebbed and flowed throughout history. By the beginning of World War II, the evangelicals, who had arguably been the largest group in the Victorian Church, had been relegated to the margins of the Church of England. The position has gradually changed since the early 1950s. Now, survey after survey points to the growth of evangelicals both numerically and in terms of influence. Gallup research for the *Faith in the City* report showed that, on the whole, evangelical parishes attract larger numbers of worshippers than most other forms of Anglicanism.

With 41 per cent, evangelicals are now the biggest grouping in the General Synod elected in late 1995. Most importantly, if the Decade of Evangelism does nothing else, it will reshape the Church of England into an organism that is more evangelical. It could be that evangelicals are set to become the biggest single force in the Church of England.

Yet it would be wrong to assume this will be the natural course, or that there need be no limits of evangelical growth as far as the future is concerned. Several times since the Reformation, evangelicals have seemed poised to inherit the Church of England, only to fail at the critical moment. In the second section I will trace these currents and the resurgence of evangelicalism in our day. Then I will be examining current debating points affecting the evangelical constituency. Finally, I will look to the future. Do evangelicals have what it takes to give leadership to the Church of England at the start of the third millennium, or are they destined for ever to be one of those movements that promised so much but ultimately never delivered?

Having set the scene in broad outline, I want now to continue by looking in more depth at the nature of evangelicalism. I will do this, first, by looking at the evangelical view of the Bible and some of the current evangelical debates about the Bible. I will then explore how evangelical self-identity is sharpened by debate with other traditions, in particular radical liberalism. Then I will outline evangelical growth over the past couple of decades, the different varieties of evangelical Anglicans, and tensions within the constituency. I will then seek to set evangelical Anglicanism in its global context within the worldwide Anglican Communion. The first section concludes with an interview with Archbishop George Carey. Here is someone with unmistakably evangelical roots who has been enriched by learning from other traditions and who finds no inherent tension between being evangelical and being Anglican.

In the sections that follow, I undertake a lightning tour of evangelical history, in the process identifying some of the roots of the tensions that exist within contemporary evangelical Anglicanism. I then move to review key current debates: Establishment, baptism policy, women's ordination, homosexuality, other faiths.

I then look to the future and key factors that will shape the contribution of evangelicalism: the evangelical social conscience, evangelism, spirituality, renewal, and the ministry of the laity. Evangelicals as much reflect what is happening in wider church and society as they shape it. What pointers are there for the future from what is happening elsewhere in postmodern Europe? Do evangelicals believe it to be their destiny to shape the future of the Church of England, or would they be more comfortable with the role of a minority ginger group?

Finally, I offer a future agenda for the Church of England. While I have taken soundings quite widely, in the end I speak as an individual.

2

WHAT EVANGELICALS BELIEVE:

THE BIBLE

Jesus loves me, this I know, for the Bible tells me so . . .

All Scripture is inspired by God [literally, 'God breathed'] and profitable for teaching, for reproof, for correction and for training in righteousness, that the man of God may be complete, equipped for every good work. (2 Tim. 3.16–17).

We have the highest doctrine of Scripture of any in the Church. We must therefore acknowledge with deep shame that our treatment of Scripture seldom coincides with our views of it. We are much better at asserting its authority than wrestling with its interpretation, sometimes highly selective and sometimes downright dishonest. (John Stott, *Obeying Christ in a Changing World*, 1977).

If the primary claim of evangelicals is that they are 'gospel people', their other great claim is that they are 'Bible people'. In fact, these two claims form part of a whole. Evangelicals hold the conviction that the Bible is 'perspicuous': its meaning is straightforward and clear enough to be apprehended by even the simplest soul. This was the motivation of William Tyndale, the great sixteenth-century translator of the English Bible. He once told a scoffing prelate that, if God spared him, in not many years he would cause even a humble ploughboy to know the Scriptures. This position contrasts sharply with other Christian traditions. Those deeply influenced by critical biblical studies tend to see the Bible as full of traps for the uneducated and unwary. And while there has been a renaissance of Bible reading in the Roman Catholic Church since the Second Vatican Council, it is insisted that personal study must always be guided by the Church's authoritative magisterium.

In this chapter, I look at how evangelicals approach the Bible. This has become the source of serious tensions in the last decade or so. I would suggest that there is more common ground than those in the heat of the battle may willingly concede, and my aim is to offer suggestions as to a way forward. I would add that I do not write as a specialist theologian: my main concern is what happens to the person in the pew who on the whole finds this whole subject difficult and at times threatening.

A 'High' View of Scripture

So what is the traditional evangelical view of Scripture? In a nutshell it is this: the evangelical is a disciple of Jesus Christ and aspires to adopt the same view of Scripture that Jesus himself held. A study of the Gospel accounts of Jesus' use of the Old Testament Scriptures suggests that he regarded the entire corpus as having supreme authority. In quoting Scripture passages he sometimes attributes its words to God himself. Since he taught that 'scripture cannot be broken' (John 10.35), he believed them to be valid for all time. The authority of the New Testament derives from Jesus and his promise of the Spirit who will 'teach you all things, and bring to your remembrance all that I have said to you' (John 14.26). In consequence, evangelicals have always insisted that they hold a 'high' view of Scripture.

But it is all very well to assert that an evangelical should have the same view of the Scriptures as Jesus. This raises as many questions as it solves. Likewise, it is all very well to agree that the Bible should have supreme authority in all matters of faith and conduct.

But how is the Bible to be understood? It is here that in recent years the evangelical constituency has ceased to appear to the rest of the Christian world as a seamless garment. For example, in 1980 a two-part series by Professor James Dunn of Durham in the evangelical theological journal *Churchman* caused a storm. The articles, based on a presentation at the Anglican Evangelical Assembly, were an attack on the doctrine of biblical inerrancy originally espoused by the late B. B. Warfield of Princeton. Dunn said Warfield's 'slippery slope' mentality, which insisted that acknowledgement of a single error in the Bible would totally undermine confidence in biblical revelation, was 'exegetically improbable, hermeneutically defective and educationally disastrous'. Dunn argued from Scripture itself for a less rigid position, citing particularly the freedom with which Jesus and the early Christians used the text of the Old Testament.

Another example is what happened in the course of the Church of England's debate about the ordination of women. Evangelicals voting on both sides claimed to have Scriptural warrant for their position. After the General Synod voted in favour, evangelical opponents claimed it had rejected 'the plain meaning of Scripture'. One said the Church of England had adopted 'a hermeneutic which is totally unacceptable'. I will be looking at the hermeneutic issues involved with both these questions in later chapters.

A generation earlier, essentially the same battle raged among evangelicals over the charismatic movement, in particular over the meaning of the Scriptures regarding the baptism and fullness of the Holy Spirit.

It is inevitable that it will flare up in another guise again in the future. For example, recent issues of *Anvil* have carried a lively debate among evangelicals about homosexuality. The sternest challenge to traditional evangelical thinking on this issue, however, has been launched with the publication of *Strangers and Friends* (Hodder and Stoughton, 1994) by Michael Vasey, a tutor at Cranmer Hall, Durham, and a member of the Liturgical Commission. It is written in a disarmingly irenic style and one strength is that Vasey is unafraid to disagree with some of the advocates of gay theologies. What is crucial, however, is his reinterpretation of biblical passages (for example, Rom. 1.26-7) most often cited as prohibiting homosexual acts, and his allegation that evangelical advocacy of the nuclear family has led them to read too much into other parts of the biblical record (for instance, the accounts of the Creation in Genesis). Conservatives have written off the book as 'flawed and speculative'. It is likely, however, that his arguments will have an impact on 'open' evangelicals who suspect that, like the issue of women's ordination, gay demands for liberalization of the Church's stance will never disappear from the scene.

On the surface, then, evangelicals appear to agree that the Bible is to be given a place of supreme authority. Underneath, however, significant differences have emerged about what this means in practice. Two generations ago, when the evangelical constituency in the Church of England was relatively small, it was possible to present a relatively united front. Now that it has grown, and positions held are more diverse, this is not so. Evangelicals can no longer claim to be a movement that is monochrome in the way it handles the Scriptures. The spotlight has moved to the field of 'hermeneutics', or how the Bible is to be interpreted. And in the process the issue arises as to whether 'infallibility' is a formula capable of serving evangelicals well.

The Hermeneutic Issue

There has been a debate about hermeneutics among evangelicals for a long time. It was freely acknowledged by John Stott in the build-up to the National Evangelical Anglican Congress held in Nottingham in 1977. Nottingham identified hermeneutics as a key issue for evangelical reflection, but the outcomes have been surprisingly slow in coming. Not long afterwards, Hodder and Stoughton published a major symposium on hermeneutics, *New Testament Interpretation*, by Professor I. Howard Marshall (1978). The work has continued, however. More recently, Professor Anthony Thiselton has produced a monumental work, *New Horizons in Hermeneutics* (HarperCollins, 1992).

For at least some, the hermeneutic enterprise is viewed with outright suspicion: they see it is a discipline at odds with the traditional evangelical conviction that the Scriptures are perspicuous, and one which can as much be used to explain away traditional interpretations.

Hermeneutics was the main theme of the Epiphany 1996 Evangelical

Anglican Leaders' Conference, reflecting evangelical anxiety about this issue. In all probability, the thinking behind it ran something like this: 'If we all read the Bible properly, we surely would all agree, wouldn't we?' So the conference was turned over to the academics and parts of the conference had the air of a lecture room. What was clear, however, was that the methodology of the more advanced thinkers on the 'open' evangelical side does not deliver a single set of answers which could thence form a platform for evangelical belief. The Dean of Lichfield, Tom Wright, and others explained the hermeneutic process as 'linking our story with God's story'. This and his five levels of interpretation were highly stimulating in the intellectual sense. But placing the emphasis as they did on 'story', by implication they were saying that no one could claim absolute precision in biblical interpretation. Moreover, they were also conceding that the Bible has more than one 'story', and thus the Bible itself contains a lot of plurality. Therefore, the whole idea of a single, unified evangelical mind based on Scripture is virtually impossible.

Criticism from Without

Evangelical thinking on the authority and interpretation of the Bible has been sharpened by criticism from without. In the 1960s, Gabriel Hebert launched a stinging attack on evangelicals and their method in *Fundamentalism and the Church of God* (SCM). It prompted a reply from J. I. Packer in a slim volume titled *Fundamentalism and the Word of God* (IVP). More recently, they had to contend with the criticisms of a former evangelical, James Barr, whose book *Fundamentalism* (SCM, 1977 and 1981) identified three pronounced characteristics of people who could be identified as 'fundamentalists': (a) a very strong emphasis on the inerrancy of the Bible, the absence in it of any sort of error; (b) a strong hostility to modern theology and to the methods, results and implications of modern critical study of the Bible; and (c) assurance that those who do not share their religious viewpoint are not 'true Christians' at all.

Barr made a monumental effort to comb the Bible to demonstrate that it contained large numbers of inconsistencies and historical errors. In addition, he aimed his sights at a number of well-known evangelical writers and commentaries which he accused of obscurantism, who refused to take note of the plain meaning of biblical texts, and even on occasions rationalized away the Bible's supernatural content. Barr's biggest problem, however, was not that his opponents mistreated individual texts and passages, but that they imposed a system of thought on the Bible that prevented it being read and understood on its own terms. Fundamentalists, he contended, squeezed the Bible into a mould of their own making.

One valuable response to Barr has come from Dr R. T. France, former principal of Wycliffe Hall, the Oxford-based Anglican theological college.[1] The irenic Dr France took it as a compliment that after years of being ignored, evangelical scholarship was at last being taken seriously by the wider world of biblical research. He took exception, nevertheless, to Barr's lumbering of conservative scholarship with 'fundamentalism', insisting that this effectively tipped the scales before the argument even began. France argued that there is a distinction between wooden, literalistic fundamentalism and the world of conservative scholarship. Fundamentalism, he insisted, was 'a perversion of true evangelicalism'. He said that like many other evangelicals of the last couple of generations, he had been able to avail himself of the tools and benefits of modern biblical scholarship without finding it necessary to move out of the evangelical world. Thanks to Barr, he said, a new mood of self-criticism was entering evangelical biblical scholarship, and this could only be for the good.

The Internal Debate

As well as occasional ructions within the constituency there has also been thoughtful, nuanced evangelical debate about Scripture. It is worth reviewing it. Early this century, ranged up against each other were the 'Princeton School' with B. B. Warfield as chief proponent of 'biblical inerrancy', and the Orr–Denney school. For Warfield and his contemporary followers, the argument ran like this: God is perfect. God is the supreme author of Scripture. Therefore Scripture must reflect God's perfection by being free from error. Scripture is therefore presented as the proverbial stack of cards. If one falls, the whole edifice must of necessity come crashing down. James Orr rejected the Princeton insistence on 'verbal inspiration'. His view nevertheless places the highest emphasis on the work of the Holy Spirit in inspiring the Scriptures.

> If there is inspiration at all, it must penetrate words as well as thought, must mould the expression, and make the language employed the living medium for the idea to be conveyed. The Scripture lays stress upon the words, often on the very form of expression. 'We speak', says St Paul, 'not in words which man's wisdom teacheth, but which the Holy Spirit teacheth.'[2]

James Denney was even more forthright in rejecting the stack of cards outlook. 'It is by no means necessary that we should know everything that is in the gospels to be true, or that we should be bound to the accuracy of every detail before they begin to do for us what God designs them to do.'[3]

While 'open' evangelical scholarship may have reached at least a temporary truce with the wider world of scholarship as a result of the Barr episode, as I have hinted, consensus has yet to descend on the entire evangelical household. During his long term as principal of the Moore Theological College in Sydney from the mid-sixties, Dr D. B. Knox developed the Warfield system further, claiming that parts of the Bible took the form of 'propositional revelation'. Over the last five years, the Southern Baptist Convention of the USA has been torn apart in an acrimonious debate in which conservatives have insisted on the dismissal of theological professors who would not assert the 'inerrancy' of the Bible. Similarly, some of what was said publicly by some evangelicals about others of their number in the context of the women's debate was shameful.

Fortunately, behind the scenes mammoth efforts have been made to face the issues and work towards understanding. It is crucial that evangelical Anglicans do not repeat the mistakes that led to splits in the 1920s. Some of the fruits of this effort were seen in a very cordial dialogue at the Anglican Evangelical Assembly in May 1995 between Graham Cray, principal of Ridley Hall, Cambridge, and Wallace Benn, the genial vicar of Harold Wood, Essex, a leading conservative voice.

The Way Forward?

1. Stop talking about 'inerrancy' and 'infallibility'

Evangelicals need to recognize that insisting on words like 'inerrancy' and 'infallibility' is a dead end. It will ensure only three things: (a) continuing (and I think unnecessary) controversy between people who in their heart of hearts want to live under biblical revelation; (b) 'unchurching' of people who want to be with the evangelical consensus but cannot be as forthright as some others about the exact form of words; and (c) relegation of evangelicals to the ghettos by the wider world of scholarship.

Evangelical history indicates that there have been influential voices who have not gone along with 'Princeton school' in asserting 'plenary verbal inspiration' as an adequate basis for the authority of Scripture. They have always admitted, for instance, that the Scriptures need not be read as a scientific work. Influential figures, such as Charles Simeon, were willing to concede that the text contained verbal discrepancies. And as David Bebbington has pointed out, the great missionary and translator, Henry Martyn, when cross-examined by a Muslim court official about the nature of the Bible, said that 'The sense is from God but the words are from the writers.'[4] In *Models for Scripture* (Paternoster, 1994), John Goldingay, principal of St John's College, Nottingham, launches an attack on the Princeton school in the light of its contribution to current controversy.

One of the factors that most challenges notions of biblical infallibility is the issue of genre. The Bible contains a variety of different literary genres. The thoughtful reader will view words and derive meaning according to the type of literature involved. A good example is how we might deal with the book of Revelation; in particular, chapter 20 which speaks of Christ's thousand-year reign, i.e. the millennium. In some parts of the world there are evangelicals who are prepared to unchurch those who suggest other than a literal interpretation. However, if you take genre into account you may well conclude that, given Revelation's family resemblance to highly symbolic Jewish apocalyptic literature, it is surely no violation of the authority of the Bible to suggest that this particular section need not be taken to prove scriptural warrant for a future reign of Christ on earth.

2. Back to Anglican Roots

It has always surprised me that evangelical Anglican societies have looked to the basis of faith of the Inter-Varsity Fellowship (IVF) when their own formularies offer more than adequate guidelines on the place of Scripture. Article VI of the Thirty-nine Articles, for instance, says: 'Holy Scripture containeth all things necessary to salvation: so that whatsoever is not read therein, nor may be proved thereby, is not to be required of any man, that it should be believed as an article of Faith, or be thought to be requisite or necessary for salvation . . .' The wording here is quite subtle. There are definite boundaries for the authority of the Scriptures. The Scriptures are authoritative in those areas where they are authoritative. So, for example, an evangelical should not feel compelled to go to the Scriptures for the last word on the laws of physics, how the earth was actually formed, or even the historical geography of ancient Palestine. Nevertheless, in the weighty matters of the doctrine of God, Christ, salvation, or practical behaviour, the Bible is the supreme guide which will never lead one into error. Anglicanism teaches that alongside the Scriptures, which have a primacy of authority, the Christian may bring to use the fruits of tradition (the experience of the whole Church throughout all the ages), and reason.

3. Willingness to Learn from Modern Scholarship

First of all, modern scholarship leaves us in little doubt about the relative quality of the scriptural material. For example, thirty years ago in his famous study, *The New Testament Documents: Are They Reliable?* (IVP), F. F. Bruce showed that there were abundant early manuscripts for the New Testament compared to the relative scarcity of early manuscripts for a great many famous classical works. And yet, the ordinary layperson is well aware when reading modern translations, particularly of the Old Testament, that at times the margin indicates that the Hebrew is 'unclear'. At this point the IVF doctrinal statement's formula of the 'infallibility of Scripture as originally given' is of little practical use, since infallibility could not have extended to the transmission and transcription of subsequent manuscripts.

Second, modern scholarship has widened our knowledge of the historical and cultural background to events recorded in the Bible and the mindset of its writers. As the Dean of Lichfield, Tom Wright, has pointed out, one important area of study has given deeper insights into the Jewishness of Jesus and the way that his teaching was in radical contrast to that of the rabbis of his day.

Moreover, the way he and the writers of the New Testament themselves interpreted the Old Testament is a model for the way the contemporary Christian will proceed with the task. We find, for instance, that they do not necessarily give equal weight to all parts of Scripture. And we discover that the teaching of Jesus and the New Testament writers is none the worse for not necessarily sharing the modern desire for absolute verbal precision.

Third, modern scholarship offers a dynamic view of revelation itself. There is much for evangelicals to learn from biblical studies: how the Scriptures are a record of God's dealing with his people, and of the reflection of his people on God in action. These reflections have their human limitations. They are steeped in the culture and history of their times. This in turn yields an important insight for the modern reader who likewise comes to the text with a worldview shaped by a particular culture. Modern studies of the Gospels and Epistles show us that the writers had particular theological motives for recording and shaping the material in the way they did. When the modern reader is aware of these different currents the rewards from the study of the Scriptures become even richer.[5]

4. Honest Preaching

One of the great tensions for evangelical preachers is how much to take lay hearers into their confidence about the fruits of modern scholarship. One of the worries of using the pulpit to talk of current theories of how, for example, the Gospels were formed, is that it may undermine the doctrine of perspicuity. As a result, some have created an artificial division between their public preaching and what they privately believe about the Bible. My conviction, having studied the Scriptures in a secular university under people who were sometimes sceptical, is that lay people *are* capable of taking the fruits of modern scholarship on board. My only regret is that over the years I found few vicars who could show me how they could be harnessed for spiritual nourishment. It was a task that I had to undertake by myself, as often as not by trial and error. To refuse to work openly with lay people on this task is itself a denial of the perspicuity principle. It would be helpful, I think, for the evangelical constituency to find a consensus of some minimum standard to which lay people should be taught about these issues.

5. Understanding Temperaments

It needs to be understood that the preference of being 'open', radical or conservative is as much as anything else a matter of temperament. I believe that the sharp differences that often emerge among evangelicals over Scripture could be mitigated if they could concede that different human temperaments tend to shape the way we see and frame answers to issues. Different temperaments are part of the glory of God's creation and in the Church they complement each other in building up the body of Christ. There are people who are by nature conservative. There are people who by temperament see things in black and white. There are people who work things out by deduction. There are others, like myself, who are apt to rely on intuition. You see the effect of temperament if you go with a tour group to the Holy Land and visit sites traditionally associated with the life of Jesus. Some will listen to the story and put their imagination to work to savour the atmosphere. Others will counter: 'But can you say for sure that this is the actual well where the angel appeared to Mary?' We see that Jesus' disciples were a team balanced by a range of different temperaments and this is one of the reasons why they were effective.

I suspect that this is one of the reasons why there are four Gospels. Mark, for example, appeals to people who like action, hence repeated use of the phrase 'and immediately'. John, on the other hand, has an enormous appeal to those who want to stand back and contemplate the mystery of the Word made flesh. There is little doubt that one of the reasons for the long enmity between Roman and Orthodox Christianity has at its roots a failure to appreciate differences in thought patterns that arise as much as anything else out of differences in culture and temperament. I believe the key to future evangelical harmony must include conceding this point, and being willing to tolerate a range of temperaments while understanding what are the key points that constitute family likeness. I am not saying that this is a cure-all. But I do believe this is one of the keys to the unity of the Church of England as a whole.

I now move to examine another factor that is crucial in evangelical self-definition. There is a case for suggesting that for evangelicals, self-definition happens as much in the way they position themselves over or against movements and schools of thought. This is happening with regard to the so-called radical liberal agenda, and it is the frontline of the battle for who will ultimately shape the future of the Church of England.

3

WHAT EVANGELICALS BELIEVE:
THE DEBATE WITH RADICAL LIBERALISM

'You should say what you mean,' the March Hare went on. 'I do,' Alice hastily replied; 'at least – at least, I mean what I say – that's the same thing you know.'

'Not the same thing a bit!' said the Hatter. 'Why, you might just as well say that "I see what I eat" is the same thing as "I eat what I see"!'

'You might just as well say,' added the March Hare, 'that "I like what I get" is the same thing as 'I get what I like"!'

'You might just as well say,' added the Dormouse, who seemed to be talking in his sleep, 'that "I breathe when I sleep" is the same thing as "I sleep when I breathe"!'   (*Alice's Adventures in Wonderland*, Lewis Carroll)

A few years ago, radical theologian Don Cupitt was invited to speak at the Greenbelt Arts Festival. His venue, The Hothouse, is the Greenbelt equivalent of Mars Hill in Athens where the Greeks would assemble to discuss new ideas. The organizers go to a lot of trouble to fit the decor to the name. Sitting amid lurid Dantesque props depicting the unbelieving being licked by eternal flames, Don quipped: 'This is just like hell. I feel quite at home.' For the next hour or so he had the audience eating out of his hands. Don Cupitt is one of those rare academic theologians who knows how to put his ideas across in a popular way. He has used television effectively to popularize his ideas. Cupitt's view is that there are no objective realities behind the language of Christian belief. Under his influence has grown up the so-called Sea of Faith movement, named after one of his television series. It now numbers several hundred clergy from various denominations.

In this chapter I want to show that a battle is on for the hearts and minds of the people of the West. It is a battle that is forcing evangelicals to think hard and strategically about what they believe and how they are called to act. It is a battle that is creating new alignments within the Christian Church because evangelicals are finding, sometimes to their great surprise, that people from other traditions who may once have been deemed 'the enemy' are keen to join with them. The dividing line is willingness to live under revelation.

In some ways, all this runs parallel to events in the late seventeenth and early eighteenth centuries when a doctrine known as deism appeared. Deism was highly influential in Germany and France, and did not leave the spiritual life of Britain untouched. Its classic statement was written by a thinker called Toland in *Christianity not Mysterious* (1696). Some deists taught that having created the world, God thereafter took no interest in it. Some deists rejected the idea of revelation and held that there was nothing beyond 'natural religion'. Certainly the system left no room for the notion of reward and punishment in what was a highly profligate age.

There is a persuasiveness about Don Cupitt and the Sea of Faith movement that is capable of attracting the interest of thoughtful people. In the end, however, it leaves most ordinary Christian people with the feeling that they have been at the tea party with Alice. Each week they are accustomed to declaring their faith in the words of the Creed. They hear and read the Bible. They know that some parts of the creeds and the Bible are more difficult to understand than others. Some wonder whether the accounts of Jesus' birth can be reconciled (and on the whole receive little help with the problem). For the most part, however, they sense that they can put their confidence in the Gospel accounts of the life and teachings of Jesus of Nazareth. They are broadly content to believe that he lived between the years 4 BC and AD 29, that he taught and healed, built up a small community of people who believed in him, that he was unjustly accused, suffered a ghastly judicial murder, that three days later his tomb was found empty and that accusations of sleight of hand by his followers never 'stuck'.

Ordinary Christians believe, too, that the Roman governor Pontius Pilate would never have crucified this harmless wandering rabbi but for the pressure the Jewish authorities exerted in the matter. The charge of the chief priests was this: 'He made himself the Son of God.' It is at this point that ordinary Christians find themselves confused by a tea party-like conversation in the Church of England between Alice and her friends.

'The Jesus of history is the Christ of the faith of the Church,' say the ordinary Christians. 'The Christ of the Church's faith is the Jesus of history. It's the same thing,' they say.

'Not a bit of it,' say the radical theologians. 'The Gospels are the inventions of the early Church. They are embellishments of a few vague memories that have been added to in the retelling.'

The Roots of Radicalism

The roots of this radical movement, among whose chief voices are Cupitt and Bishop Jack Spong of Newark, USA, can be traced to the early 1960s. In March 1963 the Bishop of Woolwich, John Robinson, published *Honest to God*. Within three years it sold over a million copies. 'Our image of God must go,' screamed the headlines.

What cannot be denied is that the early chapters of *Honest to God* pose questions to which the modern mind demands an answer. How, for instance, are we to understand ideas like God and heaven 'up there' in a culture that long ago abandoned the concept of a 'three-tier universe'? How can the message of the church be decoded so that secular people can understand? Robinson's answers, the need for a 'religionless Christianity' and a programme of demythologization, were by no means original. He largely borrowed the ideas of three German theologians, Tillich, Bultmann, and Bonhoeffer, and melted them together. It prompted Karl Barth, the great Swiss theologian, to remark: 'He has mixed three good German beers and the result is just froth.'

But evangelicals would be unwise to write off Robinson's contribution completely. His motivation, to make faith relevant in the modern market place, was much the same as that of a great many evangelicals. Moreover, he was a somewhat conservative New Testament scholar whose early dating of the Gospel of John was welcomed by a good many of them.

Just over a decade later, radical liberalism entered a further phase with the publication in 1974 by the Doctrinal Commission of the Church of England (chaired by Maurice Wiles) on *Christian Believing*. Then followed on *The Myth of God Incarnate* (edited by John Hick). Of the latter, the Roman Catholic historian, Adrian Hastings, has commented:

> If *The Myth* produced excitement it was principally the smirking excitement of an agnostic world amused to witness the white flag hoisted so enthusiastically above the long beleaguered citadel of Christian belief, the stunned excitement of the rank and file of weary defenders on learning that their staff officers had so light-heartedly ratted on them.[1]

Responses

This whole phase invites two comments.

First, as evangelical thinkers like Alister McGrath and Tom Wright have pointed out, Hick and company made uncritical use of Tillich, Bultmann and Bonhoeffer. Their ideas took little or no account of more recent developments in German theology. They appear to have ignored the fact that Bultmann's programme of demythologization had been subjected to substantial criticism.

Second, the crucial weakness is the basic assumption that the historic origins of Christianity – the revelation of God in the person of Jesus of Nazareth, his death and bodily resurrection – are either unimportant or merely symbolic. Under their system, only the teachings of Jesus count for anything. But there are two difficulties here. You cannot separate Christ's teaching from what he was and what he did. Nor is it credible to suggest that the accounts of Jesus' teaching are reliable while the accounts of the person and events surrounding them are not.

Corrosive Effects

As Adrian Hastings has commented, one of saddest and most far-reaching legacies of *Honest to God* was the demise of the Student Christian Movement. The great split in the ranks of the SCM, which gave rise in the 1920s to the Inter-Varsity Fellowship, allowed its drift into radical liberalism to progress unfettered. Up until the end of the 1950s, the SCM remained a force of national and worldwide significance. It was then that the movement removed the requirement for its members to profess any form of Christian commitment. In the 1960s, under the leadership of Bishop Ambrose Reeves who had been deported from South Africa following his criticisms of the Sharpeville massacres, the SCM put all its energies and resources into social and political action. The problem was that there were many campus organizations better placed and equipped for this purpose. By the end of the decade it had become a movement without a message. In consequence it was left without a grass-roots constituency, its material resources used up.

What happened to the SCM was a foretaste of what has happened since to the many mainline denominations that have been submerged under the radical liberal agenda. Trace, for example, the fortunes of bodies like the Presbyterian Church (USA). In 1966 its membership stood at 4.2 million. By 1991 it had shrunk to 2.8 million in a period when the US population grew from 196.5 million to 248.8 million. Interestingly, the denomination has 3,356 more ministers than in 1966, but 1,536 fewer congregations. The desire for political correctness means that a Church that consists 95 per cent of people of Scottish origin has set itself the target of having a 40 per cent ethnic minority by the year 2000, though the plan on how to get there is unclear. There is a serious and growing gap between congregations and the central structures of the denomination. At its general assemblies, staff and 'advisors' outnumber elected representatives. Says John Leith, professor of theology at the Union Theological Seminary of the Presbyterian Church's 1992 Assembly,

A commissioner who has attended many Democratic Conventions could have closed his eyes during the Assembly, even during the prayer, and imagined he was at the Virginia State Democratic Convention. The attention of the Assembly was not on the commission of the risen Christ to preach, to teach, and to baptise or on the origin of the church in the hearing of the word of God, but on its social agendas and its organisational structures. While social activism took primacy over evangelism, organisation and process over the gathering of congregations, there seemed very little awareness that apart from vigorous worshipping, believing congregations the church has no influence or power. More significantly, there seemed to be little awareness that the Gospel is what God does, not what human beings do, and that the faith in a God who reigns, who raised Jesus Christ from the dead, who sends forth the Spirit, who can do more than we can ask or think, is the source of the church's very life – not a process, organisation, or social agenda.[2]

On the whole, it is Churches with a clear message that are growing. Yet for many radical liberal apologists this counts for nothing. Take, for example, this comment by John Selby Spong, Bishop of Newark in the Episcopal Church USA. In the end it is a prescription for the abolition of the Church.

> The only churches that grow today are those that do not, in fact, understand the issues, and can therefore traffic in certainty. They represent both the fundamentalist Protestant groups and the rigidly controlled conservative Catholic traditions. The churches that do attempt to interact with the emerging world are for the most part the liberal Protestant mainline churches that shrink every day in their membership and the silent Catholic minority that attracts very few adherents. Both are, almost by definition, fuzzy, imprecise, and relatively unappealing. They might claim to be honest, but for the most part they have no real message. They tinker with words, redefine concepts, and retreat slowly behind the rearguard protection of a few pseudoradical thinkers. I have sought to live in this arena. It shrinks daily.[3]

The fire-breathing Bishop of Newark has been enormously popular with the British press, who he has charmed with his urbanity and ready wit. A year after publishing *Rescuing the Bible from Fundamentalism* in 1991, he was back with *Born of a Woman*. The British press like nothing better than a bishop spouting views that are heterodox, and prefer to ignore the critiques of theologians who insist that his views are muddled. Spong's books are based on suppositions of his own making: that Paul's attitudes to women grow from the fact that he was 'gay', and the unfounded proposition that Mary was a victim of rape. They prompted Tom Wright, New Testament scholar and Dean of Lichfield to comment:

> He rushes on, constructing imaginary, historical worlds and inviting us to base our faith and life on them. If we refuse his invitation he will, no doubt, hurl his favourite abuse word at us again. But if everyone who disagrees with Spong's book turns out to be a fundamentalist, then I suppose that all the fundamentalist churches in the world would not be able to contain the new members who would suddenly arrive on their doorsteps.[4]

Alister McGrath has commented of his writing:

> It is an utterly fantastic creation as capricious as its creator, resting upon special pleading, superficial engagement with issues, and a dogmatic

imposition of a preconceived agenda upon the New Testament material, which does not even have the merit of popular appeal. Spong runs the risk of making fundamentalism seem intellectually respectable in comparison with Anglicanism.[5]

During the last few years, there have been signs that English theology has taken a more conservative course. The liberal teachers of the 1960s have been replaced by younger, more conservative theologians like Paul Helm, David Ford, Anthony Thiselton and Robin Gill.

Dr David Jenkins, the recently retired Bishop of Durham, does not fit neatly into the Cupitt–Spong school. For a start, he had an evangelical conversion in his youth and maintains an evangelical's infectious enthusiasm for talking about his faith. He has always been a firm believer in God, in the incarnation and the resurrection. The debate with him has always been about the means through which they came about. Unfortunately his verbal communication often leaves people breathless. Just before his consecration he made headlines by publicly questioning the literal understanding of the virgin birth. Three days after his consecration in York Minster, the west front was struck by lightning, prompting some to suggest it was the judgement of God. For ten years he used his episcopacy to question many of the core beliefs of traditional Christians. He delighted the press. He managed to catch the imagination of a generation of students, prompting a Durham resident to observe: 'Go into any pub in Durham and you will hear theology being talked over the beer.'

Like John Robinson before him, and Don Cupitt, Jenkins is good at raising awkward questions. As such he did evangelicals more of a service than they perhaps realized by getting the English public talking about questions of faith. For that reason they will miss him more than they would care to admit. But there was an inherent danger. In countries where the press is hostile either to Anglicanism or Christianity in general, an un-nuanced statement by a bishop can be pure dynamite, and that was one of David Jenkins' blind spots.

OBJECTIVE TRUTH AND MEANING

The big difference between the Sea of Faith school and its liberal predecessors is its teaching that questions of truth and meaning can no longer be answered in any kind of objective manner. In his book *God in Us* (SCM, 1993), Anthony Freeman, a young Sussex clergyman, argued that 'God' is not an objective reality but an expression of human values and ideas. It is a viewpoint which shares more in common with Buddhism than historical Christianity. It boils down to a form of solipsism (the idea that nothing real exists outside my own self).

What intrigued me about Freeman's book was the fervour and intensity with which he put his case for believing that there could be no objective belief. Another area of contention was the way in which he consigned evangelical beliefs to the dustbin, without having taken the trouble to investigate what they actually stand for. One glaring example was his claim that they hold that the Bible was dictated by God to human scribes. It would seem to me that a movement that lays claim to enlightened minds needs to take the trouble to do its homework.

The other major trend of the last decade has been fragmentation within liberal thought. Gone for ever, so it seems, is any form of consensus about how key questions should be tackled. More than ever before, liberal theologians belong to small, watertight groups, each quarrying away at small, specialized disciplines. So there is liberation theology, feminist theology, gay and lesbian theology, and Third World theology. Each of these disciplines have their own presuppositions and data. Rarely are they subjected to sustained criticism from without since no outsider is deemed qualified to hold valid opinions. Only a feminist may critique feminist theology. Only a Third World person may critically review the work of another Third World theologian. Only a family member can possibly relate to 'my' experience base.

POSTMODERNITY

All this turbulence on the theological scene signals the fact that Western Christianity is being rocked by tremors which have shaken the foundations of the thought-system on which it has been based for three hundred years. Western thought drew from the Ancient Greeks a confidence that human reason could help discover and define what was ultimately true and valuable. From the Ancient Romans it drew a vision of spreading its enlightened and prosperous civilization to the four corners of the earth. In a postmodern age, reason itself is suspect. Thinkers such as Jean-François Lyotard maintain that reason and the social systems it has created are coercive and repressive. The legacy of the postmodern attitude to life is to ignore or disdain authority, to cease caring either about absolute moral values or striving towards shared, ultimate goals.

Postmodernity therefore presents the greatest contemporary challenge to the Christian Church because of its relativistic world-view stand in contrast to traditional Christian claims. The earliest Christian creed was 'Jesus Christ is Lord.' It is a statement that refuses to allow the Christian faith to be relegated to being one among many world-views, and refuses to believe that all religions stand on an equal footing.

Two Possible Responses

There have been two kinds of evangelical response to these developments, and both are valid. First of all, evangelical apologists have been on hand to debate with the radicals. I have already mentioned the work of Alister

McGrath and Tom Wright. Second, there have been interesting and valuable examples of evangelical interaction with some of these fields, in parallel with developments in biblical studies discussed earlier. Elaine Storkey of the London Institute for Contemporary Christianity has done this in relation to feminism. Another very fruitful area is interaction with Third World theologies, and the Oxford Centre for Mission Studies is an important contributor here.

There is another kind of evangelical response, too. It recently prompted the American, Dr Mark Noll, to write *The Scandal of the Evangelical Mind* (Eerdmanns, 1994). Too many evangelicals are apt to duck involvement in hard-minded pursuit of truth. A truly evangelical engagement with the liberal agenda will involve both the heart and the head. It will be as much at home in the market place of ideas as in the pulpit.

To summarize, I would suggest that there is a fundamental divide between evangelicalism and both the radical liberal and postmodern thought I have tried to describe.

1. ATTITUDES TO TRUTH

The Sea of Faith movement sees the incarnation of Christ as a symbol of the need to identify with our global neighbour and share in their sufferings, the resurrection as a summation of the hope that good will triumph over evil. But the evangelical insists that each of these events are true in themselves. Jesus Christ was God. The implications are both astonishing and life-changing. Jesus Christ actually died on the cross. He died not just as a martyr but as the One who bore the sins of the human race on himself. Jesus Christ was raised to new life. By doing that, God declared him Lord of the universe, and the eternal judge of every human being. The postmodernist says, 'You are entitled to believe whatever you want, so do me the favour of letting me believe whatever I please.' In contrast, the evangelical insists that there can be salvation in none other than Christ, because like Peter they are convinced that he has 'the words of eternal life'. This is the 'scandal' of Christianity and 'the foolishness of God'.

2. ATTITUDES TO THE CHURCH

It is no accident that, with few exceptions, the kind of liberal and postmodern thought I have tried to describe is corrosive to the Church in its local form. It has no message. Its only basis for survival is activism in central church structures.

As I have intimated, this battle is creating a new alignment within the Christian Church, and the dividing line concerns attitudes to revelation. On one side of the line stand those who hold that religion and faith are creations of human ingenuity. On the other stand those who hold that what can be known about God and the human destiny can be perceived through revelation, supremely the incarnation of God in Christ.

It is a new alignment that cuts across old party divisions. There is a place within it for those who share a catholic commitment to the historic continuity of the faith. There is a place within it for those who, in the best liberal tradition, seek to confront the hard questions thrown up by living in the contemporary world. There is a place, too, for those who share the evangelical vision to declare the Good News and make it known as widely as possible. It requires willingness to put aside disagreements that fed party strife in order to confront larger questions that require a united response. I will return to this issue in later chapters.

Meanwhile. together with the seventeenth-century clergyman and poet, George Herbert, we are invited to stand in wonder at what God has done in Christ.

> Philosophers have measur'd mountains,
> Fathomed the depths of seas, of states and kings,
> Walked with a staff to heav'n and traced fountains:
> But there are two vast, spacious things,
> The which to measure it doth more behove:
> Yet few there are that found them; Sin and Love.
>
> Who would know Sin, let him repair
> Unto Mount Olivet; there shall he see
> A man so wrung with pains, that all his hair,
> His skin, his garments bloody be.
> Sin is that press and vice, which forceth pain
> To hunt his cruel food through ev'ry vein.
>
> Who knows not Love, let him assay
> And taste that juice, which on the Cross a pike
> Did set again abroach; then let him say
> If ever did he taste the like.
> Love is that liquor sweet and most divine
> Which my God feels as blood; but I, as wine.
>
> From *The Agonie*

4

EVANGELICAL ANGLICANS
IN GLOBAL CONTEXT

The Church of England was and is a national Church, established and in part
controlled by the state. Before this body could serve as the nucleus of a
world-wide fellowship, the question had to be asked whether Anglicanism
was merely a by-product of the English way of life and constitution; or
whether it is a genuine form of Christian faith and practice, such as could
maintain itself in total independence of the soil and the State of England.
(Bishop Stephen Neill, *Anglicanism*, Mowbray, p. 278)

To understand evangelical Anglicanism fully, it needs to be viewed in a global
as well as a Church of England context. I come to the subject as one nurtured
in my faith by non-English Anglicanism, who has had the privilege of seeing a
great deal of the Anglican world first hand during six years on the staff of the
Anglican Consultative Council.

The Anglican Communion may not be the largest of the Christian denom-
inations, but it is one of the most widespread. According to the *World
Christian Encyclopedia*, it exists in over 150 countries and is growing at a
Pentecost-like three thousand a day. Evangelicalism has had a significant
stake in its expansion from beginnings in the British Isles. Broadly speaking,
Anglicanism expanded in two phases.

Origins

The Colonial Era

The first phase coincided with Britain's exporting of its own people to countries such as Australia, Canada, New Zealand, Southern Africa and the United
States. With them went clergy, the Book of Common Prayer, and a form of
Anglicanism that depended in large measure on memories of church life in the
old country. Not surprisingly, it was an Anglicanism that was conservative in
temperament. It tended to view the Church of England as the 'norm'. Lacking
up-to-date contact with the movements of reform and change that were inevitably part of the living tradition of the Mother Church, it often tended to
fossilize, clinging tenaciously to fading memories of the past and erecting
buildings in the style of parish churches left behind on the other side of the

world. For example, the twin towers of St John's pro-cathedral Parramatta, one of Australia's oldest churches, located west of Sydney, were a direct copy of the towers of the Reculver parish church on the Kent coast, one of the last glimpses remembered by passengers leaving English shores for the new world.

The Great Age of Missions

The second phase coincided with what has become known as the 'great century of missions'. Historians tend to date it from 1857 and Dr David Livingstone's famous Cambridge appeal in which he encouraged a generation of students and idealists to take the gospel to parts hitherto unknown by the white community. Anglicanism, however, had been in the process of recovering its missionary vision for a century. The closure of the monasteries by Henry VIII left something of a vacuum of social and missionary work in the English Church. The spiritual needs of the colonies gave rise to the formation in 1698 of the Society for Promoting Christian Knowledge (SPCK) and in 1701 the quaintly named Society for the Propagation of the Gospel in Foreign Parts (now USPG). Among its eighteenth-century servants was John Wesley, who had a disastrous sojourn among the colonists of Georgia. In fact, it was another ninety years before the SPG agreed that its remit should include taking the gospel to the heathen.

It was the foundation of the Church Missionary Society in 1799 that focused what had been a steadily growing evangelical commitment to world evangelization. Whereas SPG was mainly 'clericalist' in orientation, the Church Missionary Society, founded in 1799, was predominantly a lay society. Its early years were closely associated with the anti-slavery movement and it quickly became – and for that matter still is – a radical voice within the evangelical constituency.

Today the missionary movements have a host of critics. This should not be surprising. Undoubtedly many missionaries carried with them cultural baggage that held that British was best. This sometimes destroyed good things in the local culture, hindering the cause of the gospel in the process. However, mechanistic theories that insist that the missionaries were dumb tools of capitalism do no justice to the motivation, for example, of the young people who lie buried in the missionary graveyard in Mombasa, Kenya, some of them having been in malaria-infested East Africa but a few weeks in obedience to God's call.

The other issue often raised is the spectre of colonialism. While it is true that the expansion of Anglicanism worldwide is linked with British colonialism, as much as anyone it was missionaries who first saw that political independence was inevitable. Anglican mission fields became self-supporting, self-governing indigenous churches well in advance of political independence.

The benefits that accrued to the Church of England from this movement of people are often overlooked. For if the missionary movement took the gospel to utmost parts of the earth, it also changed the fabric of the Mother Church in remarkable ways. It challenged it to become missionary in character. A century of overseas missions led to corresponding missionary movements to the inner cities and other areas of deprivation. Moreover, it confronted English Christianity with its own divisions and challenged it to repair them for the gospel's sake. The ecumenical movement first began on the mission fields where missionaries discovered that denominational labels need be no barrier to cooperation with other traditions as well as being meaningless to the peoples who were being won for Christ through their labours.

There are, of course, myriads of histories and studies that trace and record these movements. Stephen Neill's *Anglicanism* stands out.[1] Rather than trace history, my purpose here is to offer analysis of the contemporary scene, and the current instruments of inter-Anglican consultation and communication.

Suffice to say Anglicanism's global expansion gave birth to something far more robust than the Church of England in chaplaincy form. As Stephen Neill has pointed out, it was based on an ecclesiology that chose not to walk in the ways of either Geneva or Rome, in the spirit of Anglicanism's celebrated *via media* or middle way. This was not necessarily a recipe for blandness or compromise. 'Anglicanism', says Neill, 'is a very positive form of the Christian faith that teaches the whole of Catholic faith, free from the distortions, the exaggerations, and the over definitions both of the Protestant left wing and of the right wing of Tridentine Catholicism.'[2] As such, it was capable of prompting great acts of heroism. Importantly, too, it gave rise to a form of Christianity that could adapt and change as culture warranted.

An Establishment Mentality

One part of the Church of England legacy that is likely to come under increasing scrutiny is what might be called Anglicanism's 'establishment mentality'. The debate about the establishment of the Church of England is a matter to which I shall be devoting an entire chapter. Here, taking up Stephen Neill's point quoted at the beginning of the chapter, I want to comment on how exporting an 'establishment' outlook has not necessarily benefited the overseas churches.

Other than the Church of England, no other national Anglican Church enjoys the status of a State Church. Some, such as the Churches of Ireland, Wales and Barbados, were once established in law. Many, however, inspired by or perhaps envious of the opportunities for service (and no doubt status) that the establishment model offers, have got themselves into difficulty. In the USA there are about 2.5 million Episcopalians in a population of 250 million (a proportion that some sociologists would say amounts to being a sect). Yet a high proportion of politicians claim to be Episcopalians and Washington

Cathedral is called the National Cathedral. The outcome is that in the field of public affairs, the Episcopal Church's headquarters staff and General Convention tend to take themselves far more seriously than is warranted. Nigeria offers another example. There the Anglican Church is known as the Church of Nigeria (Anglican Communion). Yet there is no sense in which the nation accords the status of 'Church of Nigeria' to Anglicanism.

It is recent events in Rwanda, however, that signal how the establishment mentality can lead overseas Churches into serious trouble. Taking a cue from the way the Church of England has close links with the British State, Anglican Bishops in Rwanda went out of their way to court the now-discredited former regime. They became so close to those in power that they were unable to speak out against tribalism. In due course, some were directly involved in the ethnically motivated massacres.

Authority in Anglicanism

One of the major tasks for the churches planted in both of these phases of the growth of the Anglican Communion was to discover whether there were principles enshrined in Anglicanism that had universal value and should be preserved alongside the task of speaking relevantly to the new culture in which they are set. As the Sri Lankan missiologist, D. T. Niles, once observed, Christianity is a plant that is transferred to new surroundings in a cultural pot. In order to survive and thrive, its roots must be nurtured from the soil of the new culture and inevitably there will come a time when the roots cause the cultural pot to crack.

Finding the balance between giving due deference to universal truths and the need to adapt to particular cultures continues to be a lively and at times painful issue for Anglicanism. Is there a core of belief and expression that is 'Anglican' and non-negotiable? Who decides what this should be? And should churches that are constitutionally independent be in any way accountable to Anglicanism as a whole? The issue of authority in the Anglican Communion has long been a debating point. Up until the middle of the nineteenth century, the Archbishop of Canterbury and the Bishop of London exercised some degree of 'remote control' over the affairs of the colonial churches. In the absence of their day-to-day supervision the concept of synodical government began to evolve.

But the shape of the future was determined by what happened in the United States of America after the War of Independence. In 1783, Episcopalians of Connecticut elected Samuel Seabury as their first bishop and sent him to London to be consecrated. Seabury met with a somewhat mixed reception. There was no precedent for the consecration of overseas bishops. Moreover, Seabury could not swear allegiance to the English Crown, as required under the rubrics of the Church of England. Seabury's dilemma was finally resolved in an upper room in Aberdeen in 1784. Bishops of the Scottish Episcopal Church – a tiny remnant who, having backed the wrong side during the invasion by Bonnie Prince Charlie, were subject to the Penal Laws – agreed to make him a bishop in the Anglican succession. As well as taking episcopacy back to Connecticut, Seabury took with him the Scottish Prayer Book which gave American worship a flavour distinct from churches who based future prayer books on the 1662 Book of Common Prayer.

In due course, the Westminster Parliament cleared the way for consecrations for overseas churches in 1786, and the chapel at Lambeth Palace became the launch pad for a stream of bishops all over the world. In time, there were enough bishops of the Anglican succession to consecrate locally. This mechanism meant that Anglicans were well ahead of most other denominations in turning 'mission fields' into self-governing churches.

The Lambeth Conference

Anglicans soon realized, however, that if giving these new churches autonomy had missionary strengths, there was still a need to take counsel. In 1863, a convulsive dispute in South Africa between the Tractarian Archbishop, Robert Gray of Cape Town, and the radical Bishop of Natal, John Colenso, made this a matter of urgency. The bishops of Canada began calling for a world gathering of bishops. The issues of the dispute were important in themselves but underneath there was the problem that the legal status of the colonial churches was undefined. The upshot was the first Lambeth Conference in 1867.

From the outset, Lambeth refused to style itself as a world governing body for Anglicans. To this day, while Lambeth is considered the most influential inter-Anglican body, it does not have power to bind or limit the autonomy of national General Synods. Anglicanism has always resisted creation of a Vatican and the office of Archbishop of Canterbury enjoys a primacy of honour but has no legal authority except where he remains as metropolitan of a handful of overseas dioceses that are 'extra-provincial'.

The real beneficiaries of the Lambeth Conferences are the bishops who attend. A good many work in lonely and difficult situations. The opportunity to draw strength from their peers is important. From the perspective of ordinary people, it presents a vision of the Church that transcends the bounds of parochialism. It is specially important for people in the British Isles to be confronted with a view of Anglicanism that is multiracial and multicultural. Less than a quarter of those attending Lambeth 1978 were from the British Isles and that proportion grows smaller and smaller as the years unfold and the Church overseas – particularly in the Third World – grows apace.

Occasionally a Lambeth Conference hits on a theme that catches wider imagination. Such was the 1880 Lambeth Conference's endorsement of the so-called Lambeth-Chicago Quadrilateral that spelled out the essential elements needed within a reunited church, namely the place of the Scriptures, the ancient faith of the Church, the creeds, baptism and the Eucharist, and the ministry of bishops.

Then the 1920 Lambeth Conference's Appeal to All Christian People helped make ecumenism an Anglican priority. In 1958 its thinking on the family was an important contribution. It will be interesting to see how the historians will view the impact of the 1988 Lambeth call for a Decade of Evangelism.

It is worth pointing out, however, that in each of these cases Lambeth resonated with people in the pews precisely because it caught a wave that was already apparent. The 'down' side, and this is even greater in a television age, is that great processions of mitred bishops present an unnecessarily pompous image of the Church. If there is a locus of episcopal authority it is surely to be found in the way those holding this office are the servants of the servants of the One who washed the feet of his disciples and said, 'I am among you as one who serves' (Luke 22.27).

There has always been an untidiness about the way Anglicanism deals with major issues of principle. The classic example, of course, was the question of the ordination of women. The churches of Hong Kong, America, Canada and New Zealand all went ahead and ordained women because they judged it to be right in their circumstances, rather than waiting for the go-ahead from elsewhere. But this is not the only case. Through liturgical revision, particularly, variances between the churches of the Anglican household are manifest. Whereas Anglicans worldwide were once held together by the liturgy of the Book of Common Prayer, now individual member churches of the household have created prayer books of their own. It is possible to discern a 'family resemblance' between the various liturgies spawned over the last couple of decades, but when, for example, the church in New Zealand judged it right to include material in its new prayer book that reflected Polynesian culture and spirituality and sounded distinctly 'New Age', eyebrows were raised; but the principle of autonomy stands.

The Anglican Consultative Council

In the last three decades, Anglicanism has created two other instruments of consultation that meet more frequently than the once-every-ten-years Lambeth Conference: the Primates' Meeting and the Anglican Consultative Council (ACC). The 1968 Lambeth Conference created the ACC – made up of bishops, clergy and lay people. At Lambeth 1978 it was agreed that in addition to the ACC, the primates of the Anglican Communion should also meet regularly. That in itself is an example of the checks and balances – some would say untidiness – that is the hallmark of Anglicanism.

When the first meeting of the ACC in Kenya in 1970 passed a resolution to the effect that there were no theological objections to the ordination of women, it triggered a decade of heart-searching and endless discussion over the question of authority within Anglicanism. The ACC motion was greeted with glee by those churches wishing to ordain women, but opponents wanted to know by what authority this small and under-resourced body should act in this manner. In 1968, it had been widely felt that the ACC would take the place of the Lambeth Conference. There was a strong body of opinion in favour of that development at the ACC's third meeting at Trinidad in 1976, but the Archbishop of Canterbury, Donald Coggan, thought otherwise and won the day.

There has as yet been no substantial independent assessment of the contribution of the ACC. Its staff effectively became a permanent secretariat for the Anglican Communion and a succession of secretary generals have been much loved as confidants to the Anglican leadership throughout the world. The second meeting of the Council in Dublin in 1972 devised the process now known as Partnership in Mission (PIM) which created a system where a national church would invite representatives of other parts of the Communion to take counsel with it in identifying its mission priorities. It became a very important instrument for those churches requiring outside funds to support their work. It had teeth because most major mission agencies of the older churches agreed that their funding would primarily serve priorities agreed at national Partnership in Mission consultations.

Nevertheless, PIM has never been a complete success, for three reasons. First, it was never able to control and channel all the funds likely to flow. Nor should it. Today individuals and parishes can have close relations with overseas parishes and dioceses. The idea of control is totally impractical. Moreover, creation of electronic superhighways will cut radically across the traditional instruments of partnership with churches overseas. In any case, there will always be urgent needs and charismatic individuals that will prompt church people to give directly rather than through the established channels.

Second, it led to the bureaucratization of mission. In order to plan PIM consultations and organize the flow of money and personnel, Third World churches found themselves needing to create provincial offices and staffs. This may have been a necessary development as they matured as churches, but it was not a cause that excited the rank and file supporters of mission agencies. Moreover, it cast mission agencies as responders rather than initiators. There may be a link between the decisions of the Church Missionary Society (CMS) and the United Society for Propagation of the Gospel (USPG) to support PIM priorities and their financial difficulties in the early 1990s.

Third, and perhaps most important from a world evangelization point of view, it is essentially conservative. It tends to lock the Church of England into long-standing relationships rather than opening up new missionary opportunities. Under PIM principles, the Church of England is linked mainly to areas where the Anglican Church already exists or where there are long-standing ecumenical partnerships. A map of PIM would show, for instance, that the Church of England has few official missionary relationships in the lands north of the Sahara. This partly explains why evangelicals in the Church of England readily support interdenominational missions, and why evangelical young people have flocked to get a taste of missionary work through agencies such as Youth With a Mission and Operation Mobilization.

The other dimension of the ACC, of course, is its council meetings. Viewed via their official reports, these meetings are at best a mixed bag. The second meeting, in Dublin in 1972, invented PIM and this created a significant proportion of future agendas for over a decade. While PIM arguably 'worked' for Third World churches it was much slower in having an impact on the internal mission policies of older churches such as the Church of England. Interesting enough, though, the process envisaged in a PIM consultation is very much the same as what is involved in mission audits which are now encouraged by most dioceses in the Church of England.

ACC meetings regularly monitor the progress of ecumenical dialogue, but they can hardly claim to have shaped the Anglican enterprise in ecumenism. Through the inter-Anglican budget, it has supported initiatives such as the Inter-Anglican Doctrinal Commission and the Commission on Women in the Episcopate (commonly called the Eames Commission), but again the ACC is the workhorse rather than the initiator. Except where ACC meetings have been a dry run for an upcoming Lambeth Conference, since Dublin they have tended to lack the straw with which to make bricks. This suggests that while the ACC meeting brings together a colourful and exciting array of people, it has not learned what to do with them.

It has always been the policy of the Church of England to send a 'balanced' delegation to ACC meetings. In earlier years, the evangelical layman, Sir Norman Anderson, made a substantial contribution as a member. More recently, English evangelical members included John Smallwood, Canon Colin Craston, and Dr Christina Baxter. Colin Craston, who became chairman in 1990, has long been concerned about the issue of where the locus of authority in Anglicanism lies. He was the architect of making Cape Town a joint meeting of the ACC and the Anglican Primates. Interestingly, the ACC has so far had five chairmen and the last three, John Denton (Australia), Yong Ping Chung (Malaysia) and Colin Craston are all of evangelical extraction. In no case did they try to impose evangelical agendas. They would never have got away with it.

The Primates' Meeting

Regular meetings of the senior bishops in the Anglican Communion did not actually begin with the decision by the 1978 Lambeth Conference that there be regular Primates' Meetings. For many years until 1968, the metropolitans (those with the status of archbishop in their region) formed the Lambeth Consultative Body. This body disappeared with the creation of the Anglican Consultative Council which brought laity and ordinary clergy into the picture.

While the ordination of women was not on the agenda of Lambeth 1978, it was discussed endlessly over meal tables and in the corridors. It was realized that the disappearance of the Lambeth Consultative Body had left a vacuum, and a way needed to be found to enable the senior bishops to confer regularly. By calling for Primates' Meetings, on the face of it Lambeth appeared to be saying that it wanted to put a brake on the ACC and individual churches taking controversial faith and order decisions without international agreement. Opponents of the ordination of women hoped it would put an end to this and other unwelcome innovations. ACC apologists, likewise, were suspicious that it would be supplanted, and that Anglicanism would eventually be ruled by a pontifical Archbishop of Canterbury surrounded by a college of cardinal-primates.

In reality, Primates' Meetings have never in any sense acted as a 'brake'. But the existence of a combination of the ACC and Primates' Meetings, the extensive travels of the Archbishop of Canterbury, together with the telecommunications hardware now generally available, means that communication within Anglicanism is far better than it was in earlier years. It means that actions by an individual province rarely catch the rest by surprise. As much as anything, being caught by surprise was at the heart of the problems experienced by the Anglican Communion in the years between 1970 and 1978.

The Primates' Meeting has steadfastly refused to claim a role that tells the churches of the Anglican Communion what they can or cannot do, much to the disappointment of the press. They are more in the character of a retreat than a business meeting. Each primate knows that while he has a special task as a guardian of faith and order, it is his Provincial Synod that has the power to enact legislation and initiate reforms. While I suspect that some primates, especially those from younger churches that may be numerically or economically weak, would like to be able to appeal to higher authority, the great majority would have it no other way.

The debate about authority and the Anglican Communion presents its own peculiar set of questions for evangelicals. It dovetails neatly into the debate about the evangelical doctrine of the Church. Many of the current generation of evangelicals were raised in a context that strongly emphasized the notion of 'the invisible Church'. This was summed up in a clause in the Doctrinal Statement of my own Evangelical Union at Macquarie University in Sydney: 'The one universal and invisible Church to which all true believers belong.' There were echoes of this kind of thinking in the presentation by Philip Hacking, Chairman of Reform, at the Evangelical Anglican Leaders' Conference held in Epiphany, 1995 when he said that the New Testament 'knows only the church local and universal. Respect for and loyalty to denomination must never undermine this truth and there is a great need for greater freedom for the local church.'

An evangelical raised on this ecclesiology sees no real need for denominational or ecumenical structures. In contrast, traditional Anglican polity insists that the Church is both a spiritual and temporal entity. The local, regional and national is linked to the universal Church by sharing its creeds and sacraments. It is possible, nevertheless, to operate within Anglican structures on a pragmatic basis while adhering to an 'invisible church' ecclesiology.

Ecumenism

While it may be true that rank and file evangelicals tend to be lukewarm as regards ecumenism, several individuals have played key roles in international ecumenical dialogue. Julian Charley, formerly Warden of Shrewsbury House in inner-city Liverpool and now vicar of Malvern Priory, served for many years on the Anglican-Roman Catholic International Commission. Anglican-Orthodox talks have benefited from the presence of Dr Oliver O'Donovan of Oxford. Likewise, a factor that commended Dr George Carey to other constituencies of the Church of England was his involvement with and ultimately his chairmanship of the Faith and Order Advisory Group (FOAG), the body that assesses the theological fine print of ecumenical dialogues.

Ecumenism is a field where a little evangelical heart-searching is in order. Keele committed evangelical Anglicans to the ecumenical enterprise, yet in the early 1970s evangelicals found themselves combining forces with Anglo-Catholics, with whom they had little or nothing in common, to defeat union with the Methodists.

The charismatic movement has been a catalyst for breaking down barriers both within Anglicanism and more widely. Yet evangelicals inevitably tend to stand aloof from the ecumenical agenda, in part because their priorities lie elsewhere and because inheritance of the 'invisible church' doctrine means that some see little point in the search for visible unity. There is a suspicion, too, that ecumenical representatives are not as plain-speaking in dealing with representatives of other Churches. There was a good example in the late 1970s when the results of a Church of England-Baptist dialogue produced versions of the doctrine of baptism on behalf of their Churches that rank and file people from both sides would in no way have recognized as their own. This anxiety deepens when it comes to official Anglican-Roman Catholic dialogue. Evangelicals were frankly very uncomfortable about the ARCIC *Authority* Agreed Statement, in particular its call for a universal primacy under the Bishop of Rome.

What is the future scenario for ecumenism? The days are long past when the ecumenical movement seriously contemplated creating a mega-church. At

best ecumenists hope that through dialogue and increased mutual understanding, the Churches will grow closer together, with intercommunion
and the interchangeability of ministries as tangible goals. This is laudable,
and will work in some instances. The best scenarios from an Anglican point
of view involve the Methodists and various Lutheran communities.

Yet it is surprising how the old ecumenical vision of a single world Church
persists. Even if it was possible for the major denominations to agree to a unity
package, in our postmodern culture the trends are running in the opposite
direction. In the 1970s and 1980s, international corporations swallowed up
thousands of businesses to create huge conglomerates. In the 1990s, business,
having realized the folly of this approach, is rapidly breaking up these conglomerates. The mega-trend is decentralization. Application of optic fibres to
communications points to a future where the accent is on small-scale businesses, 'virtual' or decentralized electronic offices, and cottage industries.
This is already having an impact on the life of the Church. Using desktop publishing, clergy are already creating custom-made liturgies. In the future there
will be a huge amount of material available to them as networking and
information banks develop further. Some in the Church of England may
hold on to a wish for 'common prayer'. In reality this will just be a pious
hope. Ecumenism will create common lectionaries and hail agreements on
the wording of traditional texts found in the liturgy. Parishes, however, will
regard these resources as some of many available in a growing supermarket and
will pick and choose according to their own criteria of perceived need. The
next wave of questions on authority issues is likely to grow out of the kind of
world that this trend is creating.

Europe

Over the last generation, the Church of England has experienced a significant
shift in its relationships. Interest in the Anglican Communion, which to many
represents a bygone era, is waning. With the Single European Act and the
opening of the Channel Tunnel, Europe beckons more than ever. Anglican-
Lutheran accord is currently hailed as the most hopeful ecumenical field in
which Anglicans are engaged. The Meissen Agreement signals closer links
with the German churches. The General Synod has put its weight behind
the Porvoo Declaration with the Nordic churches and closer relations with
the state churches in continental Europe are on the way.

Again, evangelicals are likely to be lukewarm about these developments.
Many, of course, have their own European networks. The Inter Continental
Church Society is a significant player, supporting both evangelical Anglican
chaplaincies and special ministries in summer-holiday resorts. It sees church
planting as an important part of future strategy and this sits uneasily with
formal ecumenical relationships that mostly frown on 'proselytism'. There is

nervousness among conservatives, too, about close relations with churches where state legislation requires recognition of homosexual unions. So far the potential ecclesiastical Euro-sceptics have had their minds elsewhere. That is not likely to continue indefinitely.

Individual evangelical parishes have been energetic in creating links with Eastern Europe following the demise of the Berlin Wall. It is mostly unilateral in character. Most of these relationships do not require central organizations as their midwife. Another growing area of evangelical mission is contact with students coming to Britain. Growing numbers are patronizing language schools, and the strategic evangelical brains readily understand that converting them will be an important hedge against the secularization of Continental Europe.

Inter-Anglican Evangelical Structures

In 1958, Anglo-Catholics attending the Lambeth Conference staged an enormous show of strength with a rally that filled the Royal Albert Hall. A procession of coped and mitred bishops surrounded the entire building. Bishop (later Archbishop) Marcus Loane, senior assistant bishop of Sydney, was at Lambeth as substitute for Howard Mowll who was ill. This event convinced him that something needed to be done both to galvanize and further the evangelical cause in the Anglican Communion. At the end of the conference he visited John Stott, Rector of All Souls, Langham Place, in central London, and Canon Talbot Mohan, Director of the Church Pastoral Aid Society. Out of these discussions emerged the Evangelical Fellowship in the Anglican Communion (EFAC).

Over the years since, EFAC has held national, regional and international conferences throughout the world. Its main strategy, however, was to provide bursaries for advanced theological studies to the brightest young evangelicals from Third World countries. A generation or so on, this policy is beginning to pay dividends and a number of EFAC bursars have become senior leaders. Probably the most notable is Dr Michael Nazir-Ali, originally from Pakistan, now Bishop of Rochester and probably the Church of England's first Asian bishop since Theodore of Tarsus (668-90).

The State of the Party

EFAC's international conference in Canterbury in 1993 provided a bird's-eye view of the relative strength of evangelicalism in different parts of the Anglican Communion.

THE INDIAN SUBCONTINENT

Most impressive of all were the contingents from the churches in India. Their tradition of theology and social concern is honed by living alongside other ancient faiths who have been strongly resistant to evangelization. Despite all that, this context has given birth to an articulate and self-confident evangelicalism.

SOUTH AMERICA

Another surprise packet were the Brazilians, who exhibited the same hard-mindedness and a thorough integration of spiritual and material concerns. The Southern Cone of South America has produced a form of Anglicanism that is full of Latin fervour, enthusiasm and eccentricities that are writ large. But in the person of Pat Harris, the Bishop of Southwell, who spent twenty years working there, lastly as Bishop of Northern Argentina, the Southern Cone has proved an important laboratory on how to make the Church of England into a missionary Church.

AFRICA

For many years, Africa has been Anglicanism's major missionary frontier and the church there continues to grow rapidly. What was clear, however, was that Asia is the fastest growing edge of both evangelicalism and of Anglicanism in its evangelical form. EFAC showed that it could accommodate representatives both from the larger Church of the Province of Southern Africa (CPSA) and the Church of England in South Africa (CESA). The split between these two bodies – dating from the Colenso affair of the 1860s – still persists and, because the Archbishop of Canterbury recognizes only one Anglican Church in each place, CESA is not welcome at the Lambeth Conference or other inter-Anglican portals.

ASIA

The Anglican diocese of Singapore is without doubt one of the most eccentric in the Anglican Communion, having espoused the charismatic movement in a substantial way. And yet it has often been far more imaginative about how to do mission in an urban-industrial complex than many of its European, Australian or North American counterparts, not least by the way it has set up churches in high-rise apartment blocks. Korean Christianity is now a major force and a sender of missionaries to Africa and South America. The Anglican Church there, which began as a creature of the Oxford Movement, now has an evangelical renewal movement which has made it more self-confident and outgoing.

AUSTRALIA, CANADA, USA

The older, Western churches offer an interesting contrast. Anglican evangelicalism in Australia comes in two distinct breeds: Sydney and non-Sydney. The Sydney form is conservative and bruisingly self-confident. When it suits its purposes it 'hangs loose' to traditional Anglicanism, but for all that, the diocese is a remarkable institution with its own publishing, radio, and television production facilities and huge involvement in social care. Non-Sydney is less clerical and copes better with Anglican comprehensiveness.

Evangelicals are very thin on the ground in the Anglican Church of Canada and they have had to learn how to work with groupings such as various renewal movements and the Prayer Book Society to get a hearing in the wider church.

Most surprising is that, coming as they do from a continent where evangelicals are legion, those from the Episcopal Church, USA, are clearly the most beleaguered and despondent. Their defensive action against the ordination of openly practising gay clergy has further isolated them in a church whose current Presiding Bishop, Edmond Browning, clearly wants to go down that route. They suffer from political naiveté as well. After the revelations that the former ECUSA treasurer, Ellen Cooke, a Browning protégé, had embezzled large sums of church money, they lost sympathy with a campaign to secure his resignation. Since a resignation would not trigger an election for a successor, it would have been far better tactics to concentrate on making coalitions to ensure election of someone more to their liking in 1996.

THE CHURCH OF ENGLAND

Compared to Anglicanism elsewhere, the Church of England has an enormous wealth of resources – both financial and in terms of talents and skill. In the comparison with Anglicanism elsewhere some weaknesses show up. For example its evangelism is over-reliant on having an institutional base in the community – a legacy of establishment perhaps – whereas other Anglicans are adept at starting something from nothing. One of the millstones around its neck is the upkeep of thousands of church buildings that are non-functional and in the wrong place. What is certain is that, given its resources and the quality of its people, in missionary terms the Church of England is an underachiever. Links with the Anglican Communion have much to offer in turning the trend of decline around.

5

INTERVIEW WITH THE
ARCHBISHOP OF CANTERBURY

Dr George Carey, 102nd Archbishop of Canterbury, is possessed of most of
the characteristics of an evangelical as identified in Chapter one.

First, he had a clear, evangelical conversion. A few days after it happened,
his vicar held an open air service outside the house where the Carey family
lived in Dagenham and insisted that seventeen-year-old George stood on
the platform to give his testimony. While some churchmen whose faith had
similar beginnings can be sheepish when recalling such experiences, having
since 'broadened out', George Carey has no such scruples; and bringing
people to faith is still one of his primary enthusiasms.

Second, studying and meditating on the Bible is the centre of his devotional life. A close family friend once told me, 'In the face of a spiritual
crisis, George Carey's first reflex would be to gather a group of trusted
people around and open up the Bible.'

Third, he is a 'doer'. He is a man of high intellectual attainment but his
concerns are intensely practical. He is an early riser. He works a punishing
schedule.

Yet, despite his impeccable evangelical credentials, George Carey has never
been a party man. By his own admission his devotional life was broadened and
deepened by application of modern methods of biblical criticism, a better understanding of the teachings of the early Church Fathers, and by coming into
contact with spiritual traditions that put a premium on meditation, silence and
Holy Communion.

Today there are forces at work that are prompting some parts of the evangelical Anglican constituency to 'Balkanize' into increasingly small groups
living in isolation. Rather than playing a full part in the life of the Church of
England, some are retreating behind the castle walls of their tradition and
pulling up the drawbridge. Dr Carey has preferred a different course. In requesting an interview with him, I wanted to know why. And I wanted to
know what had happened to his evangelicalism in the process.

*As a young person in your formative years, what were the aspects of evangelicalism that
you found most appealing?*

When I started out on my Christian journey, I was not aware that I had
started attending an evangelical church. It was only much later, when I came

into contact with other types of Anglicanism, that I became aware of the specific nature of the tradition that had formed me. As some will know, I came from an unchurched background although my mother and father were devout, godly people. My brother, Bob, was the first person to start attending church and he introduced me to the church and organized Christianity when I was about seventeen. Although the worship was quite traditional, the Book of Common Prayer alone on offer, I was impressed by the liveliness of the preaching which was thoroughly biblical, and its definite commitment to evangelism. There was no denying the clarity of the gospel message which was life-transforming. Christianity in that church was a serious business and light-heartedness was not an option.

Looking back now, I can see more clearly than ever that I was also deeply attracted by the quality of its young people's work. There was a midweek discussion group called Christian Endeavour, a youth club on Monday and, following the evening service, we all trooped round to the curate's house for more fellowship and discussion.

Are there any priorities that were acquired at that time that still remain priorities both in your personal life and in your role as Archbishop?

Soon after committing my life to Christ, I developed the habit of having a 'quiet time', centring on reading and reflecting on the Bible. That remains the basis of my spirituality, even though it has broadened out to take in silence, meditation, and the sacrament of Holy Communion. A second priority is an emphasis on preaching which calls for a verdict, as well as preaching that is thoughtful, biblical and related to questions of our day. Third, I still remain convinced that young people must be central to the strategy of the local church and, indeed, a significant element of church growth.

Have there been specific times in your life which have prompted you to build a little distance between yourself and the evangelical tribe? I am thinking of your choice of theological colleges, your choice to specialize in ecumenism as a member of General Synod (including membership of the Faith and Order Advisory Group), and your willingness to affirm modern methods of biblical criticism of which many evangelicals remain suspicious.

I still remain deeply evangelical in the heart of my being, but I have come to cherish other traditions in the Church as well. Quite early on in my pilgrimage I moved away from the view that held that one particular brand of evangelicalism was the sole repository of truth.

For example, when I was accepted for training for the ordained ministry, my vicar, the Rev. E. C. G. Patterson (Pit Pat as we knew him) wanted me to go to Tyndale Hall, Bristol, where he was sure I would get 'a truly reformed evangelical theological education'. I went to visit Tyndale Hall and was very impressed by the quality of the teaching staff and the commitment of the students, but I did not feel it was right for me. I remember feeling troubled that its distinctive focus on Reformation theology, with which I was in broad sympathy, could result in a narrow ecclesiology. So, for better for worse, I rejected my vicar's advice. I went to look at the London College of Divinity and found such a refreshing openness and sense of fun there that I went back to look at it for a second time. I sat in on some lectures and found its vigorous commitment to Scripture, together with an openness to God's truth, as found in our different traditions, deeply attractive. I had no hesitation in choosing it.

A second example comes to mind. I went to serve as curate to St Mary's, Islington, an impeccable evangelical church, with Prebendary Peter Johnston, who was then its vicar. Peter was a most remarkable pastor and I learned a lot from him. During my curacy I started to read for an M.Th. at Kings College, London, with Dr H. G. Macdonald, Vice Principal of London Bible College, as my supervisor. As I was specializing in patristic theology, I got to know Professor Eric Mascall at Kings College quite well. I found myself increasingly being challenged by non-evangelical scholarship and influenced by non-evangelical spirituality, but, rather than shaking my faith, I found it being enriched by them. As my theological awareness deepened, so I found myself resisting the narrowness, superficiality of thinking and prejudice that so often go with an unwillingness to face up to challenging ideas.

It was largely as a result of patristic theology that I began to take an interest in ecumenical theology. During the heady sixties, alongside the cultural revolution which was going on in music and the arts, the Roman Catholic Church was undergoing revolution. The supposedly 'caretaker' Pope, John XXIII, called the Second Vatican Council. By 1966 I was on the staff of Oak Hill College, and found myself representing evangelicals in several ecumenical bodies. Although I had no doubts about the rightness of the European Reformation, and my commitment to justification by faith remained real and unshakeable, nevertheless it became clear to me that God was at work ecumenically.

As I got to know Christians from other great Churches, I found myself warming to their Christian story. It was a moment of truth for me to listen to a deeply moving story of faith from a Roman Catholic nun. My understanding of faith was broadening and deepening as I encountered the faith of Christians in other Churches. This in turn was to lead to a revised understanding of ecumenism and a deepening appreciation of other Churches.

Such encounters were to lead in time to real tussles with some of my evangelical friends whose interpretation of the Bible I found too rigid. I saw no reason to avoid hard questions because if Christ is the 'Truth' then all truth belongs to him.

How did you come to terms with following illustrious evangelical names such as Jim Packer and Alec Motyer at Trinity Bristol?

It seems to be my lot to follow distinguished people. You have to remember that I came from a very unlikely background for someone entering the ordained ministry, and that I had to work at it every step of the way. One of the things I learnt early on was to trust God's grace and to look more to that than to the challenges I faced. When I became principal at Trinity in 1982, the college was facing major difficulties. It needed 117 students to break even but that year it only had ninety-six, of whom less than half were training for ordination. As a result it was facing a £100,000 deficit, and just at a time when large sums needed to be spent on improving the accommodation. What is more, the different councils of the three colleges that had merged to form Trinity were not yet working well together. My task was to build it up and give a new sense of united vision. It was a time of deep challenge and personal growth for myself, as well as, I'm sure, for others.

In the debate about evangelical identity, the terms 'evangelical Anglican' and 'Anglican evangelical' have become codes for different approaches and even ecclesiologies. What do you see as the difference between the two, and are the terms helpful?

To evangelicals, these questions about identity are central. We must be clear that we are baptized into the Church and that our fundamental commitment is to the body of Christ, not to a particular tradition within that body. To focus on a tradition as the primary point of self identity, is to make the Corinthian mistake which was to focus on parties with their respective cries of 'I follow Paul', 'I follow Apollos', 'I follow Peter', 'I follow Christ'. Paul counters these with a theology we all need to heed: 'Was it Paul who died on the cross for you? Were you baptized as Paul's disciples?' We are all baptized into Christ and are members of his body and submit to its discipline. I don't find these terms helpful because the distinction confuses a tradition with an ecclesiology. The sixteenth-century Elizabethan Settlement was an explicit recognition of the breadth of the Church of England which, at that time as now, included more than one tradition.

How would you like to see evangelicalism develop within the Church of England (and the Anglican Communion for that matter)? What special contributions does it have to offer? What problems need to be overcome in order to become more effective in making that contribution?

Since Keele in 1967, we have seen evangelicals developing in confidence and moving into significant positions of leadership in the Church. This has come about for various reasons.

First, the important work of the evangelical colleges in promoting evangelical scholarship. Here I think particularly of the contribution of people like John Stott, Michael Green, Colin Buchanan, Jim Packer, Alan Stibbs, Tom Wright and many more besides. Alongside these there has been the valuable and quiet work of places such as Tyndale House in Cambridge, where generations of evangelical scholars have been nurtured and prepared their Ph.D.s. I include myself among them because the early years of my doctorate were prepared there.

Second, the large numbers of ordinands coming from evangelical churches who are gradually changing the composition of many deaneries and dioceses.

Third, the increasing involvement of evangelical laity at the highest levels in the councils of the Church, both at national and diocesan levels. I think, for instance, of Professor Sir Norman Anderson, who died in 1994.

And fourth, the distinctive contribution of the charismatic movement to the Church. Although this movement cannot be limited to evangelicals, it is a fact that they, more than any other tradition, have embraced it and been enriched by it. Rather by surprise and somewhat unwilling, I was deeply influenced in the seventies by the charismatic movement and it revolutionized my ministry. Its contribution to the Church has not only been at the level of a new appreciation of the Spirit in theology but also 'every member ministry'; enthusiasm and joy in worship; new forms of liturgy and music; and, perhaps most significantly for evangelical charismatics, a deeper appreciation of the 'sacramental' in worship and life. In many cases, this led to deeper awareness of the importance of the sacraments of the Church.

Today, from this position of relative numerical strength, I think evangelicalism could have a deepening significance for the Church of England and the Anglican Communion if it focused still more on the following elements.

First, serious commitment to biblical scholarship. Hermeneutical questions matter. Often, there is love of Scripture, particularly when applied devotionally and in expository preaching; but there is sometimes a failure to get to grips with many of the real biblical questions. Often, evangelicals have not been able to debate adequately with their liberal counterparts because of an unwillingness to address the hard questions.

Second, a commitment to ecclesiology and the traditions of the Church. My years of study in patristic theology made me well aware that one cannot simply jump from the Bible to the Reformation period as if fifteen centuries of Christian development count for nothing. There needs to be a more serious commitment to studying the continuity of the faith and the value of traditions in worship and the life of the Church. Evangelicals have often had a firm hold on the congregational aspects of ecclesiology, but a true understanding of catholicity should be embraced with greater commitment and joy.

Third, the life, flair and excitement of authentic evangelicalism has so much to give to the Anglican tradition. In particular, in my visits to different parts of the Anglican Communion, I have become increasingly aware of the commitment of evangelicals over the years to the mission of the Church. It's a story of rich adventure and the love of Christ. It still has much to give. We need this same evangelistic zeal to be present in every part of the Church, and for evangelicals to join their insights to those of other traditions, perhaps in the pattern we have modelled with Springboard.

*In your essays on 'Parties in the Church' (*Theology, *1987) you offered the metaphor of the Church being a chariot pulled by three horses: liberal openness to current questions, catholic continuity, and evangelical proclamation. What do you say to evangelicals who lay claim to more than simply being regarded as one legitimate 'part'? Do you share hopes that* *it might be possible to get the different traditions to begin to work together based on this understanding of the Church, and how might this be achieved?*

On the first part of your question, I would say to these evangelicals, 'Each part is equally valuable.' Evangelicalism, like the other traditions, has chosen to focus on certain elements which it regards as of the *'esse'* of the Church, and to put into second place elements that those other traditions regard as crucial. Such an approach comes dangerously close to unchurching other traditions. I remain convinced that the gospel is bigger than any single understanding of it. Similarly, the Church is far more extensive than any one tradition's knowledge of it. What is required of us all is humility in the light of the wonder of the message we share; and the need to be generous to one another in discovering new insights into the Christian faith as we travel together.

The second part of the question seems to assume that we are doing nothing at the present moment. I am grateful to God that the former hostility and bitterness between the traditions has, on the whole, diminished over the last twenty-five years or so. In the present House of Bishops, there is such collegiality, friendship, and commitment to Christ that one hardly notices traditional divisions. When they do appear, there is a recognition that our common membership of the body of Christ transcends our differences, however passionate our disagreements may be.

At the heart of a deepening unity among those who most sharply stand apart is the challenge to work more closely together and confront the differences with honesty and love. I would suggest that a growth in understanding must be based, not just on the doctrine of the Church, but on the nature of the Christian faith as a whole. It is often the way that, as we worship and pray together, we are led to a deeper knowledge of the faith of the other person.

To give a personal example, soon after I was appointed Bishop of Bath and Wells I was invited to lead a pilgrimage of Anglo-Catholics to Walsingham in 1988. I was initially very uncertain about this and was minded to refuse. However, as I thought and prayed about it I became aware that I knew next to nothing about Walsingham and that most of my views had been formed through polemical writings attacking the catholic wing of the Church. I felt I had a responsibility as a diocesan bishop to affirm and build up those Anglicans who might come from a different theological background to my own. I accepted with the condition that I could lead the pilgrimage in my own style.

The pilgrimage had a twofold effect on me. First, I saw how little I had really known about Walsingham and I became aware how profoundly incarnational the place was. I learned much which has enriched my own spirituality through the visit. Second, I was given the opportunity to root the pilgrimage thoroughly in Scripture. This was deeply appreciated. All of us returning home felt more strongly a sense of being transformed into the image of Christ. This had only been possible because the two different traditions had engaged with each other. I believe that pattern has profound and exciting possibilities for the Church in the decades to come.

Comments

Dr Carey took office as Archbishop of Canterbury at the relatively young age of fifty-four. Archbishops have to retire at seventy, so should he wish to serve out his full term, he still has plenty of time left to leave his particular mark on the Church of England.

The approaching end of the millennium offers a sense of focus that is not always a natural characteristic of archiepiscopates. Dr Carey inherited the Lambeth Conference's call for a Decade of Evangelism in the closing years of this millennium. He grasped this with both hands. One initiative was to recruit Bishop Michael Marshall and Canon Michael Green to create Springboard, aimed at building up the confidence of the Church in evangelistic endeavour. Many of his weekends in Canterbury diocese are spent leading parish teaching and evangelistic missions.

There was a broad consensus, too, that the cumbersome structures of the Church of England needed a radical overhaul to bring it into the twenty-first century. The failures of the Church Commissioners and the financial crisis that followed have made it a lot easier to outmanoeuvre vested interests that would once have rendered change impossible. The upshot was the so-called Turnbull Commission whose report, *Working as One Body*, recommended root and branch reform of the Church's national structures. The report's most controversial recommendation was the creation of a National Council to co-ordinate the functions of the national Church. This was subsequently modified and now this body will be known as the Archbishops' Council, with the Archbishop of York working in tandem with Canterbury. This, nevertheless, is a path to centralization of power in an era when most large corporations and institutions find they have no option but to decentralize. Another irony is that it is envisaged that the Church Commissioners should retain their role as guardian of the Church's investments despite spectacular failures in that role.

With parishes being asked to prepare mission statements and undertake mission audits, with diocesan and national systems being re-geared according to the criteria of how effective they are in serving the mission of the parishes, the general tide in is flowing in a way that will please a lot of evangelicals. But a nagging question remains. The parish itself needs a serious overhaul if it is to be an instrument of mission. And in any case, are parishes the only legitimate mission 'front line'? By gearing its national bodies primarily to their service, it may be that the Church of England will find itself retreating from other important 'front lines' that traditionally are the responsibility of a national church.

And we need to be cautious when we speak of an evangelical ascendancy.

We are witnessing a tidal movement that rather than bringing one party into ascendancy at the expense of another, signals a paradigm shift that will affect evangelicals as much as everyone else. In the process, some people nurtured in that tradition may well feel that the 'term' evangelical has outlived its usefulness. They will seek to work alongside those of other traditions and will gladly take on board characteristics that may have been absent in their own Christian formation. But if they turn their back on evangelicalism altogether, it will be left to those who will want to define it narrowly. They will get control of key evangelical institutions and operate them in partisan ways. For this reason, it is important that the identity of an evangelicalism that is gospel- and Bible-centred but at the same time open to other traditions is not blurred to the point where it is unrecognizable. While at this stage Dr Carey is keen to take evangelicals with him into a wider experience of the Church, he may yet be called on to offer leadership to the constituency to help ensure this blurring does not happen.

SECTION 2

LOOKING BACK

6

EVANGELICAL HISTORY:

THREE STEPS FORWARD AND THREE BACK

Evangelicals in the Church of England have never been a party. They have always been obstinate individualists – this is their strength, and in part also their weakness. (Bishop Stephen Neill, *Anglicanism*, Mowbray, pp. 190-1)

Haworth in the West Riding of Yorkshire is famous as home to the Brontes. But sixty years before this remarkable family went there, its vicarage was home of one of my favourite evangelicals. William Grimshaw came as parson to this windswept place in 1742. As the evangelical historian, G. R. Balleine, records, in his younger days he was a fairly typical eighteenth-century parson. He excelled as a huntsman, fisherman and at cards. An early biographer records how he 'refrained as much as possible from gross swearing unless in suitable company, and, when he got drunk, would sleep it out before he came home.' Alongside a hectic social round, he would read prayers and a sermon once every Sunday. But events in his life conspired to change William Grimshaw. When some parishioners asked him questions about their souls he found he could not answer truthfully. Then his wife died. Finally he discovered the writings of the Puritan, John Owen. By the time he came to Haworth he was a new man. His considerable energies had found a new direction. As Balleine put it, the once mighty hunter had become a hunter of souls.

Grimshaw found that the people of Haworth had a temperament to match their harsh surroundings. They were cussed and suspicious of strangers. Their motto was 'keep thysein to thysein'. The vicarage had been vacant for three years and the town had lapsed into heathenism. Funerals were held with no religious rites and yet another excuse for a drunken 'arvill'. Sunday was market day in nearby Bradford and those who stayed at home would entertain themselves with brawling football matches played on the moors.

The people soon found that their new parson could be every bit as strong-willed as they. It is said that the hymn before his sermons was always a long one, as often as not Psalm 119. 'It was his custom', records hymnwriter John Newton,

to leave the church, while the Psalm before the sermon was singing, to see if any were idling their time in the churchyard, the street, or the ale houses; and many of those he found he would drive into the church before him. A friend of mine passing a public house on the Lord's Day saw several persons jumping out of the windows and over a wall. He feared the house was on fire, but on inquiring what was the cause of the commotion he was told they saw the parson coming.

Leading lights in the evangelical revival, including the Wesleys and George Whitefield, came to Haworth to preach. On one occasion, the parson interrupted the oratory of Whitefield, 'I pray you do not flatter them. The greater part of them are going to hell with their eyes open.' The revival produced its own version of signs and wonders. On two occasions, Whitefield had no sooner announced his text, 'It is appointed unto man once to die, and after that the judgement', than a man standing near the front fell down dead.

For people who pleaded that their shabby clothes ruled out church attendance on Sunday mornings, Grimshaw established a more informal evening service. For those who said they lived too far away he developed a form of church planting, establishing barn services in four outlying centres. He was committed 100 per cent to Anglicanism. Yet he cooperated with the Methodists, working alongside the Wesleys, visiting Methodist 'classes'. He even set up a Meeting House in Haworth to ensure an evangelical succession in the village.

Naturally enough, his colourful style provoked complaints to the ecclesiastical authorities, and twice Grimshaw was investigated by the Archbishop of York. On the first occasion, the archbishop asked him how many communicants there were when he first came to Haworth. 'Twelve, my Lord,' was the answer. 'How many are there now?' was the next question. 'In the winter three to four hundred; and in the summer, near twelve hundred.' The prelate had no choice but to back such an effective parson.

Three Epochs

It is not the purpose of this chapter to give a detailed history of evangelicals in the Church of England. That has been done well enough elsewhere.[1] My aim in this chapter is to try to sketch some historical themes to help illuminate some of the questions debated today by evangelical Anglicans.

Observers of the evangelical story have discerned as many as four distinct epochs or waves where those of evangelical temperament rose to the verge of the dominant grouping in the Church of England, only to see that influence wane almost to nothing. In our present day, the evangelicals have reached a similar crossroad. The question is whether history will repeat itself. Is evangelicalism destined to become the key force in shaping the future of the Church of England, or is it destined always to function as a reforming force that is eventually overtaken by other forces and events? In this chapter, I will attempt to sketch the first three epochs in broad brush, and lay the ground for the evangelical growth seen in the Church of England since 1945.

The First Wave 1531-1633

Most histories of evangelicalism begin with the evangelical revival of the eighteenth century under George Whitefield and the Wesleys. In fact the word 'evangelical' predates this movement. It was first used by Sir Thomas More in 1531 to describe people whose way of life and framework of doctrine was firmly rooted in the Bible, in particular in the writings of St Paul.

Evangelicalism's first martyr was Thomas Bilney (1495-1531), a fellow of Trinity Hall in Cambridge, whose conversion story shares a lot in common with that of John Wesley. Having discovered Martin Luther's understanding of justification by grace through faith, he records how, 'Immediately I seemed inwardly to feel a marvellous comfort and quiet, so much so that my bruised bones leaped for joy.' For all that, Bilney remained a child of his times. He never questioned the place of the Pope in the ecclesiastical pecking order, nor did he reject such doctrines as transubstantiation. Yet he was to become the agent for the conversion of Bishop Hugh Latimer.

The conversion of Bilney heralded a flowering of evangelicalism that burgeoned for a quarter of a century before being cut short by the spectre of martyrdom. John Frith, William Tyndale, Nicholas Ridley and Thomas Cranmer, with Bilney, Latimer and some three hundred lesser known persons, paid for their evangelical faith with their lives in that bloody era. Many more fled to the safety of Northern Europe. Nevertheless, these early evangelicals did 'light a candle in England', to echo the dying words of Bishop Latimer.

For another half century, the influence of the evangelicals continued. Throughout the period, they gained strength from the continental Reformation but always steered their own particular course, being unwilling to subscribe fully, for example, to the Calvinist church government and its political outworkings. Most resisted radical calls to get rid of episcopal leadership or reject the role of the monarchy in Church as well as State.

Following the turbulence of the reign of Mary Tudor (1516-58), the nation was far from being at peace with itself. The competing forces of catholicism and protestantism were irreconcilable and Elizabeth I sought a middle way, allowing old rites and new to live side by side. It is undoubtedly true that the Elizabethan Settlement was a compromise. Yet it is wrong to portray it as lacking in principle. It succeeded in assuring national security. Moreover, it struck a delicate balance between the opposing 'catholic' and 'protestant' temperaments that formed the English religious psyche.

The death of Elizabeth and the succession of James I set the religious tide flowing in a different direction. Puritan opposition to the king grew, and the

Church of England hierarchy became a source of uncritical support of the monarch. The evangelical cause was to lie dormant for one hundred years.

ACHIEVEMENTS

There were, of course, significant achievements. In 1604 a meeting at Hampton Court between King James I and Puritan leaders saw agreement to publish the Authorized Version of the Bible. It had a huge influence on the development of English culture and language. Nevertheless, the Stuart period saw the collapse of both the monarch and the established Church.

Then, in due course, the Elizabethan Settlement was subject to serious theological attack, first by Roman Catholics and then by the Puritans. The legacy from these attacks is the best statements of the case for Anglicanism ever made. John Jewel (1522-71) wrote an *Apology* in which he defended Anglicanism against the charge that it had departed from the one true, holy, and catholic Church. There was no doubt that the English Church had turned its back on papal supremacy, but it had not departed from the essential faith of Christ and the apostles. Richard Hooker (1554-1600) wrote *Of the Laws of Ecclesiastical Polity* (1594-7), which is the classic statement against the Puritan attack. It helped establish Scripture, tradition and reason as the hallmarks of Anglican Church government, though it needs to be pointed out that Hooker did not put tradition and reason on equal footing with the Scriptures.

DECLINE

The mood of the Restoration period was not one in which evangelicalism could exercise a major influence. Whatever the case, the Restoration Church was not spared from troubles. The Act of Uniformity of 1662 divided English Christendom between conformists and nonconformists. Unlike opponents of women priests in the 1990s, who had a Financial Compensation Measure to buffer them, some 1,750 clergy were removed from their parishes without compensation and lived in abject poverty as they sought to serve their faithful people.

After the 1688 Glorious Revolution that put William of Orange and Mary on the throne, there emerged a form of 'practical Christianity' that lived alongside a rationalistic doctrine of deism. It was a world-view that cast the Creator as a divine watchmaker who, having set things in motion, had for all intents and purposes taken his leave. Personal passion reigned but religious enthusiasm was to be eschewed, as the novels of Fielding or the sketches of Hogarth amply testify.

There is an interesting parallel between the position of the Anglican Church now and during that period. The Roman Catholic Church has thrown up powerful and popular apologists, in the likes of Aidan Nichols, William Rees-Mogg, Piers Paul Reid and others, who are telling the English public that Anglicanism is fatally flawed by theological compromise.

Likewise, within many evangelical parishes there are now many of an Independent outlook who have little grounding in Anglicanism and are often hostile towards it. There is a crying need for a latter-day Jewel or Hooker to put a fresh and cogent case for Anglicanism.

The Second Wave 1735-99

We have already met William Grimshaw of Haworth. He is but one of many colourful evangelicals who helped radically change the face of the English Church for one hundred years from the first quarter of the eighteenth century. The story begins with the conversion in 1735 of twenty-year-old George Whitefield, a poor student at Pembroke College, Oxford. Five years of spiritual search and ascetic self-denial culminated in the experience of being 'born a new creature in Christ Jesus'. At twenty-one, he was ordained by the Bishop of Gloucester and the effect on congregations of his eloquent extempore preaching was electric.

Whitefield's message of new birth as opposed to the received wisdom of baptismal grace scandalized many clergy and he soon outlived his welcome in their pulpits. Returning from a first visit to America to a tide of opposition from the parsons of Bristol in 1738, he began to preach in the open air to the colliers of Kingswood. Within a month, his congregation had swollen to twenty thousand and Whitefield was signalling for help from a friend from his days in Oxford.

The story of John Wesley is well known and need not be repeated here. He was brought up as an austere High Churchman. After Oxford, he served a disastrous missionary term in Georgia under the auspices of the Society for the Propagation of the Gospel. With his brother Charles, Wesley embarked on a four-year partnership with Whitefield that ended in a passionate theological dispute between the Calvinist Whitefield and the Arminian Wesley. The Wesleys taught that Christ died for *all*, while Whitefield, following Calvin, insisted that the atonement was limited to the *elect*.

In the present day there are some Anglicans, for example in the diocese of Sydney, who would go all the way with Calvin and the Puritans in teaching a limited atonement. In England in the last thirty years, the influence of Puritanism on evangelical Anglicans has grown in some quarters but on the whole the position of evangelical Anglicans has moved towards that held by Wesley.

Whatever the case, the split between Whitefield and the Wesleys, while resolved at the personal level, was forerunner to the parting of the ways between evangelical Anglicans and Methodists. John Wesley's decision to ordain ministers, and to give his colleague, Coke, the status of bishop for oversight of the American connexion, finally made the gulf unbridgeable.

ACHIEVEMENTS

There is an ongoing debate among historians about the impact of the Wesleyan revival on Anglicanism. Nevertheless, two generations of the eighteenth century saw the emergence of rugged evangelical individualists who changed the whole temper of the Church of England. They maintained an undying commitment to the Church of England which Grimshaw, as we have seen, said was 'the soundest, purest and most apostolical'. In contrast to the Methodist connexion, they were not organized as a unit until the emergence under John Newton of the Eclectic Society, founded in 1783, which in due course gave birth to the Church Missionary Society.

The Third Wave: The Shaftesbury Bishops

As the older generation gave way to the next, the leadership reins were taken up by John Venn and the Clapham 'Saints', and Charles Simeon who served a highly strategic incumbency at Holy Trinity, Cambridge. Simeon was the inspiration of a generation of young evangelical clergy. By the strategy of buying parish freeholds and conveying right of nomination of a suitable incumbent, he sought the consolidation of the evangelical position within the established Church.

Leadership of the movement was mostly in the hands of well-born laymen, notably Anthony Ashley Cooper (1801-85), the seventh Earl of Shaftesbury (a much less rounded personality than is suggested in most evangelical hagiography). In the period, three evangelicals – Ryder of Gloucester, Charles and John Sumner – were elevated to the episcopal bench. The achievements of the period were immense. Evangelicals were instrumental in making the Church of England into a missionary church. Wilberforce and the Clapham Sect tenaciously led the fight to abolish slavery. Evangelicals were prime movers in factory reform and social legislation.

Even so, this was a period of mixed fortunes for evangelicals. Within two weeks of the abolition of slavery and the death of Wilberforce in 1833, John Keble preached his famous Assize sermon; and the Oxford Movement which emerged as a result became a prime mover in the life of the Church of England. That is not to say that the evangelicals of the latter half of the nineteenth century were not energetic. Under Shaftesbury, there was successful campaigning for factory reform. He founded his famous Ragged Schools and his legacy included involvement in six major evangelical societies: the Church Pastoral Aid Society, the Bible Society, the Church Missionary Society, the Colonial and Continental Church Society, the London Society for Promoting Christianity among the Jews, and the Religious Tract Society. Evangelicals continued to send out a stream of missionaries. Theological colleges were founded. Towards the end of the century, evangelicals supported the revivalist missions of Americans Moody and Sankey which attracted huge crowds.

For all that, the constituency was consistently unable to produce clergy of calibre to lead the Church of England at a point where its world was at their feet.

DECLINE

By the turn of the century, evangelicals were stronger in numbers than ever before. Indeed, as Colin Buchanan has pointed out, they were the strongest single force in the Church of England. As he notes, however, the second half of the nineteenth century is now to be seen as a period of decline, 'not so much a decline in numbers as in morale and confidence'. Evangelicals were beset from within and without. They had no answers to a High Church movement that was growing in confidence, changing the outward appearances of Anglicanism by wearing vestments, introducing Romish ritual, insisting on being called 'Father', claiming that they represented the Anglican mainstream. The 1874 Public Worship Regulation Act, Buchanan notes, 'far from being the point where the discipline was reasserted, became instead the point from which it was clear that the law could not be and would not be enforced against anglo-catholicism.'[2]

The evangelical response was an appeal to the ecclesiastical courts and the trial of Bishop Edward King, of Lincoln, in 1890. The upshot was victory in the narrow legal sense. But in the wider strategic sense, as Michael Saward points out, 'To the rest of the church, evangelicals were legalistic, narrow-minded, hard-faced bigots who were prepared to put their brother clergy in prison for trivial and sartorial reasons.'[3]

The threat from without came from the world of ideas. The anti-intellectualism of the Church of the period is summed up by stories of Bishop Samuel Wilberforce's debate with Charles Darwin and his concern that he had descended from monkeys. Evolution was but one of many issues of the mind that evangelicals were ill-equipped to face. Scholars were denying the inspiration of Scripture and the traditional evangelical formulation of substitutionary atonement. Lord Shaftesbury raised many a cheer from the evangelical gallery when he denounced one such work, *Ecce Homo*, as 'the most pestilential book ever vomited from the jaws of hell', but there were no substantial evangelical contributions to the debate. On the whole, evangelicals were not equipped to enter the scholarly debate about 'higher criticism'.

Scholastically and strategically they were out of the frame. As Colin Buchanan has pointed out, Archbishop Michael Ramsey's *From Gore to Temple*, covering the period 1889 to 1944, does not even notice an evangelical writer, let alone identify one who gained respect in the wider Church. As Colin Buchanan writes,

It was hardly surprising that the tendency was for the party to go half underground. It began to find its most characteristic expression in the Keswick

Convention, or even in the esoteric literature of Brethrenist eschatology or British Israelism or other forms of Dispensationalism.[4]

A major by-product was that the evangelical social conscience, which had wrought remarkable achievements in the time of Wilberforce, gradually became quietist.

It is no consolation to add that the overall fortunes of the Church of England were little better. The Great War, 1914-18, was a great watershed. Thousands of men who went to the front urged on by the bishops came home as practical atheists. Official church attendance statistics make it abundantly clear just how much the Great War was the start of a downward spiral in church attendance. Moreover, instead of having a vision for evangelism and national renewal, after the war the Church of England devoted its energy to a decade of fruitless liturgical revision. After World War II, the Church of England similarly missed a strategic opportunity. *Towards the Conversion of England*, a report commissioned by Archbishop William Temple, became a major best-seller with a succession of reprints. But instead of applying itself to its implementation, the Church of England opted to concentrate on re-building churches damaged by the blitz, and another largely fruitless exercise – grand-scale revision of Canon Law.

Meanwhile, the evangelical household consumed large amounts of energy in rending itself apart. Disputes over the reliability of the Bible triggered a split within the ranks of the Church Missionary Society and creation of the Bible Churchmen's Missionary Society (renamed as Crosslinks in the 1990s) in 1922. For all that, 'Liberal evangelicalism', so strongly opposed by the BCMS founders, faded from the scene in little more than a generation, though the trail of bitterness took longer to heal. Interestingly enough, debate about the authority and inspiration of the Bible is emerging again, but this time at least evangelicals have the benefit of hindsight.

The other episode that has etched itself on the evangelical corporate memory was the great Prayer Book controversy. In 1927, evangelicals did not have the numbers in the Church Assembly to stop its publication. Spurred on by the veteran Bishop of Manchester, E. A. Knox, they took the battle to Parliament where, amid appeals to the dislike of 'popery' that still inhabits the English psyche, it was twice defeated in the House of Commons. For decades, evangelicals had been disturbed by growth of 'Romanizing' tendencies in the Church of England. They had fought them in the ecclesiastical courts, winning the argument at times, only to find the bishops unwilling to back them up. Now they were faced with a revised Prayer Book with a distinctly 'catholic' flavour. The corporate memory of the events of 1927-8 is without doubt a huge factor as to why, to this day, a large majority of evangelicals favour the establishment of the Church of England in law. Research on the views of readers of the *Church of England*

Newspaper conducted in late 1994 found that a remarkable 58 per cent were in favour.

So what sort of people were the evangelicals of the inter-war years? We have already noted the views of Bishop Hensley Henson of Durham, stung no doubt by the Prayer Book issue. But the picture painted by Randle Manwaring, a layman who was a young man at the time of the Prayer Book controversy, is hardly more flattering.

> They were ... a separated people and their contact with non-Christians was minimal ... their subculture was of their own making ... they contributed little or nothing to political life or social well-being ... they regarded the ordained ministry and missionary work as the highest calling ... the evangelical Anglican was a very moral person, he paid 20 shillings in the pound, was hard working and a sound family man ... he liked sport and never went to the pub.[5]

And yet the evangelical fortune in the Church of England was about to rise again.

GREEN SHOOTS

There were two particular inter-war developments that helped make it possible for evangelicals to buck the trend of decline. The first was the foundation in 1938 of the Biblical Research Committee (a satellite of the Inter-Varsity Fellowship). Its aim was to face head-on the hard questions posed by critical biblical studies. Second was the activities of E. J. H. Nash, affectionately known as 'Bash', who organized camps in which there was an all-out effort to evangelize boys from some of the country's most prestigious schools. A number of these converts in due course became post-war evangelical leaders, notably John Stott and Dick Lucas.

Among the first-fruits of the Biblical Research Committee was the *New Bible Commentary* (1951) and the even more valuable *New Bible Dictionary* (1962). As Colin Buchanan notes,

> The emergence of serious literature about the Bible had an invigorating effect upon the men and women of those years. Perhaps their position did have academic respectability. The persons themselves came through the ancient universities, usually with war service or national service behind them, and often with ['Bash' camps] experience behind them. One of the characteristic features of their experience were that they were convinced of the gospel, which often had been harshly tested and found sufficient during their time in the armed forces ... And a great proportion of them were Anglican ... they reckoned that the Prayer Book and the Articles were generally on their side, and they went to work with simple faith and simple slogans ...[6]

The Christian Unions of Oxford and Cambridge produced a stream of ordinands. Numbers and confidence were boosted even further by the Billy Graham Crusades of 1954 and 1955. Even liberal criticisms of Graham's favourite slogan, 'the Bible says', turned to evangelical advantage. There were public debates about fundamentalism. And when Gabriel Hebert wrote *Fundamentalism and the Church of God* (SCM, 1957) attacking Billy Graham and some of the early publications of the Biblical Research Committee, evangelicals – used to being ignored at worst or subject of sneers at best – suddenly realized they held a position to be refuted. Such had not happened in more than a century. Evangelical apologetics made strides, thanks to the work of Cornelius Van Til and Francis Schaeffer.

The other key factor in changing the outlook of evangelicals in the Church of England was the initiative of John Stott in re-forming the Eclectics Society. It was open to clergy aged under forty. The only membership requirement was belief in the supreme authority of the Bible. Otherwise the character of discussion was 'no holds barred'. The Eclectics, says Colin Buchanan, were not simply content to test the foundations. They were

> impatient to build new and contemporary buildings upon them. They were folk who wanted policies. They wanted their theology to be applied. They were convinced Church of England persons. They were interested in reforming the Church of England instead of harking back to the Articles and the Prayer Book.[7]

It transpired that members of Eclectics had key roles in the 1967 Keele Congress, ushering in a whole new chapter in the way evangelicals expressed their Anglicanism.

It is noteworthy, however, that these developments contained seeds that were to grow into future conflict. To begin, alongside those evangelicals who wanted to be out-and-out Anglicans, there were those whose attitude was much more idealistic. They were by nature suspicious of the doctrinal plurality of a comprehensive Church. Moreover, as evangelicals got out of their trenches and began to march forward, numbers swelled. The constituency's ranks fanned out and at times some moved in different directions. When evangelicals were small in number and up against it, unity was hardly an issue. But when the constituency began to show signs of real diversity, there were those ready to cry 'foul' and retreat into a separate, idealistic world. We will see how this unfolded in the chapters that follow.

It is worth adding a comment about the way in which evangelicals have presented their history. Contemporary evangelicals are fond, for instance, of tracing their roots to Cranmer and the Reformation. But one question that needs to be asked is whether there is as much continuity as is often claimed. To what extent can we claim that Cranmer, Wesley, J. C. Ryle were proto-

John Stotts (or whoever else serves as an icon of evangelical Anglicanism in our present day)? A fair reading of the documents suggests that, alongside a sometimes slim line of continuity, there is plenty of discontinuity as well. For some temperaments that proposition is a threat. Others welcome it as the hallmark of a living tradition. This, then, is one of the major fault-lines that exists within contemporary evangelicalism. Those encamped on either side of this fault-line offer a radically different vision for the future of the constituency.

7

KEELE:

THE FOURTH WAVE?

> The NEAC animal has now been born. On the wet and windy campus of Keele University it showed itself to be a warm, friendly animal. Before it was more than a few hours old it had got its milk teeth firmly into issues like abortion and church unity and was sharpening its baby claws on 1662 and all that. It is now safe to say that whatever repercussions there may or may not be throughout the ecclesiastical jungle, evangelicalism can never be quite the same again. (The *Church of England Newspaper*, 14 April 1967)

For the generation of evangelical Anglicans who attended the National Evangelical Anglican Congress at Keele University in April 1967, this was their Vatican II. Through it they committed themselves to full engagement with the structures of the Church of England, to working constructively 'from the inside' rather than seeing themselves as a ginger group. Likewise, they affirmed ecumenism and serious engagement with social issues. It signalled a new openness, the start of a new period of creativity and confidence. But like Vatican II, Keele triggered a reaction whose force is only now becoming fully apparent.

For the Rev. Eddie Shirras, who was chairman of the Church of England Evangelical Council from 1989 to 1992, 'Keele was the conference when evangelicals in the Church of England came of age.'[1] It is a turn of phrase oft-repeated by Keele devotees. Bishop Colin Buchanan agrees with him. 'The major contribution was that it took the Church seriously, and it took the world seriously too.' Archbishop George Carey has used this phrase as well. 'At last we were prepared to enter the cerebral life of the Church and make a contribution to it,' he added.

Others tell a different story. Dr David Samuel, the former Director of the Church Society, once told me, 'What resulted from Keele was the exchange of clear-sighted idealism for a rather pragmatic, rule-of-thumb approach in which evangelicals engaged in the general free-for-all of the Church of England without any clear idea of where they were going.' Hugh Craig, who served successively as a lay member of the Church Assembly and General Synod from 1950 to 1995, claims that evangelicals were just as well represented on these bodies pre- and post-Keele. But whereas pre-Keele evangelicals had a clear agenda, post-Keele evangelicals tended to think that it was sufficient for them just to 'be there'.

The Keele story has been told fully and there is little point in going over the ground again. However, we must return to Keele if we wish to identify the fault lines that exist today among evangelical Anglicans.

Background to Keele

Far from being a crisis summit, a response to panic, there was an air of expectation in the months leading up to Keele. A number of younger evangelicals were organizing together to open up Keele to their concerns. Eclectics, reformed in 1955 under the leadership of John Stott, had produced a new breed of young evangelicals. Many of the Eclectics were former 'Bash campers' (see previous chapter).

Northern Origins

The move to hold a national congress of evangelicals began not in London, but in the northern province. A key player was Raymond Turvey, the gifted Vicar of St George's, Leeds, whose ministry had been transformed by the influence of Billy Graham in the mid-1950s. In the early 1960s he found himself deeply concerned about the isolation of evangelical clergy, particularly those on his side of the Pennines. On the western side, the legacy of the Reformation, the persistence of influential Roman Catholic families, and the immigration of Irish people via the Lancashire ports, left a Church of England with a decidedly protestant flavour. Accordingly, there were proportionately more evangelical clergy and parishes than in most other parts of England. By comparison, north-eastern evangelicals were thin on the ground. Raymond Turvey linked up with a few clergy from the north west, and it was decided to hold a Northern Evangelical Congress in York in 1963. They were all agreed on one thing. It was important to keep it in the hands of the northern group.

There were three factors in play here. First, there was the usual northern independence of mind. Then, there was a healthy suspicion of the various 'London-based' agencies that normally claimed to speak and act for evangelicals. Finally, as always, the evangelical tendency not to work under a single, united umbrella was undoubtedly in play.

This 1963 Northern Congress was a great success, both in numbers and content. From the final plenary session came the call for another in 1965. More significantly, there came from the floor a proposal by James Ayer, Vicar of Cheadle, for a National Congress. It was agreed that Colin Craston, Vicar of St Paul's, Deansbank, Bolton, should sound out John Stott, who was due to preach in Bolton a few weeks later. Stott was enthusiastic and planning for Keele began.

The Keele Statement

Keele took place in a climate where evangelicalism was becoming more vigorous, and where individuals were becoming involved in the church structures; deanery, diocesan and national. Far from being an event that radically altered the direction of evangelicalism, it largely confirmed the course ahead.

Nevertheless, its importance lies in the inspiration it gave to younger clergy and lay people; the way it confirmed John Stott's honorary leadership; and the fact that here was a rallying point for future evangelical involvement in the Church of England.

Today, much of the content of the Keele Statement seems quite unremarkable. Some of its concerns are to do with long-forgotten episodes such as the Anglican Methodist Unity Scheme, or proposals to equalize the numbers of laity and clergy on General Synod. Its calls for modern liturgy, the involvement of Christians in social action, or its passing reference to the charismatic movement are superfluous in the 1990s where the majority have long since made progress on these issues.

Yet, there were three crucial sections of the Keele statement on which evangelicals were to influence the Church of England to move forward in the years that followed.

The World

First, 'The Church and the World', (section 3) put social justice at the forefront of evangelical concerns. Evangelicalism had a reputation for being pietistic and individualistic, unconcerned for the needs of the world, placing a greater emphasis on personal salvation. Keele set an agenda for Christian involvement in politics, welfare, education, work and leisure, and the international sphere. This was taken up widely during the years that followed. We will look at this issue in more depth in Chapter 14.

Worship

Second, 'The Church and Its Worship', (section 5) acknowledged that evangelicals had 'failed to learn from other parts of God's church'. Most importantly, this admission led the statement to call for modern language liturgies. The exclusive evangelical loyalty to the 1662 Prayer Book was abandoned and experimentation welcomed. Evangelicals like Colin Buchanan played a key national role in this development.

Another major change was the renewed commitment to the Eucharist reflected in the Statement. While it emphasized the priority of preaching, it brought the Lord's Supper back to the centre of Church life. The statement went on: '... we have let the sacrament be pushed to the outer fringes of church life, and the ministry of the Word be divorced from it ... We determine to work towards the practice of a weekly celebration of the sacrament as the central corporate service of the church...'[2]

Unity

Third, 'The Church and Its Unity' (section 6) firmly committed evangelicals to the Church of England and to ecumenical dialogue with the Free Churches and even the Roman Catholic Church.

> The chaos in doctrinal matters in the Church of England today, causes us both grief and shame. We reject the current tendency towards Christian agnosticism over the fundamentals of the Gospel. In the face of this situation, it is reform that we desire not separation.[3]

For nearly thirty years, this rejection of secessionist tendencies held evangelicals in the Church of England firmly together in commitment to unity.

Furthermore, the Statement led many evangelicals into ecumenical dialogue. While evangelical Anglicans had been involved with dialogue through the Evangelical Alliance, with evangelicals in the Free Churches, they had seldom countenanced similar discussions with the Roman Catholic Church. Yet the statement welcomed new possibilities of dialogue 'on the basis of Scripture' and recognized that Roman Catholics shared 'many fundamental doctrines in common with ourselves'.

IDEALISM VERSUS PRAGMATISM

One of the most thoughtful challenges to evangelicals made following Keele came from the Rev. David Paton, a former missionary in China, who served with distinction as Secretary of the Board of Mission and Unity. 'Have evangelicals fully grasped that to play a real part in the Church of England involves taking very seriously... the existence and views of those who are not evangelical?' The answer of Keele devotees would be 'yes'.

A good example is the part played by evangelicals in liturgical revision. During the 1970s they supported changes to the liturgy which saw the removal of Cranmer's 'protestant' presentation of the service of Holy Communion. Some would say that for their own part they are more at ease with Cranmer's theology but that the teaching of the Alternative Service Book speaks more readily to the contemporary scene. For the critics, however, the cost was erosion of principles that were distinctly evangelical and protestant.

The same thinking underlies issues like vestments and the way Holy Communion is celebrated. An earlier generation of evangelicals used the Church courts in a vain endeavour to halt the use of vestments. With their arm strengthened by agreement by the Church Assembly that vestments had no theological meaning in themselves, post-Keele clergy were happy to go to parishes where vestments were part of the tradition, and wore them instead of trying to ring divisive changes. Likewise they were willing to abandon the traditional 'north side' position for presiding at Communion. For the pragmatic, this opened up opportunities for evangelicals to be accepted in places where this would have been impossible in the inter-war years. It was a line of pragmatism fuelled by realization that while there was a finite number of parishes that were traditionally evangelical, the numbers of evangelical ordinands were burgeoning.

'OPEN' VERSUS 'CLASSICAL' EVANGELICALISM

In the old scheme of things, evangelicals saw themselves involved in battle. They saw themselves aligned with the conservatives against the liberals and with purists against ritualists. Through Keele a realignment already taking place within evangelicalism was recognized.

This realignment is certainly evident in the field of biblical studies. It is currently gathering strength led by thinkers such as John Goldingay, Tony Thistelton, Alister McGrath, Richard Burridge, Dick France and Tom Wright. They are willing to use the tools of biblical studies such as literary criticism and redaction that were created originally by liberals. It is already of enormous influence.

Likewise, a lot of sting has gone out of the ritualist debate which put a great gulf between evangelicals and the more catholic-minded. Growing numbers of 'catholic' churches have found it helpful to embrace the *Mission Praise* hymnbook, while evangelicals have seen the point of giving more attention to creation and incarnational theology. Growing numbers see the point of vestments and drama in an age that is more visual than literary. Indeed, some prefer to be called 'reformed catholics' or even 'evangelical catholics'.

ANGLICANISM VERSUS PAN-EVANGELICALISM?

Part of the immediate backdrop to Keele was the dramatic call by Dr Martyn Lloyd-Jones, Minister of Westminster Chapel in London, for evangelicals to leave their denominations and form a national evangelical Church. This call took place at the National Assembly of Evangelicals in October 1966. 'I make this appeal to you evangelical people this evening,' said the Doctor.

> What reasons have we for not coming together? Some say we will miss evangelistic opportunities if we leave our denominations, but I say 'Where is the Holy Spirit?' . . . You cannot justify your decision to remain in your denomination by saying that you maintain your independence. You cannot disassociate yourself from the Church to which you belong. This is a contradictory position, and one that the man on the street must find very hard to understand. Don't we feel the call to come together, not occasionally, but always?

The Rev. Dr John Stott, already widely recognized as the leader of evangelical Anglicans, who was chairing the meeting, rose in his place with a blunt and direct rebuke.

> I hope that no one will make a precipitate decision after this moving address. We are here to debate this subject and I believe history is against Dr Jones in that others have tried to do this very thing. I believe that Scripture is against him in that the remnant was within the Church and not outside it.

Despite Lloyd-Jones's successful worldwide Bible ministry from Westminster Chapel, and his increasing influence as a spokesman for Free Church evangelicals, his call provoked little response on the part of evangelicals in the Church of England. At the same meeting the Rev. Julian Charley, who served with distinction as a member of the Anglican-Roman Catholic International Commission (ARCIC), had suggested that Free Church evangelicals should consider becoming reconciled to the established Church.

The *Church of England Newspaper* labelled Dr Lloyd-Jones's proposition as 'barmy'. Moreover, those who knew Dr Lloyd-Jones were rightly doubtful about whether his organizational skills were up to getting the idea off the ground.

The idea of secession has emerged from time to time in evangelical discussions throughout most of this century, and significantly during the split in the 1920s. It was one of the issues discussed at the 'Facing the Future' conference of evangelicals held at Swanwick in February 1966. John Stott was present and without doubt it had a bearing on his response to Dr Lloyd-Jones.

All this had an inevitable impact on wider evangelical unity. In the years following Keele, communication successively broke down. Dr Lloyd-Jones excluded Anglicans from his Westminster Fellowship. Moreover, an alliance of Anglo-Catholics and evangelicals – for entirely different reasons – defeated the unity scheme with the Methodists in 1969.

A big loser was the Evangelical Alliance. Its influence and membership seriously waned. It did not begin to recover until the mid-1980s under the leadership of Clive Calver.

Yet for a minority of evangelicals Lloyd-Jones offered a serious option. The Anglo-Catholic party in General Synod seemed all-powerful. A small minority felt 'Romanizing' tendencies in the Church of England very keenly. The Rev. Reg Burrows of Newcastle, who left the Church of England in the wake of the vote to ordain women, always sympathized with the secessionist outlook. He wrote,

> Keele committed evangelicals to the biblical reformation of the Church of England. It also virtually ruled out the possibility of secession. What was not understood at the time, and has been little understood since, is that this

double commitment provided a very sticky wicket on which evangelicals were to bat for the next 20 years or so. The rejection of secession tended to make us too tolerant of wrong things in the Church. It sent out a signal to others that we were in to stay.[4]

Evangelicals, Burrows claimed, became negotiators rather than reformers as a result of the Keele settlement.

The emergence of the conservative evangelical grouping, Reform, may yet reverse this aspect of the Keele settlement. It openly counts itself to be evangelical first, and Anglican second. The Chairman of Reform, the Rev. Philip Hacking of Sheffield, has openly said that he and many of the members of Reform would leave the Church of England if homosexual practice amongst clergy became acceptable.

While the ordination of women vote, on 11 November 1992, seems to have dealt a death blow to conservative Anglo-Catholicism, it also threatens to divide evangelicals more deeply than ever, because members of Reform, at least, see that it opens the way to other innovations that are not consonant with Scripture.

Evangelicalism after Keele

It is worth hearing the other side of the argument. 'I wonder what sort of decline might have hit the Church of England if evangelicals had followed that call,' says Eddie Shirras. 'I think our contribution must be judged against that alternative.'

We have to conclude that Keele created an evangelicalism that could thrive in the life of the Church of England. Whereas in the 1940s and 1950s, Anglican evangelical churches were few and far between, and the number of evangelical ordinands was between 7 and 10 per cent, the growth of evangelicalism in the 1960s, 1970s and 1980s was steady and surprising.

Bishop Michael Baughen recalled:

> There was a sense of being beleaguered within a Church that seemed to be dominated by non-evangelicals. It was inevitable that there was to some extent a hard edge and a distrust of all who did not share what we felt to be the only expression of the truth.[5]

Over a period of time, the evangelical theological colleges began to grow. There was a growth of evangelical representation among the senior leadership of the Church of England. In 1987, there were just seven diocesan bishops who claimed to be evangelicals, seven suffragan bishops, three deans and thirteen archdeacons. At the end of 1994, there were thirteen diocesan bishops, thirteen suffragans, eight deans and twenty archdeacons. 'Who could possibly have foreseen the fact that we would actually have many evangelical archdeacons, deans and bishops and that there would be a strong evangelical representation within General Synod?' asks Michael Baughen.

For Bishop Colin Buchanan, the growth in evangelical numbers made penetration of the Church's structures inevitable. 'So there is little use asking whether it was a good or bad thing. On the other hand it was the only way that evangelicals could produce agendas for the whole Church of England and not simply speak shrilly to their own galleries.' An example here is the contribution of Grove Books, sometimes fondly referred to by people in the know as 'Buchanan Enterprises'. 'All the Grove Books publications have been devoted to writing an agenda for the whole Church, and not just that for defiant evangelicals,' he often says.

FAILURE OF EVANGELICALS AS A 'PARTY'
To some extent, criticisms of Keele – in particular that it failed to make the Church of England more evangelical – point just as much to a failure of evangelicals to work together for change. Even now that they are the single biggest grouping on the General Synod, they are far from cohesive. The best evangelical contributions are made by networks and rugged individuals rather than through any party mechanism. It suggests, as Stephen Neill noted long ago, that evangelicals are not really a 'party'. As much as anything else they are a group of tendencies and networks who may occasionally be persuaded to pull together, as for example with Mission England in 1984. So while Anglo-Catholics mobilized in opposition to unity with the Free Churches, and women priests, while gaining victories on liturgical developments; evangelicals appear to have been caught off guard by many of these debates.

This individualism among evangelicals has contributed greatly to the organizational problems of bodies such as the Church of England Evangelical Council and the Anglican Evangelical Assembly. Another effect is that while some evangelical elders would, for example, say that existence of the *Church of England Newspaper* is crucial for the life of the constituency, by no means all evangelicals buy and support it.

THE KEELE LEGACY
By the 1980s, it was clear that the agenda had moved on. Younger evangelical clergy and lay people took up the concerns of *Faith in the City* (1984) and made urban areas a priority for their life and ministry. Often without knowing it, they had taken up the agenda of Keele in their concern for social justice, their commitment to evangelism, and their willingness to work both within the Church of England and with other traditions. Indeed, as the number of evangelical ordinands grew, more young clergy entered the parishes of other traditions. The spirit of Keele became a permanent factor in the evangelical Anglican mindset.

IS THE KEELE SETTLEMENT SAFE?

For evangelicals under forty-five, the 1967 National Evangelical Anglican Congress (NEAC) is outside the range of memory. 'I've heard of Keele,' one young evangelical deacon told me recently. 'It is supposed to be a major evangelical conference in the sixties. But it has no influence on me, now.' Yet his commitment to ministry, to evangelicalism and to the Church of England is not to be doubted. Naturally enough, he does not share the folk memories of Keele of an older generation of clergy.

The wheel has come full circle. For twenty-seven years, the threat of secession was removed from the dialogue between evangelicals and the Church of England. In the process, evangelicals themselves have changed. Now it seems that at least a small minority is prepared to contemplate the great taboo.

Is it now time for another Keele – a mass gathering of evangelical Anglicans – to honestly face differences that have emerged since Keele, and to chart a course for the future? The issue is whether there is enough unity even to agree an outline agenda. There is a window of opportunity coming up with preparations for the 1998 Lambeth Conference. If there is another NEAC, there is little doubt that the processes, concerns and solutions will be different from those of 1967. The historic Keele Congress can never be repeated. I doubt, too, that its influence and decisiveness will ever be matched. But in every generation evangelicals need something like a Keele, to demonstrate the strength of numbers and to take counsel on what priorities they should pursue together.

8

CONVULSIVE TIMES:
IS THE TIDE GOING OUT?

Evangelicals are experiencing convulsive times . . . (Press release announcing the Evangelical Anglican Leaders' Conference, held Epiphany 1995)

The progress of evangelicalism in the Church of England has been immense in the last decade. George Carey, Peter Dawes, Patrick Harris, Michael Turnbull, Chris Mayfield, John Gladwin, Michael Nazir-Ali, John Perry, David Sheppard, Michael Baughen, Roy Williamson, John Taylor and Keith Sutton were given a place on the episcopal bench. That gave evangelicals arguably their strongest-ever representation there. Likewise there was a crop of evangelical suffragan bishops including in the present day: Roger Sainsbury, Hugo de Waal, Colin Scott, Graham Dow, Michael Gear, Ian Cundy, James Jones, John Finney, Colin Bennetts, Geoff Turner, Gavin Reid, and David Hallatt.

Moreover, the agenda of the Church of England has changed in a more evangelical direction in that period. Since Mission England (1984), which triggered initiatives in evangelism that went well beyond the usual evangelical enclaves, evangelism has been a priority subject. This culminated in the launch of the Decade of Evangelism and with it a network of people appointed to get plans for evangelism in place in most dioceses. As Colin Buchanan has noted, 'evangelicals not only found the official agenda pushing them in the right direction (which was an odd experience in itself), but also found themselves up in the vanguard helping set the route and round up the followers.'[1] The Archbishops of Canterbury and York created Springboard. Church planting – occasionally surrounded by controversy but mostly a process whereby hundreds of new congregations were created by existing parishes in places previously without a church presence – became part of the official agenda of the Church of England.

On the surface, at least, evangelicals in the Church of England seem to be enjoying the fairest wind experienced in over a century.

Yet various cracks that had been discernable within the evangelical constituency for some time are more visible. The opening of these cracks can be traced in developments since the Keele Congress of 1967 and owe a lot to the nature of evangelicalism itself.

Emergence of Reform

What made these cracks visible to the public eye was the emergence of a new conservative ginger group called Reform. It would be fair to say, however, that Reform's emergence is more a symptom than a cause of them. It was at great pains to claim that it was not a single-issue group and that its emergence after the vote for women was just coincidence. Its charter applies the concept of headship, plainly rejecting the notion of women taking charge of parishes, but it leaves room for ordained women in other spheres. Made up mainly of clergy from some of the larger evangelical parishes, Reform claimed that evangelicalism had become theologically woolly and morally flabby. It was sharply critical of diocesan policies that, they said, enlarged bishops' staffs and, through the quota, taxed theologically orthodox parishes in order to subsidize the stipends of clergy who denied key articles of faith.

Reform got off to a bumpy start. The first action to grab attention was circulation of a discussion paper by the Vicar of Jesmond (Newcastle), David Holloway, suggesting that parishes in sympathy with Reform should 'cap' quota payments, both as a protest against the tide of liberalism in the Church of England, and as a means of supporting an independent programme of evangelism and church planting.

This was a serious public relations 'glitch'. Reform was immediately seen as a campaign for quota-capping by a group of large, well-off churches. It did little to help its standing, particularly among parishes who depended on help via the quota. All this came to a head during a presentation about Reform during the May 1993 Anglican Evangelical Assembly.

There were numerous delegates who were well aware that the survival of their congregations over many years was in no small part due to the fact that neighbouring parishes of other traditions had willingly paid their quotas. That a group of big evangelical parishes were now threatening not to pay their full quota amounted to little more than a 'betrayal' of smaller evangelical churches, especially those set in poorer communities. In any case, many who were net givers to the 'parish share' system were willing to testify that doing so strengthened their position as evangelicals in the deanery and diocese. In the weeks that followed, it emerged that only a minority of the original membership of Reform were actually in favour of quota-capping.

There was anger, too, among those evangelicals who had taken the Keele call seriously. In a characteristically forthright article published in the *Church of England Newspaper* on 25 June 1993, Canon Michael Saward charged that the majority of the founders of Reform had stood at the perimeter of the Church of England for twenty-five years. They had held back when what was most needed was evangelicals who were willing to get stuck in. He chided them for what he said amounted to a sectarian outlook. 'Some have little effective link even within their deaneries. Their churches are often highly eclectic gatherings of the like-minded rather than parish church communities. That is why, to many Anglicans of other traditions, they are perceived as being basically sectarian in outlook.'

Canon Saward's piece was followed up by an open letter to members of Reform by (now Archdeacon) Pete Broadbent, a member of General Synod, then Vicar of Trinity St Michael, Harrow. Reform, he said, would have helped the evangelical cause by 'talking to the rest of us about how we might be prophetic to the Church at large without creating unnecessary dislike for evangelicals'. While being willing to concede faults on both sides, he called on members of Reform to stop calling their fellow evangelicals 'liberals', and not fall into line uncritically with an ultramontane Anglo-Catholic agenda which implied a completely different view of the Church than that affirmed by evangelicals. There was no doubt that evangelicalism had become numerically strong. The debate triggered by the emergence of Reform centred on whether that witness was spiritually strong as well.

In the wake of all this, the Chairman of the Church of England Evangelical Council, Prebendary Richard Bewes of All Souls, Langham Place, worked behind the scenes in a valiant endeavour to restore evangelical unity. One outcome was a conference called by the evangelical bishops. Held during Epiphany 1995, it attracted nearly 1,500 lay people and clergy. Whether it succeeded in clearing the air is to be doubted, but it was a promising start. Another initiative is a high-powered evangelical working party to look at homosexuality, another time bomb with implications for evangelical unity.

Since 11 November 1992, a cleavage which has been latent within the evangelical constituency for over a decade has come fully out into the open. In my view this is to be welcomed. In the past, the tendency has been not to talk. Now, for once, the different sides are confronting one another instead of merely engaging people of like mind. Some of the benefits were to be seen at the 1995 Evangelical Assembly, in particular in a public dialogue between the Rev. Wally Benn, a leading spokesman for Reform, and the Rev. Graham Cray, of Ridley College, Cambridge.

Reform and its like may still opt to leave the Church of England, but the trigger will not be women. Its leaders have put their marker down over the issue of homosexuality. We will see how that debate unfolds.

There were predictions that moves to legitimize gay relationships would follow on the heels of the ordination of women since it claimed that both causes used essentially the same hermeneutic.

Without doubt, Reform's main impact has been on the evangelical constituency itself. Up until its emergence, the prevailing dogma of the 'Keele' evangelicals was that they were poised to inherit the Church of England and that the only real impediment was an occasional local difficulty created by rather unenlightened conservatives. There was a peculiar reluctance to deal openly with divisive issues.

81

Caister

The Church of England Evangelical Council missed opportunities surrounding the 1988 Caister 'Celebration'. The *Church of England Newspaper*'s 'Taffy' cartoon summed it up. It depicted smiling people arriving home from Caister and being asked, 'But where's the beef?', an echo of a then current McDonald's advertising campaign criticizing other brands for lack of substance.

On the surface, Caister was an enormous show of evangelical strength. The attendance was twice that of Nottingham. What is clear in retrospect, however, is that it did evangelicalism no service by its failure to confront real differences. It meant, for example, that a lot of important evangelical voices – on a spectrum from George Carey to Philip Hacking – were not heard.

More importantly, it meant that evangelicalism went into the 1990s without a shared agenda. Crucially, as I have already noted, there was no evangelical preparation for the debate about the ordination of women four years later. It came as no surprise, then, that in the wake of that vote, the differences that had been simmering away came to the surface with compound interest.

Caister did, however, leave one important legacy that has continued to ring in the ears of evangelicals. Interestingly enough, the note was struck by a non-evangelical. Addressing the Celebration, the Archbishop of Canterbury, Dr Robert Runcie, challenged his hearers to take the doctrine of the Church much more seriously. The emergence of Reform, with accompanying threats by some to secede from the Church of England, has meant that at last evangelicals are taking up the ecclesiology debate and it is now a top agenda item.

Differences

During the 1980s, there were various episodes that were symptomatic of the emergence of serious differences between people who called themselves evangelical. One such event concerned the editorship of *Churchman*, an evangelical theological journal owned by the Church Society. In 1983, the Church Society decided to remove the journal's editorial team, made up mostly of 'open' evangelicals, and replace them with conservatives. The upshot was emergence of a rival journal, *Anvil*, supported by several of the Anglican theological colleges.

The rift effectively institutionalized the split within the constituency. Events in the Church of England Evangelical Council were again symptomatic of the difficulties besetting evangelicals. For almost five years, until 1993, the Council and its annual Anglican Evangelical Assembly lived in stalemate, ostensibly over constitutional issues. In fact it had more to do with a struggle for control. This effectively deprived evangelicals of a mechanism for agenda-making.

Factors creating diversity

NEO-PURITANISM

There are two distinct factors that help explain how it is that evangelicals got themselves into this situation. One is theological. In Chapter 7, on the Keele Congress, I traced the development of what might be termed 'open evangelicalism'. It is clear that since 1967 it has been the dominant influence. But it is not the only influence that flowed into evangelical Anglicanism and there are smaller, conservative groupings that possess a theological strength that is highly valuable.

One reason why Dr Martyn Lloyd-Jones could appeal to Anglicans, among others, to leave their denominations to form a pure evangelical association of churches was that he was confident that a sympathetic audience existed. For at the same time as the ecclesiology of 'open' evangelical Anglicanism was emerging, there were other evangelicals in the established Church who were eagerly quarrying Puritanism for a fresh vision of the Church.

In Dr James Packer, this new Anglican Puritanism possessed a heavyweight advocate. A generation of ordinands who heard his lectures at Trinity College Bristol are one of the discernable outcomes. Another is the emergence, under the auspices of Prebendary Dick Lucas, of St Helen's, Bishopsgate, in the City of London, of the highly influential Proclamation Trust, founded in 1986. The Proclamation Trust is cross-denominational, and through its conferences and advocates it models a modern form of the Puritan vision of the minister as Bible expositor.

A great many devotees of the Proclamation Trust are parish ministers who fairly typically stay aloof from Anglican structures. The inheritors of Keele, on the other hand, were inspired both to inhabit these structures and to work for reform from within. Little wonder, then, when the Church of England at large fails to discipline the former Bishop of Durham or take a firm stand on issues where biblical authority is seen to be at stake, that one of the reflexes of the conservative evangelicals is to insist that the efforts of their fellow evangelicals working in the structures of the Church of England are futile.

Agreeing to Differ

The other root of this turbulence besetting evangelicalism has to do with evangelical spirituality. The problem is not easy to pinpoint, but it is best illustrated by observing how other parties in the Church of England deal with differences when they emerge. At General Synod you will often see people who are broadly on the same 'side' disagreeing sharply and publicly on some issue. Afterwards you will see these same people talking jovially over a pint, having made up. There seems to be something about the nature of the evangelical psyche that finds it difficult to live with ambiguity or 'grey' areas.

Many are by nature idealists. They set themselves exacting standards. They are uncomfortable with the kind of pragmatism that is an essential requirement for those who want to 'get on' in a comprehensive Church. So, in the past, family rows among evangelicals have led to serious fractures.

Knowing that, there is always a strong temptation for leaders or representative groups to pursue a policy of appeasement rather than confront an issue and the personalities involved. For nearly a decade, until 1993, the leadership of the Church of England Evangelical Council seemed more concerned to present an image of evangelical unity than to confront differences that everyone knew existed. As recent history has shown, this has neither fostered real unity, nor has it prepared evangelicals to play their proper part in the life of the wider Church and nation.

TENSIONS WITHIN REFORM

There is an inbuilt tension over what Reform stands for. Adopting a 'reformist' stance to an institution implies being willing to stick with it in order to change it from within. At the same time, Reform has made it clear that there could come a point where it would urge its members to quit the Church of England. Its Chairman, Philip Hacking, of Fulwood (Sheffield), who is known nationally and internationally as Chairman of the Keswick Convention, has said on numerous occasions that he hopes to remain a Church of England man to his dying day. On the other hand, he is on the record for insisting that should the Church officially condone either the ordination of active homosexuals, or the blessing of homosexual unions, it would be a bridge too far.

I will discuss the pastoral issues at stake on the issue of homophile relationships, and comment on the state of the evangelical debate on this issue in Chapter 12. I simply note here that the Church of England is being pressed on two sides by two almost irresistible forces in sexual politics.

The Church's 'bush telegraph' indicates that there are numbers of clergy who live with same-sex partners. The Church has no way of knowing that they are not celibate except if they say so. At present, selectors from the Advisory Board for Ministry do not ask candidates for the ministry direct questions on whether they are gay or straight, celibate or sexually active. Even if they did, there is no way of knowing if someone is being economical with the truth. For years the Church of England has lived with a degree of ambiguity on this issue. Now the combination of conservative evangelicals who say there is no place for practising gays in the ranks of the clergy and a gay community that wants the Church to give its blessing to homophile relationships means it has little space for compromise.

There are evangelicals who are willing to live with ambiguity over the gay issue. Not so members of Reform. A leading member is the Rev. Tony Higton, of Hawkwell, Essex, who for many years has worked to see an explicit repudiation of homosexual relationships by the Church. Reform has a very low boiling point on this issue. Its apologists frequently point out, for instance, that while the House of Bishops' document *Issues in Human Sexuality* (1993) has some admirable features, it makes an unfortunate distinction between the standards of behaviour required of clergy and laity when it comes to homosexual practice.

The Lesbian and Gay Christian Movement is equally critical of that anomaly. It by no means speaks for all homophiles in the Church. It insists, nevertheless, that homophiles should be free to be open about their sexuality. Even though LGCM denies any direct involvement, the 'outing' campaign conducted by the radical Outrage! group is a direct assault on this situation of ambiguity and has strengthened the ability of the LGCM to negotiate with the leadership of the Church.

It is Reform's fear that acceptance of active homophile relationships will be accomplished by a drift of opinion and practice rather than by an explicit legislative act of the General Synod. The latter is improbable in the present climate, not least because neither of the Archbishops wants to see the national Church locked into a protracted public debate that would be far more acrimonious than the ordination of women debate. For their part, the Lesbian and Gay Christian Movement want the issue out in the open.

Underlying Tensions

Evangelicalism has been allowed to drift into these patches of turbulence without much help about how to distinguish symptoms and underlying causes. A lot of this turbulence goes wider than the evangelical constituency, and indeed wider even than the Church. It is symptomatic of wider trends in British society and the Western world in general. There are good reasons for not liking the term 'postmodernism', but it remains the best term we have to help us understand the wholesale changes we are witnessing.

First, the general landscape of Western culture has experienced a shift from what pertained over the last three hundred years, thanks to the Enlightenment. We are in a period of cultural transition and that it is accompanied by turbulence should not surprise us. Western culture has become a melting pot of new ways of thinking that are at odds with the assumptions that underpinned Enlightenment thought and lifestyle.

Second, these new ways of thinking are seriously challenging traditional wisdom and ideas about security. No longer do younger people have an implicit faith in rationalism, nor do they believe – as earlier generations did – that 'progress' is inevitable. The values of the market place prevail. Ideas about leadership and authority have changed. A generation has come along that is no longer deferential to people and institutions purely on the grounds of title or office. We have only to trace the way the public and the media have reacted to the British royal family over the past couple of years to discern this. The power of centralist institutions cannot be sustained. Future development of the electronic information superhighways will break even further the hold of institutions on individual thought and expression.

Third, religion is back. A wholesale change in attitudes to rationalism means that religion and spirituality are now more widely acceptable. But it cannot be assumed that people will necessarily embrace the faith of Christ. Truth has been relativized. The world has become a 'supermarketplace' of beliefs, and people trawl its aisles filling their trolleys as they please. Furthermore, many express the view that the God of the Christians is not good, that his cause has led to the repression of women and other minorities who do not 'fit in'.

Fourth, evangelicalism itself is undergoing changes because of this cultural shift. It could be argued, for instance, that evangelicalism as we have known it, grew out of a dialectic with the Enlightenment. You get a taste of this by looking at the style of apologetic employed by the Inter-Varsity Fellowship, an apologetic hammered out on the anvil of debate with rationalism. Now the ethos requires less emphasis on apologetics and more on issues of relationships, feelings and lifestyle.

An evangelicalism formed in the face of a rationalist climate now lives alongside a breed that has broadly the same gospel at its core but often seems to speak a different language altogether. Little wonder there are tensions about what evangelicalism is, and who will speak for evangelicals.

As far as the institutional Church is concerned, the result of all this change could be as far-reaching as the Reformation of the sixteenth century or the Enlightenment in the eighteenth. We should not be surprised, therefore, if there are more turbulent times to come. What evangelicals need is to reach an understanding of how they are going to operate and to resist the temptation of turning in anger on each other because things are difficult.

Let me offer several other brief comments.

REFORMING THE CHURCH
Reform speaks of the need to reform the Church of England. It is right. But in fact the process of reform has been underway for some time. The Church of England has already been radically changed, many would think for the better, in the last generation. There are many different 'players' and sources from which this urge for reform is derived. The question is whether evangelicals have ideas and models capable of commending themselves in a comprehensive Church that will become even more diverse as the forces of postmodernism bite deeper.

UNITY A MEANS, NOT AN END
The goal is the conversion of England and the reclaiming of Western Europe for Christianity in this generation, and a peaceful and sustainable future for the

whole earth. Evangelical unity in itself is not enough. Given the issues at stake, it will be important for evangelicals to make strategic alliances with other Christians who hold a biblical and credal faith. As Colin Buchanan has written:

> What is certain is that [evangelicals] all have to keep ... (and not taking myself too seriously) in touch with each other. And somehow the talk has got to penetrate beyond 'how can we live together in peace, and even be mutually supportive' to 'what are the gospel and basic principles which determine our ecclesiology and thus direct our practice? Can we possibly find godly springs of action which will make our being together not artificially adopted in an outward way, but truly come from the heart?'[2]

A WIDER PERSPECTIVE

If the search for unity is determined by gospel principles, then it must necessarily be wider than concern for mere evangelical unity. An interesting recent development in the United States is the emergence of Evangelicals and Catholics Together (ECT). Among the key players are Michael Novak, the Templeton prizewinner, and Charles Colson, founder of Prison Fellowship and formerly of Watergate fame. Dr J. I. Packer is also involved. Already there are the seeds of such a development in Britain.

The Movement for Christian Democracy, whose main inspirer is the Roman Catholic former MP, David Alton, is a coalition of evangelicals and Catholics working across party political lines.

In an Anglican context, Springboard – with Michael Marshall (an Anglo-Catholic) and Michael Green (a charismatic evangelical) working together – shows that it is possible to create a modus vivendi to promote the faith. It requires agreement not to be divided over inessentials. We need a version of ECT on this side of the Atlantic as a springboard for a new era of evangelism and social renewal.

Can Evangelicalism Weather the Storm?

Two initiatives have taken place to help find a way through this period of turbulence.

First, it has caused the evangelical constituency to realize that it must put its house in order. At last the Church of England Evangelical Council has got to work on shaping an agenda. It is an agenda that is grounded in a commitment to theological truth, based on the Scriptures and the creeds. It is an agenda that is willing to address clear differences: the understanding of the inspiration and authority of the Bible, the meaning and significance of ministry, the vocation of the laity, and the doctrine of the Church including the case for Anglicanism. To carry this agenda forward there will need to be a willingness to allow evangelicals to disagree over their differences on inessentials and if necessary follow different paths. The evangelical constituency has shown this to be possible; for example, in the way it dealt with the charismatic movement which in its own way threatened a split during the 1970s.

Since the early part of 1994, therefore, there have been a series of face-to-face discussions between representatives of 'open' evangelicalism and conservatives on issues like priesthood, ministry, and the place and interpretation of Scripture in the life of the Church. They have been carried out in a good spirit. Public dialogues between participants from each side have been a valuable exercise in fence mending. Differences remain, but there is better mutual understanding and a growing conviction that while evangelicals may come to different conclusions on important issues, they do so within a framework of willingness to believe what the Scriptures may be seen to teach.

Second, an important role has emerged for the evangelical bishops in offering leadership to the constituency in ways they have been loath to in the last decade and a half. We saw the first signs of this in the initiative of the evangelical bishops calling the Evangelical Anglican Leaders' Conference (EALC), held in London in Epiphany 1995. That nearly fifteen hundred evangelical clergy and laity attended was the clearest indication yet that the constituency – which in the past has tended to keep its bishops at arm's length – is now ready to accept their leadership. They were further reassured by the pledge from the Conference chairman, Bishop Michael Baughen of Chester, that he was in no mood for compromise on the gay issue. He offered a conference to discuss the issue further. He even went as far as saying it was an issue on which he himself would if necessary leave the Church of England.

The question is whether all this will be enough to see off a major split. The 1996 EALC offered a useful litmus test. In 1995, with crisis in the air, evangelicals had gathered in response to a call from the bishops for a united front. Underlying differences were discernable but the mood was optimistic. In 1996, despite a lot of behind-the-scenes dialogue, the conservatives by and large were conspicuous by their absence. Attendance was smaller and the bishops took a back seat to the academics.

It was clear that the EALC had largely become a platform for 'open' evangelicalism. What is more, afterwards both sides were openly admitting that evangelical Anglicanism consisted of two groupings. This is a point that many conservatives have been willing to concede for some time. Commenting on the conference, Dr Gerald Bray, a former tutor at Oak Hill Theological College who now teaches in the USA, said:

After EALC 1996 it will be obvious to all that there are at least two main groupings within the contemporary evangelical movement. One of these may be characterised as 'conservative' or 'traditional', and in many people's minds it is identified with Reform. The other would probably want to call itself 'open', and would include most of the organisers and principal speakers at the EALC. What is interesting and important about this year's conference is that the differences between the two groups were shown to be rooted in profound questions of biblical interpretation.[3]

Perhaps more important, however, is the fact that supporters of EALC were at last willing to concede that evangelical fragmentation was a reality. Canon John Moore, Director of the Church Pastoral Aid Society, commented:

> My guess is that those who take it that the Church of England is past repair were not there, and therefore they have been lost. Those who have some sympathy for Reform but didn't want to be too identified felt encouraged and affirmed. The rest were delighted to be associated with a movement with the quality of scholarship that was evident.[4]

It is clear that a strong dogmatic framework gives identity and cohesion to conservative forms of religion. The future of Reform is uncertain. Secession remains well and truly on the agenda. But there is another scenario. What binds those of a more 'open' outlook is not so clear. It is possible that some at least will go in various directions, in the process discarding the evangelical label. If that happens, there is every prospect that in time a conservative rump could become strong enough to take control of key evangelical institutions. I will give more attention to this scenario in the Epilogue to this book.

I now turn to a series of internal questions which are debating points within the evangelical constituency.

SECTION 3

THE PRESENT: SOME
CURRENT DEBATES

9

ESTABLISHMENT:

PRESERVING A CHRISTIAN SOCIETY?

The curiosity of the Anglican scene in the first decades of this century is that it was the old fashioned Protestant who stood for the medieval 'Catholic' view of the inclusive Church, the Anglo-Catholic who argued for the 'Protestant' view of a Church diminished by the explicit faith and commitment (signified by confirmation) of its members. (Adrian Hastings, *A History of English Christianity: 1920-1990*, Collins, 1991)

In December 1992, Waddingtons, the board game manufacturers, made national headlines. The company said it was about to update its murder-mystery game, *Cluedo*. In order to bring *Cluedo* into the twenty-first century, Waddingtons decided to drop the vicar, the Rev. Green, and replace him with a city businessman. It was a clever publicity stunt. It was also a trigger for columnists in a number of the national daily newspapers to lament the continuing loss of influence by the Church of England in national life. Much of the blame was laid at the door of the Alternative Service Book and an evangelical ascendancy which promotes 'folksy' or 'happy clappy' brands of worship.

It is simplistic in the extreme to attribute decline in church attendance and its influence in wider society to changes in its patterns of worship. Most of the critics who lambast the 'banality' of modern worship, in particular no-frills evangelical worship, have little or no first-hand experience of what they are talking about. Moreover, they cannot explain why evangelical churches which offer friendly and informal worship with good quality aftercare are growing numerically, whereas many of their traditionalist neighbours with highbrow musical traditions are not.

On the other hand, Graham Cray, the Principal of Ridley Hall Theological College, Cambridge, has pointed out that only about 40 per cent of the range of human personality types are catered for by the available range of church worship. There is therefore almost unlimited scope for experiment with new forms of worship aimed at particular target groups and personalities. Many evangelical parishes are at the forefront of experiment with new forms of parish worship aimed at reaching people who are presently beyond the fringes of church culture.

Nevertheless, the critics are right on one point: the Church of England no longer enjoys the power and prestige which it once held by right as the established Church. There have been some celebrated examples of this loss of influence in recent decades. During the monetary crisis in the late 1970s, Archbishop Donald Coggan asked to see Prime Minister James Callaghan. He was told the premier had no time to see him. There were few precedents for such a snub. The trend had been moving in that direction for most of the century. A couple of years later, 25 March 1980 was named months in advance as the date for the enthronement of Robert Runcie as 101st Archbishop of Canterbury. The government then announced the same date had been selected for Budget Day. On this occasion both Conservative and Labour politicians protested that this was going too far, and the date was changed. Prime Minister Margaret Thatcher attended the enthronement in Canterbury Cathedral.

The Church of England is 'established in law'. The monarch is its supreme governor. The rights and privileges of the Church are enshrined in law in the Act of Succession. Senior bishops have a place in the House of Lords as Lords spiritual. Every inch of the land forms part of a Church of England parish so that, in theory at least, every citizen may look to the Church of England for pastoral care, which includes the obligation to baptize, marry (where there are no legal impediments) and bury the dead. One in five of the country's children goes to a Church of England primary school.

During this century, the Church of England has become 'an internally self-governed Church'. The first major landmark in the process was the Enabling Act of 1919 which created a new Church Assembly with legislative authority delegated by Parliament. After years of neglect, since there was rarely parliamentary time for detailed church matters, a mechanism now existed to enable matters such as creation of new dioceses and liturgical revision.

It was a far cry from what the more radical voices had hoped for. 'We demand liberty for the Church of England,' William Temple declared. What the cool-headed Archbishop Randall Davidson negotiated was, 'not a constitutional change which was going to shatter the chains of an enslaved Church and emancipate us from a hampering bondage'.[1] It was, nevertheless, a workable piece of administrative machinery.

The second landmark was the creation of the General Synod, opened by the Queen in November 1970. The framework of the Synod was created by the Commission on Church-State Relations, chaired by Professor Owen Chadwick. Its recommendations struck at the heart of establishment in a way that earlier initiatives had failed to do. First, it said that General Synod, not Parliament, should have final authority in matters of worship and doctrine. Second, it sought to take away the right of the prime minister to choose bishops, suggesting instead creation of a committee made up of representatives from the diocese and the wider Church.

The former proposal duly went through without amendment. Not so procedures for the selection of bishops. Prime Minister James Callaghan insisted that, since senior bishops had a seat in the House of Lords, the premier should continue to have a say in their appointment. The result was a compromise: the creation of the Crown Appointments Commission, made up of representatives of the vacant diocese and the wider Church, whose task it was to forward two names in priority order to the prime minister, who would in turn forward one to the Queen.

It is interesting to note that the two church representatives who took the proposal to Mr Callaghan and negotiated the arrangement were two evangelicals: Archbishop Donald Coggan and Professor Sir Norman Anderson, Director of the Institute of Advanced Legal Studies of the University of London. Some contemporary critics of establishment have claimed that in their heart of hearts neither wanted the radical change proposed, certainly not if it came at the cost of losing the right of bishops to be members of the House of Lords.

Evangelical Views

On the face of it, establishment appears to be somewhat at odds with the normal evangelical view of the Church. One of the leading evangelical opponents of establishment is Bishop Colin Buchanan, now Bishop of Woolwich and one of the most colourful members of the General Synod of his generation. According to Buchanan, 'It is simply improper for the body of Christ to be so shackled to the secular state machine.' Is it right that the Church, which is eternal and stands for values often at odds with political power games and compromise, be subject to secular authority? Is it right that when the General Synod, after all the due processes, agrees changes in church rules (for example, that women can be ordained) an assortment of Ulster Unionists, members of Free Churches, Jews and agnostics should have the right to vote the legislation down? As to the choice of bishops, is it right that a prime minister who may be a member of a Free Church, or even a non-believer, should have the final say in the choice of the Archbishop of Canterbury?

While more Anglican evangelicals are prepared to openly question the establishment, the majority (and certainly the majority of evangelical bishops) remain in favour. They do so for a mixture of pragmatic and historical reasons.[2]

1. ACCESS TO THE STATE SYSTEM AND PEOPLE OF INFLUENCE

Nearly all the current evangelical bishops agree that the present system offers the Church advantages which would disappear if there was disestablishment. When asked for his views, the Bishop of Chester, Michael Baughen, drew a comparison with the prevailing situation in New Zealand where there has never been any form of establishment.

It was noticeable on my visit to Christchurch, New Zealand, that the Church had almost no involvement with the State at all. The Rotary Club there asked me to speak on 'What on earth is a Bishop doing in the House of Lords?' At the end they were frankly amazed at the amount of involvement we could bring to the political scene and somewhat envious of the position which they have lost in New Zealand.

Involvement in the state system by the Church of England is extensive. Beginning with the personal influence and contact which come of right to the Archbishop of Canterbury, it reaches all the way down the line with an official place for the Church of England in coronations, national observances, memorial services, school assemblies, and often a special place in the pecking order for the vicar on local civic occasions.

2. A SYMBOLIC FUNCTION, ACKNOWLEDGING THE SPIRITUAL DIMENSION

The former Bishop of Derby, Peter Dawes, believes that giving spiritual leaders a place as of right within the parliamentary system means that the State acknowledges that there is a spiritual dimension to life. Another advantage as far the Church is concerned, according to Bishop Dawes, is that when it wishes to voice some criticism in some secular field, it is not a critic speaking as an outsider. It is 'a critic from inside and one who basically wishes to work in partnership and support whatever the government of the day is, except where morally we feel that some issue is such that we must dissent'.

3. BREAKING THE CHURCH/STATE LINK WOULD BE AN EXPENSIVE UNNECESSARY DIVERSION

Oswald Clark, a former chairman of the House of Laity in the General Synod, believes that to completely disestablish the Church of England would require at least nine Acts of Parliament. The legislative package would have to range from revision of the way in which the monarch is seen as supreme governor of the Church of England, through to the abolition of the Church Commissioners (with loss of endowments should the Irish and Welsh precedents be followed).

For their part, most of the current crop of evangelical bishops believe that for the Church to initiate steps to break the establishment link would be a costly diversion from more urgent tasks. The former Archbishop of Canterbury, Lord Coggan, summed it up in these words:

To engage in a process of breaking the link would involve the Church in many years of debate. It would give the lawyers a field day. It would suggest to the man in the street that the Church is withdrawing from the battle, and that the historic Church of the country is little more than a sect. It would take years and I doubt whether its gains would be anything like as substantial as its proponents believe.

He further believes that now is not the time for such an undertaking, coming on the heels of a long and exhausting debate about the ordination of women and when the Church needs to focus on the Decade of Evangelism.

4. CORPORATE EVANGELICAL MEMORIES

Underlying what are essentially pragmatic arguments is a body of evangelical experience in history. While some evangelicals would want to make a distinction between their particular stance and protestantism, most see themselves as inheritors of the Reformation. In England, accepting the role of the monarch as supreme governor of the Church of England and all this entails is part of the package.

The growth of the Oxford Movement within the Church of England, beginning in the mid-nineteenth century, provoked an even stouter evangelical defence of establishment than had been enunciated in earlier decades. In the 1830s, Coleridge talked about the complementarity of Church and State. 'It is the duty of the State to establish the Christian religion,' declared an Albury Conference statement. According to the more pro-State evangelicals of the time, the priestly office of Christ was represented and made visible by the Church, while the State manifested his kingly office. This led to the creation of groups such as the Christian Influence Society (1832) and an Established Church Society (1834). Robust speeches in favour of establishment, by orators like Thomas Chalmers, attracted large London audiences. In the *Record* newspaper, evangelicals had a noisy advocate of establishmentarianism.

However, the biggest single factor which remains etched on evangelical corporate memory and still tends to clinch the conservative evangelical mind in favour of establishment is the legacy of the 1927 Prayer Book controversy. During the 1920s, there was a growing clamour for revision of the Prayer Book, particularly among Anglo-Catholics who wanted reservation of the sacrament to be regularized. In addition, they wanted to see Anglican liturgy brought more into line with developments in both the Western and Eastern Churches. For the more protestant-minded, even the thought of revising the 1662 Prayer Book was anathema. The Prayer Book was familiar in language and much loved. It represented England's protestant heritage. Any thought of subverting it with Romish ideas was enough to strike horror into evangelical hearts, suspicious already of the fact that some Anglicans were involved in doctrinal discussions with Rome in Malines in the late 1920s.

In fact, the new Prayer Book comfortably passed the Church Assembly, despite vociferous evangelical resistance. The focus of the battle to defeat it then became Parliament, and here the evangelicals had two effective lay hit men in the Home Secretary, Lancelot Joynson-Hicks, and the Solicitor

General, Lord Inskip. The necessary bill passed the House of Lords after a three-day debate. But it was a different story in the Commons where the debate was shorter, nowhere near as erudite, and the contribution of Joynson-Hicks, according to Archbishop Cosmo Lang of York, 'with great skill reached and inflamed all the latent Protestant prejudices in the House'. The House debated the Bill twice, in December 1927 and in June 1928. On both occasions a motley alliance of evangelicals, helped by Scots, Welsh and Ulstermen, saw it off.

It was a triumph for the eighty-year-old former Bishop of Manchester, Edward Knox, whose tireless efforts mustered a huge country-wide wave of opposition. More than 300,000 adult communicants signed the memorial against the new Prayer Book.

This affair created divisions among evangelicals. Once the result of the Church Assembly vote was known, some suggested that they should learn to live with the new Book. This viewpoint was upstaged by Knox, Joynson-Hicks and a more conservative group of evangelical hawks.

Defeat of the new Prayer Book in 1927 to 1928 did not greatly endear evangelicals to the rest of the Church of England and the wider Anglican Communion. And it was another generation before the green shoots of the recovery of evangelical fortune became visible. Yet there is a sizeable body of evangelicals who take comfort from the fact that if a future General Synod were to lead the Church astray over a vital matter of doctrine, then the continuing establishment of the Church of England in law means that a set of further safeguards exists which can be petitioned to defeat the offending measure. Whether that is a prudent position is another matter. A series of court judgements both here and overseas over the ordination of women have implied that the Church is a private society and that secular authority should not intrude in its doctrinal disputes.

RELATIONS WITH NON-ANGLICANS

It needs to be recorded that now, as in the last century, the pro-establishment view of influential evangelical Anglicans does constitute a barrier between them and evangelicals in other denominations. The nineteenth-century Congregationalist preacher, Thomas Binney, once declared that the established Church destroyed more souls than it had saved. Some of the statements of leaders of the so-called house churches have been of a similar flavour, though some of the stridency has gone now that the house churches are more widely accepted and have themselves taken on most of the characteristics of denominations.

While most of the current crop of evangelical bishops are broadly in favour of establishment, and would resist any attempt to bring forward a package of legislation to disestablish the Church of England, seeing such a venture as a diversion and waste of resources, most agree that future decades will see 'creeping' changes.

Most accept in principle the idea of all the major Christian denominations being represented in the House of Lords among the Lords spiritual. But bishops such as Michael Baughen of Chester would oppose widening representation among Lords spiritual beyond that to leaders of other faiths. This, they would maintain, is because the foundations of the country and constitution are primarily Christian. For the sake of consistency, if it were accepted that leaders of major denominations could become Lords spiritual, then this should open the way for Anglican clergy to be able to stand for the House of Commons, as is possible for other clergy.

BISHOPS IN THE LORDS

Another area ripe for reform is the fact that in practical terms a busy diocesan bishop has precious little time to give to parliamentary work. The Bishop of Chester favours a change whereby senior bishops, most of whom retire from their diocesan duties at sixty-five, might stay on in membership of the House of Lords until they reach seventy. Such an arrangement would create a group of experienced 'working' Lords spiritual, and give more substance to the contribution of the Church in national life and in the Parliament.

APPOINTING BISHOPS

Another area ready for change is the way bishops of the Church of England are chosen. Originally, the role of the monarch in the choice of bishops was supposed to symbolize the bishops being chosen by the laity. We have moved light years from that position.

As I have said before, what rankles from the Church's point of view is that it is possible, in theory at least, for a premier who may not be Anglican (indeed may not even be a Christian believer) to have the final choice in naming a bishop or archbishop. It is a good question whether future prime ministers will necessarily feel they must have this particular power. On such matters changes are, as much as anything, by arrangement. While there are rumblings from time to time, there are few signs that the Church is ready to launch a proposed change. For their part, most of the current evangelical bishops view the present system as a fair compromise which works well enough. That could change if, for example, there was a nakedly 'political' appointment which disregarded the Church's wishes.

A similar pragmatism on the part of the evangelical bishops has been evident about the prospect of the divorce and remarriage of the Prince of Wales as heir to the throne. Conservative Anglo-Catholics come to the subject of divorce with strong views, based on belief in the indissolubility of marriage. There is a range of views within the evangelical constituency and a great deal of the debate concerns the exact meaning of Jesus' teaching. However, the whole tenor of public statements by evangelical bishops in the wake of the announcement that the Prince and Princess of Wales had separated was that while marriage for life was God's ideal, those who fell still needed the Church's help and acceptance, not condemnation. There was a broad hint that even though the precedents are few, a way could be found to accommodate a remarried monarch and supreme governor of the Church of England. It is a sign, as much as anything else, that evangelical leaders prize the relationship with the monarchy and will not easily be persuaded to give it up.

It is certain that the attitudes of some conservative evangelicals to the monarchy and the establishment link would be sorely tested if a future monarch insisted that the coronation ceremony should have an interfaith element. The matter of inter faith worship and the monarch's involvement in the capacity of head of the commonwealth is a thorny issue. It is a major agenda item in an evangelical debate about whether or not the future strategy should be to insist on asserting Britain's Christian roots, or simply to compete for a hearing in the market place of different religions and philosophies. As evangelicals continue to debate these issues a clearer view of the future shape of establishment will emerge.

ADVANTAGES VERSUS DISADVANTAGES

While it is true that most of the evangelical bishops, however mutely, support establishment, there is a growing body of opinion among ordinary evangelicals that the disadvantages outweigh the advantages. There is a new breed of evangelical, and the overall proportion is growing, that cares little for the niceties of historic precedent. They argue that while it is cosy for the Church of England to claim to be there for the whole nation, this means very little in practice. Their view of the Church is strongly oriented to the congregation, and their leaders are more prepared to talk about 'catchment areas' than the parochial unit. They are schooled as much by ideas of church growth gleaned from the USA as by English theological colleges, and cannot see the point of parish boundaries which in demographic terms mean very little (especially in the cities). Yet these boundaries inhibit cooperation between neighbours in evangelism and allow clergy to act like little popes in their own domain.

The Church of England as established states the ideal that all citizens (even Jews, Muslims, Sikhs and Hindus) are under its pastoral care. But what does this mean in practice? Leaders of other faith communities have found it beneficial to have links with Church of England leaders in times of communal crisis. But few rank and file Jews, Muslims, Sikhs or Hindus are likely to express gratitude since such a statement contains mixed messages for them.

In a media age we see an increasing politicization of the Church. The media scrutinize every word and action of the archbishops. Because of the position of the Church in the state system, a simple statement about Christian truth suffers the possibility of having too much read into it and being made over-political. It is a heavy burden for the leadership of the Church. It fosters bland-ness on their part, and it means that the public does not necessarily have the ears to hear what is actually being said.

CONTRASTS WITH EUROPE

Finally, compared to the situation of other established Churches in Western Europe, establishment here brings all the disadvantages with few of the bene-fits. The State Church tax in Germany and the Scandinavian countries is more than sufficient for the upkeep of the Church. Voluntary giving, while not particularly high, provides a huge cash base for overseas missionary and de-velopment enterprises. In the Church of England the existence of (albeit de-pleted) endowments from the Church Commissioners acts as a disincentive to voluntary giving yielding enough to meet needs.

The debate about establishment will go on. To some, tying the spiritual work of Christ to the organs of a secular state is plainly obscene. To others, the establishment witnesses to the country's Christian roots, in an age that has largely broken free from them, and should be kept at all costs. On the level of practical politics, if it were the State that initiated the break, the Church would suffer more than if it was the other way round. So it is to be hoped that some-where someone is doing some contingency planning.

10

BAPTISM POLICY

We affirm our belief in the Scriptural foundation of infant baptism, but declare that only the children of parents who profess to be Christians are fit subjects for that rite. Indiscriminate infant baptism, as commonly practised in England, is a scandal, and is incidentally productive of much of the divisive reaction against the baptising of infants ... We must be welcoming of children, as Jesus was. But we deny the propriety of baptising the infants of parents who do not profess themselves to be Christians and cannot promise to bring up their children as Christians. (*Statement of the National Evangelical Anglican Congress*, Keele, 1967, para. 71.)

Scene: The study of a woman curate. A young, single mum from a nearby council estate has come about the baptism of her baby. The curate, who has never seen her before and senses that she possesses little or no church background, tries tactfully to steer her in the direction of a Service of Thanksgiving rather than Baptism. The features of each service are patiently explained and the young mum is asked what she thinks. 'I think I'd like the one with the water,' she says simply. The sequel to this true story, told during a General Synod debate in 1991, was that the parish concerned went ahead and baptized the baby. It did so despite the mother's distance from the worshipping community of the parish and her woolliness about the meaning and significance of the sacrament.

There is no subject more capable of creating animated debate among evangelicals than the Church of England's baptismal policy. Once such a debate gets under way, it is capable of dominating the letters column of the *Church of England Newspaper* for months on end. At the core of the debate is the fact that there are many evangelicals who in their heart of hearts feel serious reservations about way the Church of England practices infant baptism.

I believe that, when it comes to baptismal policy, the Church of England lives in a world that is completely unreal, and that the messages that ordinary people receive from its leaders on this subject are confusing. On the one hand, many bishops are saying that it is important that parents and godparents should receive proper instruction about the meaning of baptism and their responsibilities. On the other, parishes are being told to avoid baptismal policies that force people to 'jump through hoops'. (This is not altogether consistent, either, since no vicar would dream of baptizing an adult without enquiring into the person's spiritual state). How do these two principles square? The answer is that they simply do not.

The underlying issue here is not so much the meaning of baptism, but the Church of England's understanding of the nature of English society. Is Christianity the birthright of everyone who happens to have been born English? Is living within a geographical area called a parish sufficient to qualify a young child for baptism? The official policy of the Church of England assumes that the answer to both of these questions is 'yes'. The Canons and recent resolutions by the General Synod require clergy to make baptism available to all comers.

The position taken by most evangelicals, however, is that England can no longer be perceived as 'Christendom'. Over the last three hundred years, more and more people have permanently fallen out of the Church's orbit and live in virtual (and sometimes practical) paganism. For evangelicals, the Church of England has no option but to rethink its strategic position and see itself as a missionary church. That implies stating with clarity where the boundaries between belief and unbelief are, and safeguarding the original meaning of baptism as the sign of crossing the boundary from unbelief to belief.

Some proponents of an 'open' baptismal policy argue that the Church's strenuous efforts to baptize are laying foundations for long-term commitment to church attendance. The statistics do not support the case. In 1985, for example, the total population was 47.3 million. Estimates were that just over half, 26 million, had received Baptism as children and that 8 million had received Confirmation. Yet Easter communicants in Church of England parishes for that year were just over 1.6 million while average Sunday communicants were 691,400.

Stated baldly, the problem is this: How does the present-day Church's practice of baptizing children whose parents obviously are not fulfilling baptismal promises or laying the foundations for them to become active members of the Church, square with the practice of the New Testament where baptism was the outward sign of inner repentance and faith? According to Stephen Corbett, editor of the newsletter of the (mainly evangelical) Movement for the Reform of Infant Baptism (MORIB), 'The Church of England is guilty of divorcing the sacrament of baptism from the Gospel and its call to discipleship.'[1]

As Bishop Colin Buchanan has pointed out, opposition to the practice of indiscriminate baptism is not new. In 1896, Hensley Henson, later Bishop of Hereford and then Durham, said during a sermon in Oxford:

The practice that works out to this miserable confusion, the modern practice of unconditioned, indiscriminate baptising is indecent in itself, discreditable to the Church, and highly injurious to religion ... Certainly the scandalous laxity which presides over the admission of new members into the Divine Society augurs ill for the future discipline of these members ... It is not charity to indulge in the solemn mockery of their use in cases where the assumption of Christianity cannot be reasonably made ...

Buchanan likewise cites the case of the famous missionary thinker, Roland Allen, whose works came into their own some fifty years after they were written, who resigned his living as Vicar of Chalfont St Peter in 1907, having come to the conclusion that the system required him to practice indiscriminate baptism.[2]

My own view is that there is another dimension that goes even deeper. Many lay evangelicals, I believe, feel great confusion about the intrinsic value of the rite. This springs from a combination of lack of proper instruction about its meaning, from witnessing widespread Church of England fudging about baptismal discipline, and feeling on the defensive in the face of articulate (and even strident) lay people of other traditions.

The case for the baptism of children runs like this: Baptism is the New Testament successor to circumcision as the outward sign of God's covenant with his people. By participating in the rite of circumcision, parents in Old Testament days claimed all the promises of God that were available under the covenant on behalf of their children. Under the new covenant, brought into being by the death and resurrection of Christ, believing parents may likewise claim all the promises of God for their children. At the point of confirmation, those who have been baptized declare that they have personally appropriated God's promises for themselves and share the faith of their parents and god-parents.[3]

Two other considerations add weight to the argument. First, we know from the New Testament that whole households, not just individuals, were baptized and that young children were regarded as full members of the Christian community. Second, in practical terms, the only way for Christian parents to bring up their children is to bring them up as Christians.

Yet if you ask the views of lay evangelicals, many will tell you that while they are happy enough to go along with this teaching, they sense that it is one of the 'softest' of the Church's dogmas. One of the proofs that the traditional baptismal formula does not impress itself strongly on the evangelical laity, is the number of former Anglicans who have readily agreed to rebaptism in the process of joining Baptist, Pentecostal, or so-called house churches.

Moreover, in an age when people are likely to attend a church of their choice – rather than going to the local parish church, or exercising life-long denominational 'brand loyalty' – Anglican congregations contain significant numbers of articulate people from Independent Church backgrounds. Many express themselves forthrightly and are well drilled in all the arguments against infant baptism. Superficially taught Anglicans are no match for them. As likely as not these people will have opted to delay the baptism of their own children until they reach 'an age of understanding' and choose for themselves. They express strong feelings whenever the clergy seem to be 'soft' on baptismal discipline.

It is little wonder that against this background, there are many evangelical clergy who feel under pressure about conducting baptisms where the parents and godparents are not practising believers. After all, the text of the Alternative Service Book makes the position crystal clear. The priest says to the parents and godparents: 'Those who bring their children to be baptized must affirm their allegiance to Christ and their rejection of all that is evil.' Then they are required to state: 'I turn to Christ', 'I repent of my sins' and 'I renounce evil'.

Possible Evangelical Approaches

Consequently there have, broadly, been four kinds of evangelical responses and all are internally consistent.

1. Take the parents (whoever they are) at face value and offer a service of baptism in which the meaning and implications of the sacrament for the parents and godparents are made entirely clear. Those possessed of a Calvinistic 'high' view of grace would hope that in due course the work of the Holy Spirit begun in the act of baptism may bear fruit in the life of the child.

2. Offer the option of a Service of Thanksgiving as an alternative to 'christening'. If the parents insist on the latter, then the parents (if not the godparents) may perhaps be required to attend a series of baptismal preparation classes. At these classes, the meaning of the sacrament would be explained and they would be left with no illusions whatever about the obligation of parents to hold the faith professed in the baptismal vows. Such a process may well lead to the family becoming regular worshippers.

3. Insist that only the children of those who are actually worshipping members of the parish should be baptized. Parents of non-attenders may be told that the church would be willing to baptize their child if they agree to worship regularly for a specified period as well as receiving a course of instruction.

4. Operate a dual policy: baptizing babies within any one of the frameworks explained above, and at the same time making a priority of promoting baptism by immersion for non-baptized new adult believers. For the most part, Anglican advocates of adult baptism are careful to stay within ecclesiastical law and do not re-baptize. There are exceptions. For instance, when he was Bishop of Bath and Wells, Dr George Carey found that a Somerset vicar had himself been re-baptized by immersion after his ordination. As far as I know, the man concerned is still in office, which only shows there are probably no direct sanctions that the Church of England can bring to bear on clergy with the parson's freehold who are errant in this manner.

ADULT BAPTISM

Advocates of adult baptism by immersion argue that it is particularly appropriate in a society that is increasingly godless and where increasing numbers have no church background whatever. It signifies publicly through something personally embarrassing that it is the candidate's intention to follow Christ. It is both galvanizing for the faith of the person concerned, and a powerful spectacle that outsiders will come to witness out of curiosity.

Moreover, a return to baptism of professing believers by immersion represents a return to roots on the part of the Church. Its symbolism better fits St Paul's teaching in Romans 6.4 where he says that Christians are 'buried with [Christ] by baptism [and] raised [to] newness of life'. Furthermore, it fits with ancient liturgies of the primitive Church where baptism symbolized the journey from darkness into light. Candidates would stand in darkness, in dark clothing. Emerging from the baptismal pool, they would be dressed in white robes and engulfed by torchlight. All this proclaimed, in a highly dramatic manner, that they had moved from the darkness of sin and idolatry into the light of Christ. Advocates of immersion should be encouraged to make more of its liturgical and dramatic possibilities.

The General Synod has consistently rejected the pleas of the evangelicals for more baptismal rigour and has adopted the principle that the Church should baptize all whose parents request it. This 'open' policy won majority support in the General Synod in the summer of 1991. The Archbishop of Canterbury has allied himself with this view, publicly defending the Synod's decision. More recently, he told a clergy conference in Ely that the Church of England needed to take seriously the old Prayer Book's injunction to 'seek out the unbaptised'.

It is an injunction that deserves scrutiny. One vicar I spoke with believes in being generous in offering baptism to those whose parents request it. He says vicars need to take a long-term view. When it is time for confirmation classes, he studies the baptismal register and searches out those who still live in the district. He has found that a great many respond positively to an invitation to receive instruction in the Christian faith and come to personal faith. As often as not friends join with them.

On the other hand, it is easy to be over-sentimental. The Book of Common Prayer, from which this injunction is derived, is the product of what was essentially a Christian society. There were two kinds of people: the churchgoer and the lapsed. It was not unreasonable for the Church to spend a lot of energy searching out the children of the lapsed and offering them baptism. The whole situation is different today. To begin, is offering baptism the best possible strategy for people who have lost all contact with the Church (and perhaps this has been the case in their family for some generations)? One thing is certain: The Church of England is unlikely to ever agree a policy to 'seek out' Muslims, Jews, Sikhs or Hindus.

Baptism Policy

The Case for Open Baptism

The former Archbishop of York, Dr John Habgood, is a formidable opponent of the stricter evangelical outlook. During the General Synod debate in the summer of 1991, he took a swipe at Canon Michael Saward, a leading evangelical, commenting that there had been more baptisms in the rural village of Plumpton than under his former incumbency at St Mary's, Ealing, in West London. More important was his observation that the evangelical view of baptism, founded as it is largely on the theology of the covenant, is deficient because it has little or no place for the baptism of Christ in its scheme of things. On this he has a point. On the other hand, there is a world of difference between the baptism offered by John the Baptizer and the Christian form of it that we encounter in Acts and the Epistles. Here, as well as involving the element of turning from sin, baptism is the symbol of incorporation into a new community of believers.

Bishop Colin Buchanan has cogently spelled out the other side of the argument: Circumcision was given to members of the household and through 'the children of promise' it was handed on to succeeding generations. In the New Testament era, baptism related to children who were born into Christian households and grew up as believers in the context of a believing home. Baptism of households (for example, 'the household of Stephanus' in 1 Cor. 1.16) springs from the baptism of believing parents. Children baptized in New Testament days were without doubt from Christian homes.

The conclusion drawn is that 'the only biblical case that has any substance is one which can take for granted the standing in Christ of the parents of the infant or child candidate'. Buchanan argues, convincingly, that the consequence of not following these biblical principles – making the meaning of baptism more and more obscure to biblically-minded Christians – will unwittingly create a groundswell of opposition to infant baptism rather than support for it, and will weaken the Church of England by making such people prey to joining Baptist, Pentecostalist, or house churches.[4]

One of the frustrations for the evangelicals is that they feel that they won the argument against indiscriminate baptism at General Synod in 1991, but failed to carry the vote. So what is to be done? One way forward, and it is being pursued by MORIB, is to encourage evangelical parishes to create clear statements of baptismal policy, or baptismal codes of practice. Creating a parish baptismal policy is a complex business. Opponents of baptismal rigour say that the Church does parents a disservice when it creates large numbers of 'hoops' they must jump through. On the other hand, many baptismal rigorists who have set up such 'hoops' find that even the most demanding process of instruction in the faith will not necessarily change the hearts of people who are determined to have their children 'christened'. One vicar told me, 'I found that whatever "hoops" we required, parents would jump

107

through them. It didn't necessarily ensure that they came to faith or became members of the worshipping community. So we have reverted to a policy where we only baptize the children of church members.'

THE CASE AGAINST RIGIDITY

While the Church of England is in a muddle about baptism policy, it would be unbiblical to go along entirely with the rigorists who would stop baptizing the children of people on the fringe of the worshipping community. The reason is theological. A study of the Old Testament prophets shows how they constantly railed against Israel's breaking of the covenant and never shrank from pronouncing dire consequences. But at no time did they say that having broken the covenant the nation should cease the universal practice of circumcision as its outward sign. The prophets knew the compassion of a God who did not snuff out the thinly smoking flax, no matter how feeble the flame.

There is undoubtedly evidence that large numbers of people pray. Gallup's European Values Survey found that three-quarters of the nation wanted some sort of religious dimension to accompany the key points of the life cycle – the birth of a child, marriage and death. The opportunity is there for the Church in the market place of ideas and competing spiritualities. And if it does not take it, there are many other forces at work that will, as a visit to places like Glastonbury will make abundantly clear.

I would want to add a footnote to the whole discussion. If evangelicals are consistent and hold the position that only the children of people who are regular attenders of worship should be baptized, then sooner or later they will need to face the issue of whether or not these children should receive the sacrament of Communion. We baptize children, knowing full well that they do not understand what is happening to them, on the assumption that God's grace is at work in their lives. So is it consistent to deny them access to Communion which we claim is the means of grace?

11

ORDINATION OF WOMEN
AND ITS LEGACY

Women are here to stay. (George Bernard Shaw)

Whether women are better than men I cannot say – but I can say they are certainly no worse. (Golda Meir)

'Divide.' Whenever the General Synod of the Church of England takes an important vote, this order by the chairman is the signal for members to leave their places and file through the respective 'yes' or 'no' lobbies. When, on 11 November 1992, Archbishop George Carey called 'divide' at the conclusion of a day-long debate on the motion to give final approval to the ordination of women as priests, the word had more than the usual resonances. The effects of the 11 November vote on Anglo-Catholics in the Church of England have been well publicized. Less widely reported is the impact on the evangelical constituency.[1]

Evangelicals: A Key Factor in the 'Yes' Vote

The loss of the 11 November vote was a shock to opponents of the ordination of women. Straw polls of members' voting intentions had always put the numbers in favour just short of the required two-thirds. At the York sessions of the Synod the previous July, a 'dry run' suggested that the legislation would fail by a handful of votes in the House of Laity. Five members changing their minds would have been enough to change the outcome. It is significant that by July 1992, opposition among evangelicals in the House of Clergy had almost disappeared. Only three voted 'no'. It was clear, therefore, that the outcome rested on whether some of the evangelical laity might be persuaded to change their minds. Several did and that remains the biggest factor in the final outcome.

I suspect that the opponents of women priests, both evangelical and Anglo-Catholic, misread the evangelical constituency. Evangelicals had a lot to gain from a vote to ordain women. Their theological colleges were the biggest producers of women clergy. Bringing them fully into the ranks of the clergy would strengthen the overall position of evangelicals in the Church of England.

Moreover, once women were admitted to the office of deacon their priesting was almost inevitable. The Church of England's only agreed understanding of the diaconate is that it serves as the final part of the apprenticeship for a priest. Anglo-Catholic traditionalists like the Bishop of Portsmouth, Timothy Bavin, tried valiantly but without success to get the Church of England to consider the case for a permanent diaconate. In contrast, few evangelical conservatives gave serious thought to what might be offered to the many evangelical women in deacon's orders if priesting was unacceptable.

Debate Not on Evangelical Terms

The Church of England had been debating the ordination of women as priests for over two decades, but this debate was rarely conducted in terms that engaged the serious attention of evangelicals. To begin, most evangelicals are not specially happy with the word 'priest'. At the *Church of England Newspaper* I sanctioned its use reluctantly, mainly on grounds that it was the only shorthand that would work for purposes of headline writing.

Most evangelicals are taught that the New Testament knows little of a Christian priesthood in the sense the Anglo-Catholics express it. They do not think of their vicar as a 'priest'. Traditionally, they have identified their clergy with the role of the 'presbyter' in the early Church. The 'presbyter' (or elder) was technically of the same status as the rest of the congregation, but 'set apart' for special tasks such as preaching and teaching the faithful. On the term 'priesthood', the starting point for evangelicals is the concept of 'the priesthood of all believers', an important slogan from the Continental Reformation.

All this has important implications. Anglo-Catholics place great emphasis on the role of the priest presiding at the Eucharist, in particular being able to pronounce the words of consecration. This is based on the so-called 'iconic' and 'representative' role of the priest. According to the iconic view, the priest is the representative of Christ who was male, so the priest likewise should be male. For those favouring women's ordination, the representation is of the ascended Christ, who encompasses the whole of redeemed humanity.

Such a formulation makes little sense to most evangelicals. For many of them, presidency at Holy Communion is functional rather than representational. What is important is that the teacher of the word is well trained and properly authorized.

The other major argument advanced against women priests was its effect on ecumenism. The ecumenically minded were concerned that ordaining women meant creating a serious barrier to unity prospects with the Roman Catholic and Eastern Orthodox Churches. Those of a more strongly 'catholic' frame of mind argued that while they were agnostic on the question of whether or not women could be priests, they were certain that the Church of England did not have the authority to make such a change independently of these ancient Churches.

For most evangelicals, neither of these considerations carried a lot of weight. To begin with, by temperament most do not set a lot of store by officially sponsored ecumenism. Evangelicals, for example, are among the strongest critics of the Anglican-Roman Catholic International Commission, and many are incredulous, for example, about the Agreed Statement which insists on the need for a universal primacy exercised by the Bishop of Rome. They would claim that there is neither a biblical nor practical warrant for it. They would argue that it would be a much better investment of time for the Church of England to get alongside some of the newer churches to see what lessons in evangelism and mission can be learned from them.

As I have indicated, none of the arguments advanced by Anglo-Catholic opponents represented the views of evangelicals. The debate among evangelicals turned on the issue of 'headship'. The two key biblical passages are 1 Corinthians 14.34–5 and I Timothy 2.8ff. Opponents took both to assert the 'headship' of the male in the life of the Church. The logic ran as follows: God is the head of Christ, Christ is head of the Church, and men are given the status of head in church leadership.

'Headship' rejected

Many opponents saw the rejection of the 'headship' argument by evangelical members of Synod as a sign of a refusal to live under Scripture. The issue is more subtle than that. A great many evangelical members of the General Synod who voted in favour at one stage or other adhered to this formulation but had changed their minds by the time of the crucial vote.

Two 'senior statesmen' who came into this category were Canon Colin Craston (Bolton) and Canon Michael Saward (London). Both would say that their original position was to go along with the evangelical consensus about 'headship' that prevailed for many years until it began to be questioned in the late 1960s. The trigger in both cases was personal contact with the ministry of women. Canon Saward recalls how, having appointed a deaconess to his staff, he found that she was in every way – as pastor, teacher and preacher – more gifted and effective than all the men who had been his colleagues up to that time. That, he said, forced him to rethink his theological position, asking what God was doing in the distribution of such giftedness. Many more would tell a similar story.

In the end, two factors persuaded evangelical members to reject submissions that 'headship' constituted a barrier to the ordination of women to the priesthood of the Church of England:

1. This view emphasized two passages over against what they perceived as the entire thrust of the Bible where the essential equality of men and women is asserted, and where teaching on spiritual gifts turns human structures on their heads.

2. This view misunderstood 'headship' in two ways:

(a) In biblical anatomy, according to C. K. Barrett and the great Brethren scholar, F. F. Bruce, 'head' meant not intellectual leadership but 'source'. This was contested by American Wayne Grudem, who combed classical literature to prove otherwise, but he failed to successfully cite biblical material in favour of his case.

(b) The 'headship' of God the Father over the Son cannot be taken to mean that the Son is in any way subordinate, and, in parallel, 'headship' in Paul's teaching cannot therefore be taken to assert the subordination of women to men in the life of the Church.

3. In practical terms, there is not a lot of evidence that there were many evangelical Anglicans who seriously applied 'headship' in the relationships of husbands and wives.

All this represents a hermeneutic shift. It reflects an approach to the Scriptures that is shared with other traditions including narrative criticism and liberation theology. As well as being willing to wrestle with the meaning of particular texts, it is concerned with the whole sweep of biblical theology and what it might say to the issue in question. The critics claim it was a case of buying into the spirit of the age and then going to the Scriptures for justification. But evangelicals of all varieties are at heart 'people of the Book' and they do not lightly realign their thinking on major issues in theology. Not all evangelical members of Synod studied the Scriptures with equal rigour, but by 11 November 1992 they had reached a consensus that the Scriptures supported a 'yes' vote. As convincing as arguments about equality are, if they had not been at ease with themselves about the biblical case in favour, the legislation would have never been passed.

An Unprepared Constituency

Even if the debate about the ordination of women was not cast in evangelical language, it is nevertheless surprising that the constituency was under-prepared when it came to the 11 November vote. The debate among evangelicals about the meaning of these passages only emerged in earnest in July 1992, when members of the Evangelical Group in General Synod (EGGS) met for a day in York ahead of the Synod sessions, in what by all accounts was a less than satisfactory affair.

This in its own way reflects the weakness of the institutions which are supposed to foster communication among the loose collection of groups which make up the evangelical constituency. Since 1980, there has been an annual Anglican Evangelical Assembly (AEA), drawing together representatives of diocesan evangelical unions and key evangelical agencies like the Church Pastoral Aid Society and the Church Mission Society. The normal pattern is that the Assembly should tackle one particular theme in depth. The topics tackled over the last five years included the Church, episcopacy, and interfaith relations. Despite the ordination of women being potentially the most divisive issue facing evangelicals during that period, this topic never became an Assembly theme.

Was it that the evangelical constituency as a whole preferred to duck the issue? It may be, though the evidence points in another direction. Throughout the same period the AEA and the Church of England Evangelical Council (CEEC) were in a state of constitutional paralysis. Suffice to say, this ensured that neither of these bodies was able to exercise clear leadership on this issue. Indeed, in 1990, the Church of England Evangelical Council made the subject the agenda for a residential meeting. For some mysterious reason the outcome of that debate was never communicated to the wider constituency.

The other lost opportunity was the National Evangelical Anglican Celebration held at Caister in May 1988. This celebration, attended by over two thousand evangelicals, was supposed to be in succession to the Keele (1967) and Nottingham (1977) Congresses of Evangelicals. It was termed a 'celebration' because the CEEC reasoned that the only way to persuade large numbers to attend was by encouraging different networks to come and do their own thing. That ruled out a Congress format or serious discussion of an agenda for evangelicals in the way that Keele had operated around the main themes of the 1968 Lambeth Conference, galvanizing evangelicals and feeding into the debates of the wider Church.

On 11 November 1992, evangelicals on the General Synod endorsed the ordination of women with a blend of principle and pragmatism. As well as the substantive theological issue, there was a feeling that the question would never disappear from the Synod agenda until a vote in favour was achieved. Better to decide now and get on. The underlying consideration was the Decade of Evangelism. Evangelicals sensed this was their big moment of opportunity to make the Church of England more evangelical. An interminable debate on women's ordination stood in the way, a point made a week before the vote, in a letter to the *Church of England Newspaper* by the former Archbishop of Canterbury, Lord Coggan.

One strong indicator that the 11 November vote had caught out many evangelicals was the letters column of the *Church of England Newspaper*. Even though the issue had been decided, for months there were scores of correspondents who wanted to debate the issue from first principles. Debate about 'headship' and the meaning of the teaching of St Paul raged.

Once again, hermeneutics were at the centre of the stage. For opponents, by rejecting 'the plain meaning of Scripture' the Church of England had taken a decisive step towards apostasy. It had adopted an attitude to Scripture which would inevitably lead down a slippery slope to all manner of aberrations, including the ordination of those living openly in gay relationships.

The Strength of Opposition

All this needs to be put in context. In the years that have followed, the numbers in opposition to the ordination of women have tended to be out of proportion to the vociferousness of their voices. At the *Church of England Newspaper*, we had taken soundings as to the views of evangelicals on the ordination of women for a period of nearly five years. All our research pointed to an excess of two-thirds in favour. I still remained baffled as to why they left it until after the final vote before they got organized.

What is more, I believe that the decision of the Church Society to test the matter in the courts made the position worse. Like court rulings on the subject in other parts of the Anglican Communion, the main thrust of the various judgments was that the Church is essentially a voluntary or private society and that it is inappropriate for the State to be involved in its internal affairs. That is a serious challenge to people who have traditionally set great store by the establishment of the Church.

The Directions *Supplement*

Given the above, people familiar with the *Church of England Newspaper* will wonder why it was that, as editor, having devoted the editorial ahead of the Synod session to urge a vote in favour, I gave opponents space after the vote through the *Directions* supplement. There are several reasons:

1. Care for minorities is important in a Church that claims to be comprehensive. In other parts of the Anglican Communion some opponents of the ordination of women found themselves increasingly on the margins. I wanted to see if the Church of England could be different.

2. I believed that the disappearance of conservative Anglo-Catholics would represent a loss to the Church of England. They share in common with evangelicals a willingness to try to live under revelation and this could be important in the context of how evangelicals deal with the radical liberal agenda.

3. I wanted to foster dialogue between conservative evangelicals and conservative Anglo-Catholics, and explore whether there was more than mere opportunism at the root of their cooperation over several key issues in the last couple of decades. The jury is still out on that issue.

4. I am committed to evangelical-catholic dialogue for many other reasons, and the *Directions* initiative was but one strand. Bringing Bishop Michael Marshall into the paper's orbit was another. As I indicate in several places in this book, I believe that this dialogue will be increasingly important for the future of world Christianity.

No Evangelical Exodus

There was never any question that evangelicals opposed to the ordination of women as priests were going to leave the Church of England in numbers, at least in the short term. To begin, there was no place for them to go. More importantly, few believed that the move touched on matters of fundamental doctrinal orthodoxy.

The emergence of the ginger group, Reform, founded early in 1993, has reopened debate among evangelicals about their identity and wider role in the Church of England. I have already discussed Reform in some detail, and I raise it again now because it has reopened an important debate about ecclesiology. There has been ongoing discussion as to whether members of the constituency owe primary allegiance to Anglicanism or to evangelicalism. Are they Anglicans first and foremost? Or are they evangelicals who happen to be Anglican, perhaps for the pragmatic reason that the Church of England is still 'the best boat to fish from' (to use a phrase from Archbishop Robert Runcie in his address to the National Evangelical Anglican Consultation, NEAC, in 1988)?

Reception

Now that women are in place as vicars, it is worth offering an assessment of their 'reception'. It is clear that, on the whole, evangelical parishes have moved quickly to affirm women as priests and deacons. Surprisingly few evangelical parishes (even those linked to Reform) took up the option available under the Act of Synod to signal that they would not accept women clergy.

What happens in the next couple of decades will be very interesting. A Methodist report published in 1993 found that after twenty-five years there was still a reluctance on the part of many congregations to put a woman in charge. At least some felt they had 'done their bit' and reverted to male ministry. In the Episcopal Church, USA, where women have been ordained over nearly two decades, a great many find it hard to obtain full-time posts. A large proportion are not in parish work despite their wish to be so.

The matter of the under-deployment of women is bound to emerge as an issue for the Church of England. One of the hard facts is that when faced with the choice, parishes tend to appoint a vicar who is a married, family person, over single candidates, be they male or female.

How are women clergy faring in the new role? The fact is, of course, that as soon as the way was clear for women to be deacons, some senior former deaconesses took charge of congregations and even entire parishes. So the idea of women in charge had been track-tested in different parts of the country before 1992.

Robert Warren, the National Evangelism Officer, has claimed that there is no parish where there is a woman in charge that is not growing numerically.[2] I suspect it is too early to suggest that this represents a trend. We will simply have to wait a few more years.

The ministry of women will undoubtedly have an impact on the style of ordained ministry exercised in the Church of England. Advocates argue that it will offer a new, more collaborative style of ministry, geared to recognizing and releasing the gifts God has given to all his Church. This in fact is the preferred model for the ordained ministry at this present time, and resonates with ideas about leadership in secular management theory.

What I suspect, however, is that when many of the devotees of the 'headship' argument view the matter with the perspective of years and experience of women in the ordained ministry, many will wonder why they pressed the argument as hard as they did.

Gains and Losses

As well as winners, there have been losers in this debate about the ordination of women. I, for one, believe that the weakening of the Anglo-Catholic wing is a loss, although the roots of the problem predate the ordination of women debate. From the mid-1960s onwards, many in this tradition suffered an increasing loss of confidence. Having eagerly embraced the radical theology of that period, Anglo-Catholic vicars discovered to their cost that it cut the ground from under their view of the gospel and the doctrine of the Church. By the time the ordination of women debate came along, the Anglo-Catholic constituency was a shadow of its past glory. They were poorly led in the years running up to the vote.

The other loser, I believe, has been the laity. For nearly a decade and a half, the Church of England's concerns about ministry took on a shape that was almost entirely clerical. Justifiable concerns that women should have the opportunity to fulfil their calling in priestly ministry eclipsed the far more important issue of how the ministry of the 99 per cent of Christians is to be exercised. As much as anything else, this is an indictment of the Church of England's cumbersome decision-making structures and the way they can be tweaked to create paralysis and stalemate. The loser here is not just one party grouping, but the entire mission of the Church.

12

THE DEBATE ABOUT

HOMOSEXUALITY

There are few new sins. And it's the old sins that get all the publicity. (Anon.)

The scene is St Michael's Parish Church, Chester Square, in London, 1991. The parish's new Associate Vicar, Christopher Guinness, is about to begin his first sermon when a stranger comes to the front and begins to speak. Members of the congregation squirm uncomfortably. Is it going to be one of those trendy sermons that starts by using drama?

Then they begin to take in what the intruder is saying: 'This man persecutes homosexuals by saying they need to be cured. Many who have tried his methods end up in despair and even suicide.' Suddenly the intruder is joined by about twenty placard-waving, whistle-blowing gay activists. It turns out that they are from a militant group called Outrage! that regularly uses these tactics against people they disapprove of. Outrage! promises they will continue to disrupt services at St Michael's until Guinness closes down the Living Waters programme to which it objects. It takes quite a few minutes for order to be restored.

We will pick up Christopher Guinness's personal story first of all. During the mid-eighties, as a vicar in South Lambeth, he grew increasingly depressed at the number of AIDS funerals he found himself conducting. Was there any way that gays could break free of the lifestyle which led to such tragedy? he asked himself.

He discovered a Californian programme called Desert Stream. Its creator was Andrew Comiskey, a Christian believer, who had been through his own personal struggle with homosexuality. He devised a thirty-week programme where participants were encouraged to pursue 'sexual wholeness through the Cross of Christ'.

Living Waters is a pastiche of psychotherapy and instruction in spirituality. As well as attracting Christians who are unhappy to be in a gay lifestyle, it has proved helpful to victims of sexual abuse and dysfunctional families. Under Christopher Guinness and his wife Lisa, Desert Stream was Anglicized and launched in Britain under the name Living Waters.

117

The Wider Scene

Now I want to move to the wider Anglican scene. The subject of homosexual relationships is a time bomb that has been ticking away for many years. There was a time when it was possible for the Christian churches to blink at homosexual relationships that did not cause a scandal, but that is changing because of pressures from two sides.

First, there are gay activists who will settle for no less than the Church fully legitimizing homosexual unions and ordaining people who say openly that they practise gay sex. Second, there are conservative evangelicals, particularly, who believe that a gay lifestyle is incompatible with the Christian life, that homosexual acts are a mortal sin, and that those who engage in them should not be in positions of leadership in the Church. There is no room for compromise between these two agendas.

The Roman Catholic Church and most evangelicals have generally stood firm on the view that all sexual acts outside marriage fall short of God's standard. On the other hand, as W. S. F. Pickering noted in his study of Anglo-Catholics, there has been a long-standing association between members of this constituency and homosexuality. 'Some of the first clergy to declare publicly that they were homosexuals were Anglo-Catholics,' Pickering writes. In 1987, a Gallup poll asked three hundred Anglican clergy for their views on a statement 'The Church can never approve homosexual acts'. Some 28 per cent of the high church group disagreed, while just 1 per cent from among evangelicals disagreed.[1] There is also a constituency who are neither evangelical or Anglo-Catholic who would question whether the Church's traditional taboo on gay sex is warranted.

The Gloucester Report

A decade earlier, in 1979, the Church of England published a report by a working party led by the then Bishop of Gloucester, John Yates. It was debated by General Synod in 1981. The report argued for a liberalization of Church attitudes. Under certain circumstances, for example when a stable and loving union exists, homosexual genital acts should have the same status as sexual relations within a heterosexual marriage. The report prompted *Time* magazine to suggest that the Church of England was abandoning traditional morality without putting anything clear in its place. In the end, the Synod declined either to endorse fully the Gloucester report or to make a clear statement to the contrary.

Enter Tony Higton

The issue re-entered the spotlight towards the end of 1987. A private members' motion by the Rev. Tony Higton of Hawkwell, Essex, challenged the General Synod over the presence of active homophiles among the clergy and called on it to reaffirm traditional biblical teaching on sexuality. (The word 'homophile' signifies a person living in or aspiring to a gay lifestyle. 'Homosexual' may simply mean someone of that disposition.) Higton strongly objected to the sale of gay literature – which he said was pornographic – at St Botolph's parish church, Aldgate, in the City of London.

An amendment moved by the evangelical Bishop of Chester, Michael Baughen, toned down the sharpness of Higton's motion. The result was nevertheless clear enough. By a big majority, Synod voted that homosexual acts fell short of the standard of behaviour required by God. The gay community felt betrayed when they found that some Synod members who had privately pledged their support voted for the amended motion.

What had prompted Higton to act as he did at that stage? The answer is that he had wind of another working party on the homosexuality question, authorized by the House of Bishops. He and his supporters did not want another official Anglican document taking a similar line to the Gloucester report.

Interestingly enough, this new working group included a number of well-known evangelicals. The working party, chaired by June Osborne, an East London deacon, reported to the House of Bishops in 1989. Higton's hunch was right. But Higton had delivered a joker card. It was politically impossible for the House of Bishops to authorize a document taking a substantially different view from the Higton motion as amended. They saw no alternative but to bury it.

Its contents, nevertheless, became widely known when copies were leaked to the press. When given the opportunity to voice their viewpoint, a poll of the mainly evangelical readers of the *Church of England Newspaper* rejected a version of the report's submissions by a ratio of nine to one.

Issues in Human Sexuality

There were an influential number of Synod activists who believed that the Higton debate should not be allowed to be the last word. The House of Bishops was persuaded to commission its own report, *Issues in Human Sexuality*, published in 1992. Its architect was the then Bishop of Salisbury, Dr John Austin Baker. It called for a period of reflection on the main debating points, offering a lot of good material on wider questions in Christian sexual ethics. However, it did contain a glaring inconsistency, which has been criticized by evangelicals and gays alike. It said there was no place for gay sex among the clergy, but it did not condemn it as a lifestyle for lay people.

A Debate that Simmers on

Subsequent events have kept the debate alive since that time, not least among evangelicals. First, in the United States of America, it was the top agenda item at the General Convention of the Episcopal Church in the summer of 1994. Debate centred around a highly controversial report on sexuality by the House of Bishops. Opponents seized on the report's failure to provide a cogent case for traditional marriage, while advocating church recognition of gay unions and the ordination of openly practising gays. They fought a tenacious rearguard action to prevent its adoption. English traditionalists believe that the American scene is a foreshadowing of things to come on this side of the Atlantic.

A second factor was events in England surrounding the so-called Turnbull affair. There is no need to repeat the full details. Suffice to say, even though Bishop Turnbull has denied that he is a homosexual, the affair has signalled that sexuality is an issue among evangelicals.

Then, shortly afterwards, there followed revelations of an attempt by Outrage! to 'out' the then Bishop of London, Dr David Hope. His episcopal neighbour, the evangelical Bishop of Southwark, Dr Roy Williamson, was drafted into the media fray that followed. He was asked by the Radio 4 *Today* programme, 'Would you be happy to ordain a priest who was open about his sexuality and told you he was not celibate?'

It was an ambiguous question. An unambitious response would have been to reply 'No'. Instead Dr Williamson said, 'I would be happy to ordain a priest if his life was a life of holiness and godliness and acceptability in terms of Scripture and tradition and the present teaching of the Church.' That left him open for more grilling. 'And that can be compatible with what in the jargon we call "a gay lifestyle", I mean in having a homosexual relationship which is open?' His reply, 'Well, it entirely depends upon whether that relationship may be stable or not . . .'

Later, Dr Williamson issued a further statement to clarify his position but the damage was done. For all intents and purposes an evangelical bishop had at least hinted that there may be conditions under which he might condone ordination of actively gay clergy. For Reform, it was a clear example of the kind of drift that it feared may be in process. The outcome was Williamson's resignation as Chairman of the Council of the Church Pastoral Aid Society.

A few days later, Reform's temperature rose even further when it became known that a pastoral letter, issued by the Primates of the Anglican Communion meeting in Windsor, contained a call for a wide-ranging reappraisal of the traditional Anglican attitude to sexuality. At a press conference, one of their number said he wanted to see ordination open to people in gay relationships, and the blessing of gay unions by the Church. News of these developments dominated Reform's annual conference held a few days later. Reform pundits had predicted a crisis over homosexuality. What surprised so many was that it had come so soon. Its members stopped short of announcing that the time had come to quit the Church of England. Reform nevertheless said it was time to think through what possible lifeboats existed for leaving the ship.

The Evangelical Debate

A sharp debate is underway within the evangelical constituency. In 1993, it had a 'dry run' in the columns of *Anvil*, the theological journal supported by the main evangelical Anglican theological colleges. It indicated that there were at least some evangelicals claiming to hold to the authority of the Bible who are now less than sure that St Paul's condemnation of homosexual acts in Romans 1 applies directly to the modern gay lifestyle.

But the sternest challenge yet to the traditional evangelical view was issued with the publication in December 1995 of Michael Vasey's *Strangers and Friends*.[2] Vasey's premise is that he holds to the authority of the Bible. From there he proceeds with a highly plausible demolition job on traditional interpretations of the biblical material. He insists that there is not one homosexuality, but many. He argues that homosexuality has been present in many forms in many societies throughout history and has not necessarily been incompatible with heterosexual marriage or undermined it. He insists that the sexual practices condemned in the Scriptures are not necessarily the same as those in modern homosexual relationships. Equally important is his view that evangelicals misunderstand the creation narratives by imposing the model of the nuclear family on them.

It is too soon to venture how important Vasey's work will turn out to be. The application traditionally drawn from some Scriptures, for example the story of Sodom, may indeed not be valid. But for evangelicals the key question is whether or not the behaviour condemned in the biblical records is in essence the same as the contemporary gay lifestyle. There will be evangelicals who, having read Vasey, may well entertain an element of doubt and that could prove crucial in the longer term. It is certain to soften up the attitudes of middle-of-the-road evangelicals who would prefer a different tone than that of Tony Higton on gay issues.

I suspect that evangelicals remain 90 per cent in agreement about the substantive issue, but a once-monochrome constituency looks set to break into several different viewpoints or emphases on how the Church should respond.

Challenges Ahead

There are two significant challenges that evangelicals will find themselves needing to address in the future.

The first is how to cool-headedly address the issues raised by Vasey and the North American researchers on whose work in part he depends. Then there is the issue of how evangelicals will react to research which is seeking to show that gay preference grows from hereditary causes. At present the data is contradictory but it is a latent threat to programmes like Living Waters who follow studies that claim that a gay preference grows from a deficient relationship between the person and their same-sex parent.

THE 'EX-GAY' DIMENSION

The theological framework and claims of the so-called 'ex-gay' movements, including Living Waters, need to be subjected to careful review. Claims of 'healing' by the ex-gay movement need to be scrutinized as well. Ironically, the operation of ex-gay programmes in evangelical churches is in its own way changing the shape of evangelical attitudes. Programmes such as Living Waters mean that for the first time gay people are allowed to be 'visible' in evangelical churches. That they are involved in a programme of Christian discipleship is a key factor in ensuring their acceptance. That in its own way is altering some of the perceptions that exist among evangelical people.

This movement nevertheless has it own inbuilt 'time bomb'. Will its healing claims hold up? Will it produce people who can truthfully testify, 'Once I was gay but now I am straight'? As a result of events at St Michael's, Chester Square, which happens to be my own parish church, I have taken a lot of trouble to question ex-gays on this point. Martin Hallett, leader of the True Freedom Trust, is quite clear that he himself has not been changed intrinsically. It is simply that he lives a contented life as a non-practising gay Christian.

Much of the ex-gay literature says that any 'healing' will be a gradual process. That certainly puts it in a different category from the instantaneous miracles of Jesus as recorded in the Gospels. I wonder, too, why – if what the ex-gay movements are offering is 'sexual wholeness' – so much of their instructional literature emphasizes controlling homosexual feelings and desires?

A Personal Reflection

I would add another personal word. As architect of the *Church of England Newspaper*'s readers' poll in the wake of the Osborne report, in the short term I was delighted with the response and attendant publicity. Our poll made headlines. The *Daily Mail* gave it prominent billing. On reflection, however, I came to the conclusion that it was relatively easy to set up a confrontation. It was another thing entirely, and much more demanding, to find a Christ-like way to respond to the issue.

A Gospel for Gays?

Can evangelicals speak of the gospel to gay people? Here in Britain, there have been two remarkable evangelical initiatives that have done this. One is the work of the Mildmay Mission Hospital at Shoreditch in London's East End. The Mildmay dates back to the Victorian era and is one of many examples of the evangelical social conscience offering practical help, in this case medical care, to the poor. The need for it became much less clear with the development of the National Health Service. For some years there was uncertainty about its future. Then, in the mid-1980s, the board of the Mildmay took the decision to devote all its resources to tackling AIDS, the toughest health-care problem of our day. Today the Mildmay is a state-of-the-art facility and hospice, an evangelical foundation doing its work in the name of Christ but in an entirely non-judgemental manner.

Another example is the emergence of ACET (AIDS Care and Education Trust) founded by Dr Patrick Dickson. ACET has led the way with objective educational materials for use in schools and elsewhere and is much in demand for consultancy and advice in Third World countries where AIDS has reached epidemic proportions.

What about parish life? One realistic evangelical model operates at All Saints Church at Beverly Hills, Los Angeles, where the rector is the Rev. Carol Anderson. Beverly Hills, of course, is located close to the epicentre of the Los Angeles gay scene. It has an opportunity to offer ministry both to gay people who drop in off the street and increasingly to people who have been casualties of ex-gay programmes.

Carol Anderson says that the parish's starting point is to accept gay people as they are into its community. Gay people have told her that being part of such a Christian community immediately reduces the need to be sexually active, since much of such behaviour is driven by loneliness.

She admits that this approach is more open-ended than is comfortable for some evangelical temperaments. She nevertheless rejoices at how it has been possible to gather a diverse group ranging from retired army colonels to men who are clearly gay and, for example, go on retreat together to the Holy Land. It was, she says, a powerful witness to the Church's claim to be a new community.

The Future

What, then, might be a positive evangelical response to the gay debate?

1. Everyone falls short of God's standards. Sex is but one area where people succumb to temptation, and sexual sins are not the only ones that kill the soul. That is why it is important to teach and practise Christian discipleship. In teaching the duty to 'subject all things' to the will of Christ, the Church is offering a radical alternative to a postmodern world-view where the first reflex is to speak of 'rights'.

2. The Church must be willing to abrogate and condemn violence against gay people, past and present. Judgement is God's prerogative.

3. There needs to be much more cool-headed theological discussion. It is clear enough that the Bible condemns certain activities. But can we say for sure, when we use the words 'homosexual' or 'homosexuality', that we are not reading back into the Bible something slightly different from what occurred in biblical times and was condemned?

4. Ex-gay programmes, Living Waters and the like, require more theological scrutiny. A key question is whether their analysis of the causes of homosexuality is universally valid, or is so merely for some homosexualities. Whatever the case, accusations of abuse levelled at the ex-gay movement demand that these programmes should be conducted within a framework of theological reflection and adequate pastoral oversight.

5. The Church must be willing to offer a quality of community that fulfils the social and family needs that often are sought through the gay scene for lack of something better. Like those evangelical parishes who baptize the children of parents who appear to be at best 'nominal', it will need to find ways to operate a policy of 'charitable assumption' about their intentions. It will simply witness that all people need to be transformed into the image of Christ, and that this is a lifelong process.

6. The last thing the Church of England needs is a long-drawn-out debate on this issue. Protracted public confrontation in the same proportions as the debate about the ordination of women would do the Church of England no good. But it is unlikely that the issue will go away.

13

OTHER FAITHS

The international community has already created transnational, transcultural and transreligious legal structures (without which international treaties would in fact be sheer self deception). But if a new world order is to exist, it needs a minimum of common values, standards and basic attitudes, an ethic which, for all its time conditioned nature, is binding in all senses of the word on the whole of humanity, in short a global ethic. (Hans Kung, *Christianity*, SCM, 1995, p. 788)

Trevor Cooling, of the Association for Christian Teachers, tells the story of Helen (not her real name), a young evangelical who is a dedicated special-needs teacher. She works with pupils who have serious behavioural problems. In the course of her work, she became close to a Hindu girl who, as well as being troublesome in school, caused her family countless problems at home. Helen worked hard. She willingly took on 'extras' in her own time. She gradually won the girl's confidence. Soon everyone could see an improvement. The girl began to fit in better at school. And her behaviour at home got better too. Her parents were delighted and invited Helen to the family home to share a meal.

But that raised problems for Helen. She knew that eating in a Hindu home meant more than merely sharing food; it meant taking part in religious rites too. When Helen shared her concern with colleagues at school she was met with incomprehension. What harm could there possibly be in sharing in a social occasion? How could she be so rude as to even consider not going? When she sought guidance from her evangelical church, the reaction was much less sympathetic. Her home group leader 'rebuked' her for even thinking of joining in the worship of false gods. He said that for a Christian believer to accept the invitation and participate would be to deny the uniqueness of Christ.

A story like this illustrates the complexity of relationships in the modern school. But more important for our purposes, it is an example of the tensions felt by a good many evangelicals. And these tensions raise vital issues about the way evangelicals understand how they should relate to the world around them.

Defining British Identity

Evangelicals share, in common with many people in modern Britain, the problem of how to define the nature of their society. In the past, the answer was unequivocal. Britain formed part of Western 'Christendom'. Even if some individuals did not fit in, it was assumed that the underlying value system was 'Christian'. As we have seen, evangelicals traditionally have placed great store in the establishment of the Church of England. In the past, it served both as a safeguard from doctrinal error, and signalled that no matter how heathen the leadership of the nation had become, there persisted various symbols which kept alive 'a rumour of angels' (to use Peter Berger's phrase). These symbols proclaimed an unchanging Christian foundation. They were given visibility by a monarch who was supreme governor of the established Church, which in turn received special status and privileges.

But today the definition is not nearly so clear. Britain is home to a visible and often voluble minority who were brought up in faiths other than Christianity. They amount to little more than 5 per cent of the population. But in some communities, like the one in which I live, the local Anglican-run primary school has a 95 per cent Muslim enrolment. The power of television, films, and all the trappings of international culture, have helped British people to see themselves in the context of the 'global village'.

DEBATE AMONG EVANGELICALS

Among evangelicals, fierce debate rages. Should evangelicals assert that Britain is at core a Christian country, where symbolic trappings – such as the coronation, or membership of the House of Lords by senior bishops – serve as reminders of Britain's Christian roots? Or should they concede that this is a pluralist culture, in which Christians have no inherent right to special privileges? Should they assert special rights based on historic precedent, or like everyone else earn a hearing in the market place of voices and ideas? What does current British culture most resemble; that of a truly Christian nation, or a culture like the one to which Christ came and in which the Church of the New Testament was born?

I have already looked at this question in the context of evangelical debates about establishment. In this chapter I will look at one particular example of how this debate has manifested itself, try to identify the strategic and theological issues at stake, and attempt to draw tentative conclusions.

The Open Letter

In November 1991, nearly two thousand clergy and a number of lay people signed an Open Letter addressed to the leadership of the Church of England. Nearly all who signed were evangelical clergy, though they were joined by some leaders of the Church's Anglo-Catholic constituency. I was among a handful of laity who signed. It was, arguably, one of the biggest grass-roots revolts in the Church in generations and it attracted widespread media attention, including the front page of *The Times*.

'We are deeply concerned', said the Open Letter,

> about gatherings for interfaith worship and prayer involving Christian people. These include the Interfaith Commonwealth Day Observance in Westminster Abbey and other such events in some of the cathedrals and churches of England, whether they refer to Jesus Christ or whether such references are minimal or excluded. We believe these events, however motivated, conflict with the Christian duty to proclaim the Gospel. They imply that salvation is offered by God not only through Jesus Christ but by other means, and thus deny his uniqueness and finality as the only Saviour.

It contended that the events in question 'conflict with the Christian duty to proclaim the Gospel' and were 'deeply hurtful to those in this country who have come from other religions into the Christian faith ... especially where such faiths are unwilling to tolerate conversions or the existence of minority Christian communities.' It appealed to the leadership of the Church of England 'to oppose, and where possible, prevent such gatherings'.

THE CONTEXT

The immediate backcloth to the Open Letter had two parts. The first was that 1991 signalled the start of the Decade of Evangelism. The call by the 1988 Lambeth Conference for such a Decade at the end of the millennium had caught the imagination of the Church of England in a remarkable way, but it did not go down well with other faith communities in Britain.

The second was growing unease, especially among some evangelicals in the Church of England, about the growing popularity of services of interfaith worship and prayer. Two events became the symbol of this unease: the annual Commonwealth Day Observance held in Westminster Abbey, and a Festival of Faith held in Canterbury Cathedral in September 1989.

The Commonwealth Day Observance (the Abbey authorities are careful not to call it a 'service') is attended by the Queen and some members of the royal family. The biggest proportion of those attending are school children. The Observance consists of readings from the sacred writings of the main religions within the Commonwealth, prayers, periods of silence, and music. The great concern of evangelicals has been that in order not to be in any way offensive to the various faith communities present, the Christian segment offers a toned-down and bland version of Jesus Christ. It highlights his moral teaching, while avoiding the Christian claim that he is the only saviour.

Canterbury Cathedral's Festival of Faith in September 1989 brought together representatives of the main faith communities in Britain. Its main theme was the environment. It was an attempt to follow up what had been set in motion when the Pope called together world religious leaders in Assisi to express concern about the future of the planet. It brought Christians together with representatives of most of the other faith communities in Britain. What particularly got up the noses of those who ultimately were to organize and sign the Open Letter was a dramatic presentation in the Cathedral on the Saturday evening which was openly syncretistic in tone. At one stage it said: 'The trees have power. We worship them. *Yanomamo.*'

Some Reflections

I watched it. To be fair, this was not worship. Moreover, the presentation was intensely dull. Only the most dedicated of conservationists, or parents whose duty was to support the thespian activities of their offspring, would willingly have given up their Saturday night for it. But evangelicals – as people who are life-long students of the Scriptures – care intensely about the meaning of words. If these words meant what they appeared to be saying, then it had to be concluded that people were using the Mother Church of the Anglican Communion as a stage for ideas that were sub-Christian and unacceptable.

There is a further dimension. A great deal of what happens on the UK religious scene appears in the press all over the world. If a bishop appears to have denied part of the Creed or if there are reports that the Church of England is sponsoring interfaith worship in ways which appear to suggest that all religions add up to more or less the same thing, then minority Christian communities, especially where there is a high proportion of converts, feel very vulnerable.

Such reports deeply hurt Christians in Pakistan, where the government recently instituted the Muslim Law Code (*Sharia*) 'as the highest law, against which there is no appeal'. They are not helpful in Northern Nigeria where there are periodic outbreaks of violence between Christians and Muslims. They are no comfort in Malaysian cities where Muslim authorities have banned church bells and the singing of Christian hymns. Nor are they much comfort even in Australia, where recently a wayside pulpit carrying the message 'Jesus is Lord' was banned on the grounds that it destroyed social harmony and was offensive to other religious groups.

It needed a campaigning activist to turn pent-up passion into concerted action. The evangelical constituency had such an activist in the person of the Rev. Tony Higton, Vicar of Hawkwell in Essex. Higton had shot into the headlines in 1987 when he moved a motion at General Synod condemning homosexual practice among the clergy (see Chapter 12).

Higton had been active on the issue of the Commonwealth Day Service for some years. Attempts to put the then Archbishop of Canterbury, Robert Runcie, on the spot by asking questions at General Synod were unsuccessful. His next move had been to organize a petition to the Queen, which attracted over 100,000 signatures. Rather than persuading Her Majesty to think again about the Commonwealth Day Observance, it prompted a royal show of strength. The 1991 Observance was attended not only by the Queen and the Duke of Edinburgh, but by the Prince of Wales as well.

Having been effectively brushed aside, Higton had another card up his sleeve: a proposal for an Open Letter to the leadership of the Church of England. As a piece of publicity it was brilliant in its conception and cost-effectiveness.

Reactions to the Open Letter

Even before it reached the public domain, the Open Letter ruffled feathers. The Archbishop of Canterbury, who was shown an advance copy, pleaded with those concerned not to publish it. Despite his own evangelical roots, Dr Carey totally rejected the thinking behind it. He set out some of his reasons in a Presidential Address to the October 1991 sessions of General Synod. 'It failed to define inter-faith worship and prayer. It divided me from my predecessor. It played on Christian fears about encounter with people of other faiths. It was likely to lead to an assumption that they were an unwelcome presence in our society.'

He went on to quote a comment by the Roman Catholic Weekly, the *Tablet*:

> What is missing from the Open Letter is the whole dimension of the human family. There is no sense of the shared crisis facing humanity as a whole. All the world religions today are challenged to ask each other what they most deeply believe, and to see how far they can share, so as to draw strength from each other on behalf of the human family so as to save it from failure.

Its timing upset the church leadership. The Church's Board of Mission, whose Secretary, Canon Philip King, a former General Secretary of the evangelical South American Missionary Society, expressed frustration because his board had a major report on interfaith worship well in hand.

Publication of the Open Letter brought an immediate howl of anger from other faith communities. Dr Zaki Badawi, chairman of the Imams and Mosques Council of the UK, and Principal of the Muslim College, said: 'I hope these people will reconsider their views. This will rebound on them.'

Many of those involved with the Open Letter had not bargained for the way other faith communities interpreted their words as potentially racist. Nor, on the whole, had they thought through how their words would go down in situations like Bradford where all the faith communities came together to offer prayers in the aftermath of the disastrous football-stadium fire.

EVANGELICAL CRITICISMS

There was criticism, too, from among the ranks of the evangelical constituency. Dr Christopher Sugden, director of the Oxford Centre for Mission Studies and a former missionary in Bangalore, India, commented:

> The important issue is what other faith communities heard with the Open Letter. For them, worship and religion cannot be separated off from life. They see life as a whole. They hear our rejection of any possibility of meeting to worship jointly as a rejection of everything they hold dear. It would be like hearing someone say that we are welcome to a party, our wife and children must not come.

In Sugden's view, to say to other faith communities that Christians can do social work with them, though we may not worship together, is to separate religion from the rest of life in a way more characteristic of Enlightenment culture than a world-view formed by the Bible.

Interfaith relations was the topic of the 1992 Anglican Evangelical Assembly held in May. The Open Letter was not debated directly. Nor for that matter was the General Synod report on interfaith worship. What did emerge from the Assembly and subsequent events, was that despite intense discussion, there was more than one evangelical 'school' on the subject.

A CHANGING MISSIONARY CONTEXT

In this debate, evangelicals are struggling to come to terms with a missionary world different from that which existed in earlier decades. One important consideration is that during the days of Empire, missionary work was done from a position of power. Where Empire held sway, there was no great necessity to relate to other faiths on equal terms. But where white Anglo-Saxon British Christians share their neighbourhoods with adherents of other faiths, power does not come into it. They must relate as neighbours on more or less equal terms, with a Christian apologetic that is neither strident nor arrogant.

Trevor Cooling, of the Association of Christian Teachers, told the 1992 Anglican Evangelical Assembly about an exercise he uses in seminars for evangelical leaders. Each person in the group is given a piece of paper with one question on it. They are not allowed to look at their neighbour's piece of paper, and each person must give either a 'yes' or 'no' in answer. The two questions are: 1. As a Christian parent, would you object if a teacher influenced your child away from faith in Christ? 2. As a Christian teacher, would you seek to influence children in your class towards faith in Christ?

'Half the group have question one and half question two, but almost invariably 100 per cent answer "yes" to their question,' Cooling reports.

Usually there is a pregnant silence as the penny drops and participants appreciate the import of this result, namely that as evangelical Christians they are prepared to do unto the children of others what they are not prepared for others to do unto their children. The Golden Rule is contravened.

THEOLOGICAL QUESTIONS

Where, then, does all this leave evangelicals? There are at least two areas needing to be addressed.

The first is fundamental because it has to do with the nature of God, the meaning and purpose of the work of Christ, salvation and judgement. The second concerns the nature of British society, and how we are supposed to get on 'down here'.

In the wake of the Open Letter, most of debate has focused on community relationships. But the presuppositions we bring to that discussion grow out of our theology. And here evangelicals still have a lot of work to do. Do only Christians go to heaven? Is it possible for someone who has not heard of Christ, or who may even have conscientiously rejected Christian presentations of him, to still possess 'saving faith'? How are we to understand the teaching of Hebrews 11 about those who pre-date Christ but are clearly saved through faith in him?

The Mystery of Salvation, the report of the Doctrinal Commission published late in 1995, helpfully defines the key questions in the debate. Exclusivists, it notes, see salvation 'exclusively through explicit faith in Christ, or through the Church'. Inclusivists, on the other hand, see salvation as 'ultimately through Christ, but inclusive of all, or of people who follow other faiths...'[1]

For many years, a broad evangelical consensus operated, based on the thinking of Canon Max Warren, a former General Secretary of the Church Mission Society, where Christians chose to live, work and witness alongside other faiths and seewhere the Spirit led. The Open Letter reopened that whole issue.

'CHRISTIAN' OR PLURALIST

This brings us back to the questions posed at the beginning of this chapter. Should evangelicals be asserting that this is a nation which is at core Christian, and fight for the accompanying privileges? Or should English Christians accept that theirs is a pluralist society, and be prepared to argue the case for their faith in the market place of ideas?

In considering the first option, evangelicals will need to take into account that this is precisely what is happening in many other countries and Christians are among the first to condemn the outcome. In India, where the Ayodhya

Mosque was destroyed, triggering an outbreak of communal violence, radical Hindus were saying, 'Since we are the majority, we will define what India is.' We have seen these same forces at work in many Muslim countries.

For evangelicals in Britain, it is reasonable to register concern about interfaith worship, held in buildings consecrated for Christian use, which compromises the uniqueness of Christ. That is the reason why I signed the Open Letter. I suspect, however, that like many a Euro-politician, some of us signed and only afterwards began to discover the full implications of the fine print. Were we by implication saying, 'We are the majority so we will define what Britain is'?

PEACE BETWEEN THE CULTURES

The gospel of Christ transcends all nations, thought-systems and cultures by announcing a new humanity. According to Ephesians 2, in Christ the human race is made one. His blood has 'broken down the dividing wall of hostility'. Members of the new humanity 'are no longer strangers and sojourners, but you are fellow citizens with the saints and members of the household of God...'

And the mega-issue for the future of the human race is to discover how harmony between the races and cultures can be found. Hans Kung has commented that, if there is to be peace between the great culture blocks of the world, it will be because the religions that underlay them have found a way to live together.[2] All this requires that evangelicals discover a more profound approach to the interfaith issue.

THE FUTURE:
WHAT EVANGELICISM HAS
TO OFFER THE
CHURCH OF ENGLAND

14

THE EVANGELICAL
SOCIAL CONSCIENCE

Now what use is it, my brothers, for a man to say he 'has faith' if his actions do not correspond with it? Could that sort of faith save anyone's soul? If a fellow man or woman has no clothes to wear and nothing to eat, and one of you say 'Good luck to you,' . . . what on earth is the good of that? (Jas. 2.14-16, J. B. Phillips' translation)

We affirm that every Christian congregation must turn itself outward to its local community in evangelistic witness and compassionate service . . . We affirm our duty to study the society in which we live, in order to understand its structures, values and needs, and so develop an appropriate strategy of mission. (Affirmations 16 and 18 of *The Manila Manifesto*, statement of the Congress on World Evangelization, 1989)

A young man with the world of cricket at his feet opts to be ordained and live in the East End of London. He gathers around him a talented team and together they work to establish a church that is indigenous to Canning Town. David Sheppard and his team discover that to be credible the church must possess a 'holistic' gospel that not only saves souls but confronts deprivation and social need.

A young woman, rejected by various missionary societies and voluntary service agencies, goes to Hong Kong under her own steam. For the next twenty years she serves her fellow human beings in a drug-infested part of the colony. Jackie Pullinger's motivation: to share the love of God that she has found through her personal faith.

A young Anglican member of the staff of the Evangelical Alliance is given the task of coordinating the EA's small overseas relief fund that had existed for many years. George Hoffman sets to work with doggedness and vision. In a little more than a decade, TEAR Fund is one of Britain's top charities.

The human race has always made a habit of putting individuals and groups into categories and boxes. Often as not, it is on the basis of the most cursory perusal of the evidence. In St Paul's day it was said that all Cretans were liars. In ours it is said that all Australians are brash. Like their present-day descendants, the greater majority of Cretans of two thousand years ago were probably amiable and honest citizens. Likewise, today there are at least a few Australians who do not live up to their national stereotype.

In our present day, the image of the evangelical social conscience suffers from being stereotyped. As often as not, it is by people who have taken little trouble to inform themselves about it. Evangelicals have been variously labelled: a tambourine-shaking and arm-waving cultic movement that diverts the poor from their misery with promises of 'pie in the sky by and by'; blind followers of the right-wing ideology of the moral majority; rigid fundament-alists whose highly personalized and privatized religion is of no earthly use, or an anti-intellectual stream that flatly denies the fruits either of science or modern biblical scholarship.

Lessons from History

It is fair to say that some evangelicals have sometimes exhibited some of these tendencies. It has therefore required evangelicals both to review their history in order to confront their mistakes, and to look outward and forward to how their faith may be applied in the contemporary world. As we saw in Chapter 6, it is equally fair to say that the achievements of evangelicals in Britain in the period between 1830 and 1880 were considerable. The Clapham Sect, a group who surrounded William Wilberforce, not only saw off the slave trade but won better conditions in the factories and mines. Then there is the factory reform and ragged schools of Ashley Cooper, the Earl of Shaftesbury. The legacy of that work is still visible today in the Shaftesbury Society. Evangelicals are aware, equally, that for some that vision for social involve-ment was somehow lost in the late Victorian era.

Clive Calver, Director of the Evangelical Alliance, has made this issue the subject of a major study. He believes that there was a period, beginning in the latter part of the last century, when evangelicals opted for 'fundamentalist ghettoism', brought on by buying into a doctrine of dispensationalism that led to withdrawal from the cultural mainstream. Martyn Eden, former Dean of the London Institute for Contemporary Christianity and now Public Affairs Director of the EA, likewise cites dispensationalism as a major cause of this shift, together with an evangelical 'defensiveness in the face of liberal theo-logy'. John Stott offers an interesting variation on the theme. 'The chief theo-logical cause of its loss was a vision of God as too religious, instead of a God of creation and Lord of all.'[1]

David Bebbington has made a series of helpful suggestions as to the causes of this loss of evangelical vision.[2] He agrees with Calver about the impact of premillennialism in creating evangelical quietism. By implication it taught that there was little point in Christian intervention in public issues since the imminent return of Christ would set things to right without human help. But Bebbington cites a number of other factors. He suggests, for instance, that in the latter part of the nineteenth century and much of the first half of the twentieth, evangelicals lacked substantial contacts with parliamentarians and opinion leaders. Moreover, the Anglo-Catholic ascendancy, which supported collectivist solutions to social problems, left evangelicals who traditionally emphasized the improvement of the individual on the margins. Only as the Inter-Varsity Fellowship began to produce evangelical graduates throughout the professions and the business world did their position begin to improve.

Recovering the Vision

During the last two decades, evangelicals have been reassessing that situation. For evangelical Anglicans, one of the major turning points was the Keele Congress (see Chapter 7). For evangelicals in general, the Lausanne Congress on World Evangelization (1974) stands out as a turning point. At Lausanne, the quietist outlook of Western evangelicals was radically questioned by Third World evangelicals; in particular by South Americans, Samuel Escobar and Rene Padilla, for whom the gospel was a mandate for political and social involvement. An important follow-up was the Willowbank statement on gospel and culture (1975).

A key figure both at Keele and Lausanne was Dr John Stott. By the late 1970s, he had embraced a whole range of social questions – for example, astounding the constituency by embracing nuclear pacifism. His social thinking is spelled out systematically in *Issues Facing Christians Today*, first written in 1984 and revised in 1990.

Concern for the need to recover the evangelical social conscience led to the foundation of the Shaftesbury Project, whose first director, Patrick Dearnley, later became the Archbishops' Urban Officer following publication of *Faith in the City* (1984). His successor was John Gladwin, who went on to be the Secretary of the Church of England Board for Social Responsibility, Provost of Sheffield, and then Bishop of Guildford. One of John Stott's main concerns was the need to develop a 'Christian mind', where the individual's involvement in work, social issues and leisure were informed by biblically based presuppositions. In pursuit of this concern, he helped found the London Institute for Contemporary Christianity which merged with the Shaftesbury Project in 1988.

Gradually, older evangelical social agencies like the Shaftesbury Society were joined by organizations such as Care, ACET, the Jubilee Centre and TEAR Fund. With the Evangelical Alliance, these agencies have combined to make the evangelical voice a significant one on the national scene.

It is interesting to reflect on how far this sea change within evangelicalism, and evangelicals' growing strength in national structures, has affected how the Church of England now deals with social and public issues. It would be unthinkable if evangelicals were not fairly represented. Moreover, it is almost a matter of formula that each official report includes a section that reviews biblical foundations.

The Biblical Framework

So what are the biblical foundations that inform the evangelical social conscience? Two towering biblical themes give evangelical thinking its shape: the doctrine of Creation and the reality of the cross. At the beginning of the Bible, we are told that God made the human race in his image. It is a view of humanity that runs a collision course with systems like apartheid that discriminate on the basis of race. But it is made even more profound by the fact of the cross. As Patrick Dearnley, puts it, 'The bottom line for me is that if God thought we were worth sending his son to die for us then we should do everything we can to remove the things that spoil and to help that redemptive purpose.'

The Hebraic Tradition

The Hebrew tradition insists that, while in God's sight there is a profound difference between what is sacred and what is profane, there is no place for dualism. Social wrongs are moral wrongs. It is a point that has sometimes been lost on the Western Church which followed classical tradition in making a distinction between the material and the spiritual. This point had its own peculiar effect on some forms of evangelicalism, with concern to separate from 'the world' and to cherish the quest for personal salvation over and above a more holistic understanding of the biblical faith.

The key element in the social teaching of the Old Testament is to be found in the Hebrew word *mishpat* (justice). It prompted the prophet Amos to thunder against those who grew rich by oppressing the poor. 'Let justice flow down like waters, and righteousness like an ever-flowing stream' (Amos 5.24). It established the Year of Jubilee as a remedy for inequality.

The New Testament

When we turn to the New Testament, we find the same passion for justice. The heart of its story is that 'God so loved the world'. The New Testament is well aware that there are forces at work in human society that prevent it flowering into the full potential that is the will of the Creator. Among them are poverty (Luke 6.20), war (Jas. 4.1), discrimination (Col. 3.11), superstition (Gal. 4.9), immorality (1 Thess. 4.3), slavery (Rev. 18.11–13), and oppression (Mark 10.42).

Perhaps the most inspiring of all scriptural passages on this theme is the Magnificat of Mary (Luke 1.46–55). Although it is regularly read and sung in church, it is not necessarily understood. One reason is that the English translation has rendered Mary's poem in the past tense. This does it a disservice because, as various commentators point out, in fact it speaks of God's victory as if it has already happened:

he has scattered the proud in the imagination of their hearts,
he has put down the mighty from their thrones,
and exalted those of low degree;
he has filled the hungry with good things,
and the rich he has sent empty away.

Early Christian Centuries

Evangelicals, particularly, are fond of celebrating the place of apologists and evangelists in winning the Roman Empire to the faith of Jesus Christ. That is only part of the story. It is true that the intellectual arguments of the likes of Tertullian and Justin strengthened this fledgling faith in the market place of ideas. But the actions of the early Church spoke even more loudly than its words. The Church's commitment to helping the weak was a key reason why pagan Rome finally made Christianity its official faith.

Christian values were in sharp contrast to the social mores that operated in the pagan world of the first three centuries of the Christian era. A widow in the first-century world was vulnerable to poverty and exploitation. Clement of Rome records that, by the beginning of the second century, the Christian Church was caring for hundreds of widows. When the plague hit the ancient city of Carthage, pagan households would throw those infected on to the streets. In contrast, the Christian community, led conspicuously by their bishop, would take these people in and care for them. In the fourth century, the Emperor Julian the Apostate, who tried to reintroduce pagan worship in an empire that was now officially Christian, wrote that the only way that paganism could ever make a comeback would be for it to learn to care even more than the Christians.

Issues for Evangelicals

In the remainder of this chapter, I wish to address four issues that illustrate what are the current strengths, questions and opportunities for the evangelical social conscience.

The 'Sunday' Debate

In 1986, evangelicals were at the centre of a coalition of interest groups who successfully lobbied Parliament to defeat the Shops Bill. The Keep Sunday Special campaign managed to get together groups as disparate as the Mothers' Union, the Lord's Day Observance Society and the Shopworkers Trades Union. Six years later, the government piloted through an amended package. Why did it succeed, having been defeated earlier?

I need to comment, first of all, on the evangelical preoccupation with 'Sunday'. The idea of the sabbath was part of the Jewish roots of Christianity, but from early on, the Church celebrated the first day of the week, the day of resurrection, as the Lord's Day. The evidence seems to suggest that while it was a day for worship, it had few sabbath accretions and work went on more or less as usual. As time went by, and particularly after Christianity became the official religion of the Roman Empire, there was a considerable amount of 're-Judaizing'. So 'presbyters' became 'priests', 'the Lord's Table' became 'altar', 'offerings' became 'tithes' and 'the Lord's Day' once again became 'sabbath'. For reasons as much of temperament as of history, Anglo-Catholics have largely appropriated the first two, while evangelicals have tended to emphasize the latter two.

Contemporary evangelicals have a more relaxed Sunday pattern than operated even a generation ago. Indeed, Keep Sunday Special's REST principles, which allowed for the possibility of playing some forms of sport, reflects this. Nevertheless, they were roundly criticized by the more conservative Lord's Day Observance Society. In the end, of course, evangelicals were unable to win their case. In the first instance they were unable to persuade the government to invoke the law against supermarket chains who chose to defy it. Second, they were unable to muster the needed support for an Act enshrining even the REST principles. The reasons were threefold: the commercial interests wishing to change laws that were in fairness highly inconsistent (you could buy a pizza, but not fish and chips, you could buy a Sunday paper but not a Bible) had infinitely more financial resources to fight their case; the coalition that saw off the 1986 Shops Bill did not stay together; and an incumbent government that is successively re-elected has time on its side to pilot changes through the Parliament. I will return to that point later on.

I believe that the fight to keep the traditional Sunday was worthy, but in the end it masked deeper issues for evangelicals about how they themselves live. It is not so much that there is no respite from work, but what to do with leisure time. Leisure can so easily be filled up with a hectic round of activities that are more a treadmill than a recreation.

School Worship

In 1989, the efforts of Baroness Caroline Cox saw to it that the House of Lords passed an amendment to the Education Act that required that state schools should hold regular assemblies where there was an act of worship. It specified that in these acts, and in religious education (RE) courses, the content should recognize Britain's cultural heritage, with content that was 'predominantly Christian'. It was a move hailed at the time by evangelicals as a major victory against secularization and against those humanists who sought to make RE a mishmash reflecting the market place of religion and non-religion that exists in postmodern Britain.

In the succeeding years, however, the subject of school prayers and the content of RE has continued to be a subject of sharp division among evangelicals. There has been consistent concern that the position of Christianity is being eroded in model RE syllabuses. Moreover, evidence abounds that the provisions of the law about assemblies is being consistently broken in a significant proportion of primary schools and the majority of secondary schools. In 1994, for example, the Headmasters' Conference took up the issue, making it plain that the present system was just not working.

In the face of this, evangelical ranks divided. On one side stand lobby groups such as the Tyneside-based Christian Institute, organized by Colin Hart, which cites parental views in support of traditional arrangements. On the other stand organizations like the Association of Christian Teachers, and its General Secretary, Richard Wilkins, who make the point that people who don't believe the Christian faith cannot be compelled to lead Christian acts of worship, and that it is unreal to expect that unbelievers can worship 'in spirit and in truth'.

At the heart of the publicly aired differences between evangelicals on this issue are different perceptions about the nature of British society and how its Christian heritage should be affirmed. For people like Colin Hart, and his mentor, David Holloway, the outspoken Vicar of Jesmond, the number of people of other faiths in Britain is relatively small and the predominant influence on British culture was and will always be Christianity. For others, British life has taken on the character of a market place, and resorting to the law to try to preserve Christian privileges will ultimately be futile. The only course is to try to win hearts and minds by reasoned arguments.

Many of the objectives of Christian Institute bear a close resemblance to those of the American evangelical lobbies that for more than a decade have been waging a campaign to reinstate prayers in state schools. Despite helping President Ronald Reagan into power and being courted by a succession of other administrations, the legislative achievements of the American Christian 'right' on schools and pro-life issues have been negligible. There is presently no substantial evangelical 'right' here in Britain.

It remains to be seen what shape future evangelical action will take in the field of education. What is certain is that evangelicals have a considerable stake in that future and through the London-based Christians in Education, organized by Ann Holt, they have substantial links with the Department of Education. One of their major objectives is to work for a much greater presence of evangelicals in the diocesan and the national Church of England boards of education.

Underneath these issues is a larger one. What is the objective of the Church of England for its enterprise in education? One thing is certain: one in five children in Britain attend Church of England schools. The pastoral and missionary opportunities springing from this are immense, but there seems to be no clear agreement either among evangelicals or in the wider Church as to what the approach should be.

Shaping the Future

What is certain is that evangelicals are moving into the political arena and are becoming sophisticated in the way they lobby politicians and the government about public issues. Just before the last two general elections, a group of evangelical agencies got together to issue a list of questions to elicit the stance of candidates on what were regarded as key issues. How much influence this had we cannot measure, save to comment that it is only possible to achieve broad-based evangelical action by concentrating on a fairly narrow agenda of moral questions such as pornography, abortion and euthanasia.

As we saw with the Sunday debate, for better or for worse evangelicals were outflanked. A party capable of staying in power for a full term or more has almost unfettered power to get its desired legislation through. By the time draft legislation is being discussed, it is nigh impossible to win radical changes. On the whole, however, it is only when Parliament begins to debate that Christian people are alerted to the issues.

What evangelicals therefore need is a means whereby they can anticipate the future and thus play a proper part in shaping the agenda. At the *Church of England Newspaper* we began to lay foundations for a more proactive approach. In 1994, in conjunction with the Evangelical Alliance, *CEN* launched a newsletter called *Westminster Watch*, which keeps its finger on the pulse of national politics, not merely in Parliament but in the political parties and think-tanks. But this only scratches the surface. If evangelicals believe that they have a crucial part to play in bringing British society back from the abyss, they will need to devote far more energy and resources to undertakings of this kind.

Writing in *Christianity Today*, Tom Sine has commented:

> A leading futurist predicts that we will experience as much change in the next ten years as we have in the past three decades. Such rapid change means that the church can no longer plan as though the future were going to be an extension of the present. We will not only need to do a better job of anticipating the future, we must become even more imaginative about responding to tomorrow's challenges.

New Alliances

One political development that has caught a great deal of evangelical imagination is the Movement for Christian Democracy (MCD). The inspirational figure is Roman Catholic MP, David Alton, who is due to leave politics after the next general election following the abolition of his seat. The MCD is unique in that it draws membership from right across the parties. It is also unique because it has created a growing political coalition between Roman Catholics and evangelicals. It began with a relatively narrow agenda, notably pro-life issues and anti-pornography. It has gradually widened its range of concerns to include issues like broadcasting standards, debt, and even how to sort out London's traffic hassles.

The MCD has steadfastly set its face against becoming a political party in its own right, in the manner of continental groups under the influence of Dutch Reformed thinking. Its strength is that it can draw ideas from across the political spectrum. This is refreshing in a country that is frankly bored by much of the petty pointscoring of party politics. Its prospects of having a significant political influence would be transformed if proportional representation were adopted in either the British or European Parliaments.

But the MCD is important for another reason. As I have already said, I believe that the full recovery of the evangelical social conscience will be a key factor if the tide of secularism, disorder and disintegration is to be reversed in Britain. I do not believe, however, that evangelicals can achieve this on their own. They have neither the numbers, the experience, nor the ideas to work single-handed. They must be willing to do what even ten years ago would have been unthinkable: work strategically with Roman Catholics. Evangelicals and catholics broadly agree on the moral agenda. Evangelical Anglicans share the catholic creeds with Roman Catholics and have common baptismal vows. As I have indicated already, a significant evangelical-catholic accord now exists in the USA.

Three Further Issues

In concluding, I would like to raise three further issues that are still major debating points among evangelicals and need to be resolved.

1. The Tension between Evangelism and Social Action

The underlying problem is that some evangelicals have a mistaken dualist understanding that divides nature from grace and the spiritual from the material. There is still a tendency for some evangelicals to regard the material world and the world of the spirit as either/or. Others see the point of social action only as a means to evangelism. For a holistic model, we have only to read about the ministry of Jesus. Jesus is good, both as a 'sign' of the coming kingdom and out of the sheer goodness of his heart.

2. Disagreements about 'Kingdom' Theology

As I have tried to show above (and I will pick this up again when I look at the Decade of Evangelism in Chapter 15), a proper understanding of 'kingdom' is crucial. Nevertheless, a number of evangelical debates remain. There are some who 'spiritualize' kingdom to the exclusion of its use as an inspiration for political and social action. Others, particularly those influenced by dispensationalism (mistakenly, I believe) locate the coming of the kingdom some time in the future to the detriment of contemporary involvement. To confuse the picture further, some evangelicals (particularly those in the so-called house churches) have embraced a form of postmillennialism, which posits the creation of a future Christian society. All these issues need open debate within the evangelical constituency.

3. Right-Wing Politics

Evangelicals are largely drawn from the middle classes. Right-wing parties everywhere have tended to view them as a constituency to be colonized and used for their ends. This process is nakedly obvious in American politics but more subtle here in Britain. In the end, it is an issue for representative bodies of the evangelical constituency here in Britain to keep in review.

15

AN EMPHASIS ON EVANGELISM

This Conference calls for a shift to a dynamic missionary emphasis going beyond care and nurture to proclamation and service. (Resolution 44, Lambeth Conference 1988)

The only hermeneutic of the gospel is a congregation of men and women who believe in it and live by it. (Bishop Lesslie Newbigin, *The Gospel in a Pluralist Society*, SPCK, 1989, p. 277)

Parishioners at a west country village, where the parish church is comfortably full with about one hundred people attending each week, undertake a mission audit. They discover that the bulk of worshippers come from the end of the village where the parish church is located. In order to reach out to the other half of the village they resolve to transplant part of the congregation to the British Legion hall at the other end of the village. Very soon there are one hundred people attending services in both places.

Parishioners at Wensleydale decide to hold what they label 'The Wensleydale Feast'. They pray that 140 people will turn up and they do. Towards the end of an enjoyable evening Canon Michael Green of Springboard talks for ten minutes to explain what the gospel is about. Those attending are invited to fill in a card if they want to learn more. Thirteen people who were not church attenders complete the form. They become part of a nurture group and are brought fully into the life of the Church.

If there is one issue on which all evangelicals agree, it is the priority of evangelism. If there is one thing on which most will unite, it is in support of some major evangelistic effort. As we have seen in Chapter 1, this is fuelled by a white-hot emphasis on the need for personal conversion. According to the great missionary statesman of the fifties, the late Canon Max Warren, the call to conversion is 'the very heart of the evangelical approach, the citadel of its doctrine, the key to its pastoralia, the method of its evangelism'.

This emphasis has created an essentially activist movement where, as David Bebbington has observed, 'a natural implication is a constant quest for fresh converts'. Charles Haddon Spurgeon, one of the great Free Church preachers whose writings and sermons are still an inspiration to countless evangelical preachers, once said he would never preach a sermon which did not make clear the way of salvation. One of evangelicalism's strongest preoccupations is the training of lay people in apologetics and various methods of bringing people to personal faith. It is no coincidence, therefore, that evangelical Anglican parishes devote a great deal more resources than other traditions to youth and children's work.

In this chapter I want to spell out what this core evangelical commitment has to offer the wider Church. At the same time, we should not underestimate how much the decision of the Church of England to embark on a Decade of Evangelism has effected evangelicalism. First of all, it has created an opportunity for evangelicals to offer what is their greatest strength for the benefit of the wider Church. Second, it is challenging evangelicals to reflect more deeply on their theology and practise of evangelism.

What Is Evangelism?

Because evangelicals are essentially practical people, they have tended not to put a lot of emphasis on either a definition or a theology of evangelism. At the various Lausanne Congresses on World Evangelization, workshops on new methods of evangelism always attracted large numbers whereas those on theology tended to attract only a minority.

Trying to find and agree a definition and theology of evangelism is a dangerous undertaking. The Church of England was conscious of this in its planning of the Decade of Evangelism. In the early months, the aim was to obtain the broadest possible base of support for the undertaking. Adoption of any single definition would, of necessity, have narrowed rather than broadened this base. In any case, since the advent of big evangelistic crusades from D. L. Moody to Billy Graham, it has proved possible to obtain wide participation in the absence of a clear definition which in the end was provided by the actual proclamation.

Nevertheless, in the context of a Decade of Evangelism, where the emphasis is as much on the reshaping of the Church for its missionary task as it is going out to win new converts, working on the creation of a shared understanding of what the gospel is, and of the meaning of 'evangelism', is imperative.

I want to venture that evangelism is 'proclaiming the kingdom of God', and in doing so I gladly acknowledge my debt to Canon John Chapman who was for many years Head of the Department of Evangelism for the Diocese of Sydney.

The Kingdom

The coming of the kingdom is the keynote of Jesus' teaching, as recorded in the Gospels. Mark, for example, is an extended gospel tract. Its natural divisions give us an outline of the teaching of the early Church about what is the nature of the gospel. Jesus' first recorded words are, 'The time is fulfilled, and the kingdom of God is at hand; repent, and believe in the gospel' (Mark 1.15). The work of evangelism is to invite people to become citizens of the kingdom, by acknowledging the place of God as the king through personal repentance of sin and belief in his Son.

Mark's Gospel spells this out in detail. Having sounded this keynote, a long prelude unfolds. Jesus engages in a period of public ministry accompanied by healings, signs and wonders. Then at about the halfway point of the document, Jesus takes his disciples away from the crowds to a quiet place in Caesarea Philippi. He first asks who the crowds say he is. Then he asks for their own view and we have Peter's confession: 'You are the Christ' (Mark 8.29). That is the turning point. Mark says that from then on Jesus began to teach his disciples that being the Christ meant suffering and death at the hands of the authorities. At the end, when all has been accomplished and Jesus has breathed his last, a Gentile centurion delivers the final verdict: 'Truly this man was the Son of God' (Mark 15.39). The reader is left with the opportunity to make their own judgement.

Gospel and Kingdom

All sorts of implications for the practice of evangelism grow from linking it to proclamation of the kingdom. An emphasis on 'kingdom' suggests that evangelism does not belong merely to the private domain. The coming of the rule of God places the existing human order under judgement. That understanding is encouraging evangelicals to search for their historical roots in an endeavour to discover, for example, why a movement that achieved so much in the field of social justice in the time of Wilberforce and the Clapham Sect later became 'quietist', giving the impression that faith was essentially a private, individual matter.

Another consequence is the opportunity to explore the place of the prophetic in church and national life. Earlier generations of evangelicals were generally more interested in the 'foretelling' than the 'forthtelling' dimension of prophecy. We are now seeing a recovery of the 'forthtelling' dimension. Nevertheless, proclamation of the gospel will always be directed to the call for conversion, and everything springs from it. As John Wesley once said, 'The soul of improvement is the improvement of the soul.'

Church as 'Sign' of the Kingdom

Likewise, the need to reorder the Church to be truly missionary in purpose is prompting evangelicals to look more seriously at the nature and role of the Church. As I have already noted, in the past evangelicals have tended not to take ecclesiology seriously. They have at times tried to conduct programmes of evangelism that were largely divorced from the life of the churches. Evangelicals are now more likely to see the point of the Roman Catholic dictum that there is no salvation outside the Church. Thus the Church exists both to proclaim the kingdom in word and deed and to be a 'sign' of the Kingdom. In the process, there is a wider understanding of proclamation which can be through worship, the quality of relationships within the life of the Church, the evident work of the Spirit in the life of the Christian community, or practical demonstration including care for the poor.

Hallmarks of a Missionary Church

An international Mission Issues and Strategies Group, convened by the Anglican Consultative Council, has observed that for generations Anglican parishes worked primarily according to a pastoral model. They are reasonably proficient at nurturing existing believers, but few were geared to reaching beyond the confines of their congregations to make new Christians. The primary task in the Decade, then, is to trigger a radical overhaul and rediscover what it means to be a missionary church. So where do we look to discover what the hallmarks of a missionary church might be?

One of the tasks the Church of England should set itself is to look more closely at why the so-called house churches have grown so rapidly in the last decade and a half. I believe that a study of the rapid growth of Pentecostal Churches in traditionally Roman Catholic South America, where it is estimated that new people are being added at a rate of 400 per hour, would yield similar results.

1. SPIRITUAL IN OUTLOOK

These churches are unashamedly spiritual in their outlook. In contrast to so many Anglican clergy, their leaders are not embarrassed to talk about God in public. They may address political issues as required, but they do not politicize the gospel. They realize that people want spiritual answers to spiritual questions. They are bathed in prayer. In most of these churches there will be a group of intercessors who commit themselves to meet regularly, often very early in the morning, to pray for every aspect of the life of the church and its people.

2. THEY ARE 'POPULAR'

The leaders know how to speak the language of the people. Worship is informal. Undoubtedly an underlying liturgical form exists, even if it is not immediately discernible, but there is space for human contact and spontaneity. The style of music is unashamedly popular. Whereas much Anglican music is akin to Radio 3, visitors to these churches will hear strains more like Radio 1 or Radio 2. Archbishop George Carey once commented that the Church of England risked 'dying of good taste'.

3. THEY MOBILIZE EVERY MEMBER

In almost every case, leadership is expressed corporately. Most have created organizational structures where people work in teams on every aspect of church life from organizing worship; visiting the neighbourhood, the sick and elderly; planning evangelistic strategies; leading children's and youth work; through to administration and finance. Undergirding this is a commitment to train people for these tasks. The result is an articulate congregation of Christians, each of whom is equipped to 'give a reason for the hope that is within them'.

4. THEY CREATE COMMUNITY

Networks of mutual help are established that are in no way dependent on the clergy or leaders. In many ways, they develop the character of an extended family. If the homemaker in a family unit is sick, they rally round with practical help with cooking, shopping, and collecting the children from school. If a member is in financial difficulty through unemployment, there will be gifts in cash and kind until they get back on their feet. Some have developed credit unions to tackle the insidious problem of family debt. There are indications, too, especially among the Black Churches, that they are committed to helping individuals to become more effective economic units.

There are some implications to be extracted for the Anglican Church as it seeks to reorient itself to become a missionary Church. For too many Anglicans, 'church' has come to mean 'building'. Linked to that, the office of vicar conveys such powerful prerogatives that the building becomes their church. It is all too human in these circumstances for clergy to assert their rights and for parishioners to stand back and let them 'get on with it'.

To truly be a missionary church, however, one further ingredient is needed. It is very easy for a church to be little more than a social club. A missionary church, however, will consciously limit its activities and will make sure that everything that it does is geared to serve its call to mission. As Robert Warren, the National Officer for the Decade of Evangelism has said, 'The pastoral and maintenance church seems to be marked by doing different things (church groups and activities). A missionary church will be marked by doing the ordinary things (work, leisure, family life) differently.'

The Decade

We have now passed the mid-point of the 'Decade'. Why a Decade of Evangelism in the first place? How effective has it been so far? What is to be said of the evangelical contribution to it? And are there new questions for evangelicals emerging from it?

Why a Decade?

The cynic could say that there should be no need for the Church to contemplate a Decade of Evangelism on the grounds that evangelism should be a normal part of its life. This is a fair point. Yet it can be argued that when only about one million out of forty-seven million attend Sunday services of the national Church, there is a strong case for giving priority to recalling the lapsed and reaching out with the Good News to people who have not heard it explained clearly.

Top-Down or What?

There was a lot of debate about how the Decade should be launched. Early on, it was thought that each diocese should send a representative to a great service in Canterbury and light a torch that would be carried, Olympic-style, to the other forty-two cathedrals throughout the country from where each parish in turn would ignite its own torch. This was ruled out for good reasons. First of all, the idea that Canterbury is the cradle of the evangelization of England is contentious to say the least. When St Augustine came to Britain in 597, he found that a Celtic church with its own robust brand of evangelism already existed. Second, it was realized that in recent years few 'top-down' efforts at nationwide evangelism have actually worked. Third, and most important, it was realized that the real need was not a set of activities but a basic reorienting of the life of the Church of England.

Mid-Point Evaluation

So now, having passed the mid-point of the Decade, what tentative conclusions can be drawn about its effectiveness? There are, of course, some who have already written it off as yet another passing fad. That is less than fair. We have only to look at the way the Decade has reshaped how many of the dioceses define their priorities to see that it has had much more effect than most resolutions passed by Lambeth Conferences.

A good example is the diocese of London where Bishop David Hope, while voicing the wish that it should be labelled the Decade of 'Evangelization' (to connote a wider agenda that included social action as well as promotion of personal conversion), nevertheless launched an Agenda for Action in which he asked the parishes to conduct a mission audit and set themselves clearly defined mission priorities. A similar process has occurred in most dioceses.

Likewise, we have seen a lot of rethinking about the actual role of bishops. Across the river in South London, Southwark diocese has reordered its diocesan administration so that it is geared for mission. Each of its bishops leads an area mission team which is available both for formal mission events and for training the clergy and laity in the work of evangelism.

NEW MODELS

The Decade has thrown up new models for evangelism, such as the Alpha course, now in use in over 1,200 churches. The process is akin to the ancient catechumenate. Participants attend a series of meetings where the rudiments of the faith are explained. The menu includes: Who is Jesus? Why did he die? Why should I read the Bible? Who is the Holy Spirit? What about the Church? No sceptical questions are unwelcome. On the way, a great many who began professing no faith find themselves becoming active believers.

SHIBBOLETHS QUESTIONED

Even here, certain evangelical shibboleths are being re-evaluated. Since the Moody and Sankey missions of the late Victorian era, evangelicals have tended to set great store on 'instant' conversion in the manner of Saul on the Damascus road. Alpha demonstrates that conversion can be a process that takes place over a period of time, in contrast to the long-held evangelical notion that it had to be a single, climacteric event. Likewise, Alpha integrates evangelism and instruction in the faith in a healthy way, whereas many evangelical groups were previously stymied in evangelical parishes because of a perceived need to 'build up the Christians first.'

MINISTRY TO CHILDREN

There is similar rethinking in the area of children's ministry. In earlier generations, evangelical parents were often deeply concerned that their children made a 'decision' for Christ. It is now more widely understood that Christian parents should treat their children as not potential but actual members of the Church, quietly encouraging them to enter the full inheritance of faith promised in their baptism.

Robert Warren, the National Officer for the Decade of Evangelism, has offered a mid-term report of the Decade in *Signs of Life*, published early in 1996.[1] It contains a lot of encouraging anecdotes. It claims that the Church of England's decline has 'bottomed out', though it is somewhat short of statistics. But it raises two other important questions: 1. Is it not fair to say that much of the activity attributed to the Decade would have happened anyway? 2. Is it not fair to say that any church that preaches a 'message' will experience growth, Decade or no Decade?

An Unfinished Agenda

I would suggest, however, that there remain some unfinished agenda items.

1. The Market Place of Ideas

It is clear, as the Archbishop of Canterbury has acknowledged, that during the last century and a half the Church has fared very badly in the market place of ideas.

The Church emerged from the encounter with Darwin and Freud as the loser because of its mental rigidity. The centre of intellectual life moved away from its long association with religion. And religion responded – at least at first – largely in a negative spirit. It lost an opportunity to absorb new insights, not least because it was too firmly wedded to a science of an earlier age. Worse, the Church failed to grasp the significance of the new intellectual challenges to the Christian faith, and when it began to do so at the turn of the last century, most of the damage had been done. The conditions had been created for the growth of an implicit agnosticism, which was largely the consequence of the steady erosion of a dynamic and speculative approach to theism. The discoveries of the eighteenth and nineteenth centuries (made by those who were, in the main, practising Christians) were vitiated by the Churches which found new ideas deeply shocking.[2]

SCIENCE AND FAITH

While it may be true that science and religion are no longer at war, and a great many scientists and theologians believe that these disciplines complement each other, the Church is still losing out in the encounter with science. MARC Europe has claimed that British young people are deserting the Church at the rate of one thousand a week. While the figure has been disputed the point still stands: the Church is facing an uphill battle for the minds of the next generation. Is it a coincidence that the age at which most youngsters leave the Church is the age at which they begin to encounter some of the hard questions that science poses for faith? Yet among the plethora of study materials produced for Sunday schools, youth fellowships, and religious education for youngsters at these ages, there is hardly any that deal adequately with the questions of faith and science.

FREUD'S LEGACY

Equally important is coming to terms with the legacy of Sigmund Freud, the other tower of influence in modern Western culture. 'A theological dogma might be refuted [to a person] a thousand times,' he once wrote, 'provided, however, he had need of it, he again and again accepts it as true.'

Evangelicals, of course, depend on truth claims as the core of their apologetic. They claim that their faith can be validated by the appeal to history. Belief in God and the claims of Christ hinge, ultimately, on actual history, with the bodily resurrection of Christ as the ultimate proof. (Little wonder that there was an evangelical outcry when Dr David Jenkins raised questions about the bodily resurrection.) Thanks to Freud and his legacy, the modern person is no longer impressed by the appeal to historical 'proofs'. Today, rather than being confronted by an unbelieving rationalist, the evangelical apologist is more likely to encounter the modern person who says, 'What you believe is fine for you, but so what?'

AFTER THE ENLIGHTENMENT

Most apologetics in current use reflect the debate between faith and the rationalism of the Enlightenment. Postmodernism has thrown up a whole range of new preoccupations. It is no longer a case of persuading people to believe in the 'spiritual' but instead to forward the case for Christ in a supermarket of competing spiritualities. In such an environment, the Christian faith is as much caught as taught. There is much to learn from the missionary endeavour of the early Church, where the care for the poor, the sick and the widow, and attractiveness of worship were of equal importance in propagating the faith by the apologists.

2. Understanding the Generations

Another important dimension is to understand that this generation has created what Michael Sack has labelled 'the multiplex congregation'. Anglicanism has always aspired to a common liturgy and a common lectionary, but every parish consists of at least four distinct audiences and these do not fit together harmoniously. These are outlined here:

GENERATION X

Age range sixteen to twenty-five, Generation X. They are the 'feed me' generation. They have been hard hit by changes in the economy and many have never had a 'proper job'. Their self-esteem is low, and they tend to retreat into tight, self-contained groups. They look to the Church for unconditional love and acceptance, and a very short list of what is right and what is wrong.

BUSTERS

Age range twenty-five to thirty-five. This is the 'why me?' generation. Unlike Generation X, many got a start in the formal economy, but are falling out of it as it retracts. They dislike mingling with other generations, and are sceptical of guarantees, either from politicians, clergy, or other authority figures.

BOOMERS

Age range thrity-five to fifty. This is the 'entertain me' generation. They are faddish and intellectually lazy. Nevertheless, they are looking for clear spiritual definition. They want to talk about meaning, self-definition and worth. They are restless for new models of church life, and fascinated by the media.

OLDER ADULTS

Age range fifty and up. This is the 'need me and show me' generation. They often possess skills and material resources. They want to do something worthwhile. They need positive mentoring from peers, and appreciation.[3]

Evangelicals instinctively understand the need to focus evangelism and worship for the different generations, according to temperament and their stage in the lifecycle. The Church of England needs to understand that concern to order worship and parish life in that manner need be no threat to 'Anglican order'.

3. Internationalism

One of the lessons gradually dawning on the Church of England is the benefits that can accrue from relationships with the Churches of the so-called Third World. The Church of England is finding that the deployment of people from these Churches can make breakthroughs for evangelism that do not normally come otherwise. People from the Third World have a spirituality that makes no distinction between the sacred and profane. They are therefore able by example to encourage English people to talk naturally about their faith. Another benefit is that for some reason they are able to break through English reserve about speaking on topics that are regarded as private or personal. In addition, their world-view enables them to speak openly and naturally about social issues in a way that is not in conflict with holding a personal faith. It is to be hoped that the Decade will stimulate even more Christians from the Third World to come here and to other parts of post-Christendom Europe as missionaries.

4. Academic Research and Statistics

What is truly surprising is that there are few academic institutions here in Britain which offer advanced studies in mission. In consequence, apart from the work of the Association for Christian Research, there is a paucity of statistical information and reflection on what is undertaken by the Churches in the name of mission. We do not know enough about the conditions under which British churches grow, nor are we in a position to evaluate claims of churches that they are 'growing'.

Evangelical churches, particularly, need to be more hard-minded about distinguishing between 'transfer growth' and growth as a result of evangelistic outreach. Likewise, they need more insight on the distinction between 'revivalism' (recalling lapsed Christians to faith) and 'evangelism' which must of necessity mean 'making new Christians'.

5. Models for National Events

One reason why the critics say the Decade is dead is that it appears to have had little impact on the national consciousness. As yet, it has turned its face against staging events aimed at making the entire nation sit up and take notice of clear proclamation of the gospel. In 1997, there will be a series of national pilgrimages to mark the coming of St Augustine and St Columba to these shores, but it is a good question whether these events will serve such a purpose. Without new models for getting the ear of the entire nation, a Decade of Evangelism remains essentially a case of the Churches doing much the same as they always have done.

154

16

EVANGELICAL SPIRITUALITY

Worship is not the prelude to a sermon; it is a lifestyle that is to be nurtured every day. (Alvin Slaughter)

Begin each day with private reading of the Word and prayer. Sin will keep you from this book, or this book will keep you from sin. (John Bunyan)

In the bar at the General Synod, I found myself in conversation with a leading member of the catholic group. Suddenly the conversation took a serious turn. 'Do you know why I could never be an evangelical?' she asked. I was on the edge of my seat. 'You people have no spirituality!'

Spirituality: A Problematic Term

Not all evangelicals like the term spirituality. For the more protestant, it carries the connotations of ritual and even superstition. For others, it suggests New Age attitudes, a supermarket of beliefs and rituals where the individual is free to 'pick and mix' according to personal preference. Not all spirituality is Christian. As Alister McGrath has noted, 'The Buddhist idea of meditating by emptying the mind of all its thoughts stands in contrast to the Christian idea of allowing the mind to focus in Jesus Christ.'[1]

Nevertheless, spirituality is a buzz word these days. While the sales of most kinds of religious books have plummeted in recent years, sales of books about spirituality continue to grow. There is a great demand for anthologies of 'classics' of spirituality from the Eastern churches as well as the West. Publishers that once traded solely in evangelical titles are eager to add 'catholic' spirituality titles to their range. Anthony Bloom's *School of Prayer* is as much read among evangelicals as it is among the Orthodox. Courses on spirituality are in great demand. Retreat venues report record bookings.

Ten years ago, few evangelical vicars would have dreamed of suggesting that their parishioners should go on retreat. Now retreats are being promoted as an accepted and necessary part of life. As well as being encouraged to take part in formal retreats, evangelical laity are taught to create their own informal retreat days, making use of silence and the standard techniques of meditation and contemplative prayer.

There is much that is healthy about these developments. In part it grows out of wide dissatisfaction over the standard evangelical approaches to devotional life. The reason is that while contemporary evangelicalism encourages mammoth efforts to discover the Bible on an informational level, it is less skilful at valid use of it to address the heart and emotions. When I was growing up, I had the privilege of hearing excellent public exegesis of the Bible, but there was a widely held view that application was a personal, private matter. Many evangelicals are retarded in their spirituality, thanks to Bible teachers who made a false distinction between Word and Spirit.

Issues for Evangelicals

Word versus Spirit

One of my abiding memories is of my father reading the Bible at the dinner table every evening. He was very keen that we learn portions of Scripture off by heart. When I was nine, Billy Graham came to Australia for his first crusade there and my father drilled us on all the verses prescribed for counsellors. The outcome was that I absorbed a simple but profound framework for personal faith that has never left me. I can still recite all these verses (in King James English, of course).

Later, I did several courses in biblical studies at university level. At the same time I bought a copy of Alan Stibbs's evangelical classic, *Search the Scriptures*, and worked systematically through practically every book of the Bible. Added to that, I benefited from the my university Evangelical Union's tradition of offering weekly public lectures, many of which took the form of exposition of biblical books and themes. In my second year at university I read *The Kingdom of God* by the American Presbyterian, John Bright (Abingdon, 1963). It was highly important because as well as unpacking a theme that is at the core of Jesus' message, it put the Scriptures into a framework. When I went to university I resolved that my knowledge and skill with the Scriptures should be at the same level as my ordinary academic study. It is no boast to say that by my early twenties I achieved that. Despite this enormous effort, I still had few skills in prayer, silence or stillness. I had a faith that required a punishing round of activism.

The 'Quiet Time'

For generations, the central plank of evangelical spirituality has been the daily quiet time. It consists of subscribing to daily notes published by a variety of publishing houses. The common format is a short Scripture selection, accompanied by a few 'thoughts' by the author of the series, and points for prayer and reflection. Like many who aspired to having a daily quiet time, I found there were two problems. First, having been so thoroughly schooled in the Bible, I found that the notes rarely did more than scratch the surface of the daily portion. Second, and more significantly, I found difficulty in making a regular space in my busy lifestyle for a quiet time. Failure to keep this discipline is a major source of evangelical guilt trips. A friend of mine, who was for many years a missionary in Africa, told me recently how despite the fact that she rarely read them, she would leave her Scripture Union notes in a highly visible place in the living room, open at the day's portion, in hope that none of her colleagues would suspect that she was 'backsliding'.

More than it knows, modern evangelicalism is a creature of the Enlightenment, and its contention that only reason really matters. As Alister McGrath has pointed out, many Christians

> limit their spirituality to understanding the biblical text: reading it, making sense of its words and ideas, and understanding its historical background and thus its meaning for today. Thus the emphasis continues to be on reason. Yet we need to reach behind the Enlightenment, and recover older and more authentic evangelical approaches to spirituality ... The Enlightenment placed an embargo on any *emotional* involvement with the Scripture, or any use of the human faculty of imagination – two approaches which earlier evangelicalism had treasured. Scripture was to be read as if it were a religious textbook, not a narrative of the love of God.[2]

Back to Classic Roots

That the spirituality of protestants and evangelicals has been affected more by the legacy of arid Enlightenment rationalism than a great many other Christian traditions helps explain a long-standing evangelical defensiveness in the face of a century of confident Anglo-Catholicism. Now, however, evangelicals are sharing in the cultural mood swing against Enlightenment rationalism. In the process, many are eager to discover tools and models of spirituality used in other traditions, not least those of Roman Catholicism and Eastern Orthodoxy.

This, of course, has its benefits. The Churches of the Reformation cannot claim a monopoly on truth, and in seeking to rid the Church of unhelpful accretions, it is just possible that it discarded things of value.

There is, however, a danger. In this generation there are evangelicals embracing other traditions, turning their back on evangelicalism, for the reason that they have come to believe – like my friend at the General Synod – that evangelicalism lacks a robust and satisfying spirituality. They are misinformed. But the fact that so many people brought to faith through evangelicalism have come to believe so, indicates that somehow evangelicalism has let them down. It has done so by losing touch with its own classic roots and it needs to rediscover them.

I will now try to enumerate what to me are some of the hallmarks of evangelical spirituality.

1. A World-Affirming Faith

As well as shaking the institutional Church, the Reformation led to radical changes in individual spirituality. The spirituality of the medieval Church was cloistered behind monastery walls and the spiritual fare of ordinary people was meagre. In order to be a serious Christian, the only option was to leave the world and join a religious community. It was a spirituality that was celibate, ascetic and elitist.

The Reformation offered a completely fresh focus. The inheritors of the Reformation spoke of living the Christian life. The Reformers showed that devotion did not require withdrawal from society. It was possible to engage in mundane living, to live every moment in the presence of God, and to order one's affairs according to the Word of God. It was a holistic faith. The life of the family, work on the farm, the workshop, the kitchen, carrying out one's profession or trade, were all endeavours to be organized in a way that conformed to God's will, and were to be done with all a person's might.

A major theme from the Reformation, that forms a key part of classic evangelical spirituality, is stewardship. The Reformers reacted against the asceticism of medieval spirituality by emphasizing the teaching of Jesus about being good stewards of talents and money. They encouraged merchants, artisans, farmers, housewives and bankers to discover the spiritual value of their work. This, they insisted, was a sphere for vocation. It was a faith that equipped the Christian for life in the market place. The protestant work ethic grew from the Reformed understanding of stewardship. It partly explains the essentially practical mindset of the evangelical. Family life, the raising of children, and the care of the old, were sacred trusts. Family prayers became a cornerstone of Christian devotion.

2. The Primacy of the Word

Evangelicals inherit from the Reformers a spirituality of the Word. The Reformation brought a renewed emphasis on it. It can be argued that, as much as anything else, this was a recovery of the Church's primitive roots. Meditation on the Word is at the foundation of the Gospel of John. Jesus is revealed as the Word. He is the revelation of the Wisdom of God who made the world and held it together by his power. The very centre of the Christian life is hearing this Word, receiving it through faith, and living it in daily experience.

This spirituality happily draws on the Church's Jewish roots. The Psalmist spoke of meditating on God's law. Studying and caring for the sacred books, copying their texts, preserving a history of interpretation, and using them as a source for preaching was a huge enterprise for the Jewish people. Much emphasis was given to learning to recite texts. The apostles put premium on prayer and the ministry of the word (Acts 2.4).

The Reformation led to a recovery of the preaching of the word. John Colet (1467-1519), Dean of St Paul's, was one of the early exemplars of a fresh approach to the Scriptures that sought to uncover the direct meaning of the text. Later, Luther, Calvin, John Knox and others put aside the official church lectionary and preached sermon series on biblical books. This is still the staple diet of many evangelical churches.

The advent of the printing press made it possible for the ordinary person to read, and study the Scriptures for themselves. Belief that the Scriptures were perspicuous, that even the simplest ploughboy could understand their meaning, made this study a serious, almost universal exercise. Today, evangelical churches put a premium on Bible study at all levels: its exposition from the pulpit; as the centrepiece of weekly meetings in churches or homes; and for the individual on a daily basis.

Yet it is precisely here that during the last century many evangelicals have unwittingly bought into the Enlightenment's agenda, though without some of the excesses in which others indulged. Of course, they have not done so to the extent, say, of some other protestant traditions. I suppose the epitome of application of Enlightenment influence on biblical studies was the old 'International Critical Commentary' series. Most contained highly complex technical analysis, then followed the briefest of notes on the text's 'religious significance'. A combination of a need to be seen as meticulous in the exegesis of the biblical text, and an understandable desire to distance themselves from some of the more woolly elements in their own tradition, left a great many evangelical Bible exegetes in a not dissimilar position, making a false distinction between Word and Spirit.

There are plenty of signs, however, that evangelicalism has moved beyond this phase. The Inter Varsity Press's 'The Bible Speaks Today' series is a good example. What is more, evangelicals are discovering that application of the tools of modern critical scholarship opens up fresh possibilities for use of the classical evangelical approaches to meditating on the Scriptures.

The psalms are the great sourcebook of evangelical spirituality. The earliest Christians treated the psalms as the prayers of the Holy Spirit. When they had their backs to the wall and faced persecution they drew comfort that the yearnings of the psalms had been utterly fulfilled in the coming of Christ. The psalms helped them pray when they could articulate no words. They were a manual that gave them permission to speak frankly to God of their pain, their anger and about the iniquity of injustice. Little wonder, then, that Isaac Watts, the first great hymnwriter in the English language, based many of his hymns on the psalms. Likewise, Charles Wesley both produced metrical psalms and dotted many of his other hymns with allusions to them. In our own decade, the popularity of *Psalm Praise* witnesses to the endurance of the psalms as a devotional sourcebook. For this reason, I believe it is one of the great tragedies of Church of England worship that the regular reading or singing of the psalms in worship has been phased out.

3. Living in the Presence of God

Evangelicals inherit from the Reformers the conviction that no intermediary is needed in the prayers of the saints. Believers are themselves a kingdom of priests who may at any time enter boldly into the presence of the heavenly Father. For the Reformers, it meant teaching ordinary people that they did not need to wait until Mass before they could bring their petitions before God, nor pay a distant religious community in order to have their concerns added to a prayer diary.

Today, it means that when I am under pressure in the workplace I can silently send an arrow prayer and say 'Your calm, Lord', or if my temper is apt to boil over at someone who is being impossible, I can say 'Your patience, Lord'.

Evangelicals are essentially 'doers', and hence intercession is at the core of their prayer life. It is here, however, that it is possible to see evangelical spirituality at its worst as well as at its best. Human selfishness and self-centredness know no bounds, and the art of intercession is getting our desires in line with God's purposes. The starting point is realization of our need for the Spirit to 'teach us to pray'.

Because prayer is communication, it can take many different forms. It may just be saying a word, 'God', or 'Lord', to acknowledge that I am in the presence of the divine. A lot of my personal prayer takes the form of singing as I walk, using the words of hymns and spiritual songs I know by heart.

SUPPLICATION

Supplication is essentially a prayer of request. In his evangelical classic, *Prayer*, Ole Hallesby (IVP, 1948) says of supplication, 'It is the will of our heavenly Father that we should come to him freely and confidently and make known our desires to him, just as we would have our children come freely and of their own accord and speak to us of the things they would like to have.'

THANKSGIVING

Thanksgiving is a difficult form of prayer because Anglo-Saxons, particularly, are not good at being effusive in thanksgiving. I have been in many a meeting for extemporary prayer where the leader has suggested that a period of time should be given over to praise. Within moments, prayers are being punctuated by the phrase, 'And we ask . . .' Prayer of thanksgiving invites us to keep an inventory of the good things God has given us: health, work, shelter, family ties, friends, food and clothing. The Bible, too, is a storehouse of reasons for praise: recital of what God has done in the history of salvation, the person and work of Jesus, and the creation of the community of the

Church. Some of the psalms serve as an excellent focus for praise. Another helpful way to sustain praise is to have a collection of hymn books and dip into them regularly.

CONVERSATION

Two other helpful metaphors for prayer commonly used by evangelicals are breathing and conversation. Of the latter, Hallesby writes,

> To pray is to let Jesus into our lives. He knocks and seeks admittance, not only in the solemn hours of secret prayer when you bend the knee and fold your hands in supplication . . . He knocks and seeks admittance into your life in the midst of your daily work, your daily struggles, your daily 'grind'. That is when you need him most.

SILENCE

Silence does not always come easily to evangelicals because by nature theirs is a talkative Christianity. Silence in prayer is a skill that is cultivated in the same way that it is possible to be silent with people who we know very well. One way into silence is use of the Church's liturgical offices. I personally find the use of Evening Prayer extremely helpful. Likewise, I have cultivated use of the Jesus Prayer, and in this I benefit from knowledge of a vast range of Scriptural doctrines and phrases that can be included in its repetition: 'Jesus, bearer of our sins . . .; Jesus, friend of the friendless . . .; Jesus, Saviour and Redeemer . . .' to name just a few. I myself have never prayed in tongues, but friends with that gift witness to it as a way of communicating 'with groaning that cannot be uttered'.

In the remainder of this chapter, I want to briefly draw attention to some of the other hallmarks of evangelical spirituality.

THE MYSTERY OF PROVIDENCE

The Reformers re-emphasized the nature of God's providence. They were confident that God's providence governed every area of life. As their inheritors, evangelicals take seriously how God's providence and guidance embraces every part of their lives. In making key decisions they think, pray and listen to the Word as they try to discern how God is leading. They draw heavily on the stories of how God guided Abraham and the patriarchs as examples of how God intervenes to shape the lives of the believing individual. There is a strong conviction that everyone has a God-given purpose and vocation in life. The devout life is one given to his service.

Not surprisingly, then, one of the main concerns of an evangelical person is to discern the will of God for their life. Given their belief that God does guide, and that in his providence he has a purpose for every believer, key decisions – such as career, marriage partnership, business relationships – are the subject of sustained prayer. The Puritans used to say that there were three aspects of discerning God's guidance: what sayeth the circumstances, what sayeth the Scriptures, and what sayeth the Church. The scriptural dimension is not a superstitious search for a text that might confirm a particular course of action, but the study of God's general purposes in the world.

MENTORING

For over a century, the so-called Great Commission (Matt. 28.19-20) has been taken by many evangelicals to signal an imperative to missionary service. In fact, the imperative here concerns not 'going', but the call to 'make disciples'. A classic evangelical spirituality involves a commitment to being a mentor, both in being committed long-term to helping specific people along the journey of faith, helping them to bring their life in line with the will of God, and providing godly counsel in the weighing of key decisions. It recognizes that in the life of every Christian there needs to be a Paul (a wise and knowledgeable senior person), a Barnabas (an encourager), and a Timothy (a younger person to be nurtured and built up with an eye to the future). Mentoring was at the heart of John Wesley's system of 'classes'. In our day, the evangelical parishes that are experiencing numerical growth practise various forms of mentoring: in particular home groups and prayer triplets.

THE LORD'S DAY

Recovering the spirituality of the Lord's Day was important to the Reformers. It is a tradition that has been inherited by evangelicals. It explains in part why supporting campaigns like Keep Sunday Special have been a natural evangelical reflex. It has to be said that this is an area of evangelical spirituality that has been badly obscured by some of the worst excesses of sabbatarianism. Yet when we go back to the New Testament there is something profound about keeping one day a week special. The early Christian sign of the eighth day (John 20.19, 26) is a celebration of God's new creation in Christ. It also celebrated the resurrection.

Sadly, as I have already noted in Chapter 14, 'Sunday' has suffered from an over-abundance of evangelical legalism. The rules became myriad. A better way to understand the tradition of the Lord's Day is to focus on its positive elements. Lord's Day 'manuals' that date from the Reformation and Puritan eras indicate that this was a day for prayer and meditation. But it was not to be observed as narrowly spiritual or individualistic. It was a day for hospitality, for table fellowship, for doing good and caring for the poor, as well as being a day of quiet and retreat.

QUIET DAYS

A few years ago, John Pearce, vicar of Limehouse in East London, wrote a Grove Booklet called *Advance by Retreat*. It was a sign of a willingness among evangelicals to use approaches to spirituality traditionally thought to be 'catholic'. In fact, the tradition of retreats and quiet days belongs to the entire Church and grows from the example of Jesus, who regularly took his leave from public ministry for periods of prayer and reflection. John Stott, among many evangelical leaders, has testified publicly to the benefits of regular quiet days, and this is being emulated in increasing numbers by evangelical laity.

THE LORD'S SUPPER

The Reformers taught that the celebration of the Lord's Supper is the sign of God's covenant of grace. The sacrament not only brought people into communion with God. It was something that brought the individual into the Christian community. As well as celebrating the atoning death of Christ on the cross for our redemption, the Lord's Supper was a foretaste of the banquet of heaven 'until he comes'.

In recent years, growing numbers of evangelical churches have begun to insist on making Communion, or the Lord's Supper, the centrepiece of Sunday worship. This, however, is not universal. Some of those who resist this trend would prefer to make it a 'special' occasion, with a high level of preparation. Others believe that public worship should always be accessible to all. Emphasizing Communion for the family of the church gives an unhelpful signal to people on the fringes. In counselling members of churches of an Anglo-Catholic tradition on how to be more effective in evangelism, Bishop Michael Marshall of the Archbishop of Canterbury's Springboard team constantly urges greater emphasis on services of the Word.

My friend in the bar at General Synod had a point. The spirituality of some evangelicals, not least those existing solely on a daily quiet time diet, is threadbare. As I have tried to show, the evangelical tradition has a distinct and robust spirituality. It is simply that many evangelicals seem unaware of its full range and depth. I find it sad that some are looking elsewhere for help in their spiritual life, mainly, I suspect, because no one has introduced them to the classical roots of their own tradition.

17

THE EXPERIENCE OF
RENEWAL

For myself in assessing this new phase of the charismatic renewal I stick to
what I have long thought about the other phases and about many other
Christian movements besides – they are about two-thirds phoney and one-
third God *but* a third, with God in it, is a lot. (Tom Smail on the 'Toronto
Blessing' in the *Church of England Newspaper*, 3 February 1995)

In 1963, St Mark's, Gillingham, accepted the gifts of the Holy Spirit in one of
the first manifestations of the charismatic renewal in the Church of England.
It did so without demur or amazement. The vicar, John Collins, wrote in the
quarterly bulletin of the Anglican Prayer Fellowship for Revival in March of
that year:

During the last two months, we have had the joy of seeing the Holy Spirit
working in a new way within the Church. So far, it is the inner nucleus (some
40 or 50 in number) who have been blessed. I am anxious not to exaggerate,
though it would be easy to do so. This is not revival. But I should certainly
say that those who have been affected show all the signs of being filled with
the Holy Spirit: and very attractive and wonderful it is.

The hallmark of charismatic renewal for his church was an increased boldness
in evangelism which he called 'a loosening of tongue in witness'. Other manifestations included increased 'love and joy', 'spiritual understanding' and
'healings'.

John Collins believes that this movement came as a result of deep dissatisfaction within the congregation with the quality of both their personal lives
and the work of the Church. 'It was not that there was no blessing. But it was
all so different from the Acts of the Apostles.'

Clergy and laity set more time aside for prayer, and their eyes were opened
to 'fresh understanding of Romans 6 ... with the promise of deliverance from
sin'. Surprisingly enough, it was six months before the gift of tongues was
exercised in the congregation, confounding the view of many charismatics
that the 'baptism' or 'blessing' of the Holy Spirit is validated initially by
tongues.

John Collins told me:

> Whereas in the rest of the country the issue [of tongues] was raising much excitement and controversy, after a week or two we scarcely talked about it. It simply became part of the devotional life of many of our leaders to their great benefit; and I suspect this is what happened in the Acts of the Apostles.

Baptism, Fullness and Tongues

I believe we have reached the stage where 'charismatic' Christianity has come to represent the centre ground within evangelicalism, not least evangelicalism in an Anglican form. Even churches that do not allow manifestation of the gifts of the spirit in public worship have been changed radically by its influence. The concept of every-member ministry, widely affirmed by evangelicals, is fuelled further by an understanding of the gifts of the Spirit. But the process of getting there has sometimes been fraught.

American Roots

One of its earliest outbreaks was in 1963, when a Lutheran pastor visiting London met with Michael Harper, then a curate at All Souls, Langham Place. Harper, whose main job was chaplaincy to the retail stores of Oxford Street, first encountered charismatic renewal through the Full Gospel Businessmen's Fellowship. Soon he was speaking in tongues and was quickly acknowledged as leader of this new movement in England.

But renewal needed an extra ingredient to get fully into the Anglican bloodstream and this was provided through the ministry and writing of Dennis Bennett of Seattle, whose influential testimony was published in a highly popular book called *Nine O'Clock in the Morning* (Hodder).

According to participants, the first phase of charismatic renewal in the early 1960s through to the 1970s was characterized in the main by the sort of humble surprise, indicated by John Collins. They claimed it revolutionized the spiritual life and public ministry of many gifted clergy. Tom Smail recalled how his first experience of renewal in 1965 followed a period of 'disillusioning disputes' in his church which left him 'low and depressed'.

'I found my relationship to God refreshed and intensified, a new pastoral closeness to people, a fresh self-confidence and – never central for me – a beginning of a new experience of spiritual gifts, including tongues,' he told me.

GEORGE CAREY'S EXPERIENCE

Similarly, Archbishop George Carey recalls his experience of renewal in 1977 on a visit to Canada, which was to revolutionize his prayer life, and renew his ministry, leading to many greater things.

I found myself on my knees saying: 'Lord, you know the mess I am in right now. And yet I owe you so much. I thank you that you met me years ago when I was a lad of seventeen. And I thank you that you called me into Christian ministry and empowered me for your service. But Lord, I have become so busy in your service that I have lost you somehow. I have been so self-centred and interested in doing what I want that I have forced you out of my life. I cannot live a hypocritical life any more. Unless you fill me again with your Spirit, I cannot go on!' Such was my prayer, and nothing dramatic happened – no thunderclaps, no wind, no fire; but it was 'Elijah-like' because God spoke to me in a still small voice. In the calmness of that Sunday evening there was an amazing quality of peace about the room.[1]

Inevitably, this new movement that blew freshness into the lives of clergy and lay people aroused controversy. First, evangelical Anglicans found themselves engaged in a passionate debate between intellectualism and emotionalism. John Collins again told me:

After all, since the war, with a rise of evangelical scholarship, great and successful efforts had been made by John Stott, Jim Packer and many others to present evangelicalism as acceptable to thoughtful men and women, especially in the student world. Speaking in tongues therefore seemed to them to be irrational, emotional, uncontrollable.

One of the factors that increased the temperature was that some devotees seemed to be opting for Pentecostal theory rather than the theology of their own tradition, giving a greater emphasis to 'tongues' than to other spiritual gifts. In fact, an increasing number claimed that the charismatic experience was a 'baptism in the Spirit' and that this 'baptism' was authenticated by speaking in tongues.

Their critics would have nothing to do with 'second baptism', arguing that it was biblically unwarranted. What is wrong with your first 'baptism' that you need a second? they asked. A plethora of alternative names were suggested to describe the experience, including 'blessing' and 'freshness'.

All Souls, Langham Place was at the epicentre of the debate. Its highly influential rector, John Stott, took it up, publishing a thoughtful booklet, *The Baptism and Fullness of the Holy Spirit* (IVP, 1964, 1975). The first point he makes is that no one can claim to be a Christian without the Spirit of God. In this sense there are no first-class or second-class Christians. Second, the 'baptism in the Spirit' is a characteristic of the evangelical conversion. Third, John Stott's insistence does not rule out further experiences as the Christian comes into the fullness of the Spirit.

Although, as ever, John Stott was courteous and firm in his rebuke, this did not hide a bitter war of words waged for many years within the evangelical

Anglican constituency up to the early 1980s. In 1964, Michael Harper resigned from All Souls. Soon afterwards he helped form the Fountain Trust which put the charismatic movement on an ecumenical basis. For the most part, charismatics were as polite and gracious as Stott in their language, yet they could not hide the fact that they believed Christians needed this second experience of God's blessing – be it called 'baptism' or 'fullness'. The conservatives could draw only one conclusion from their arguments: that there were first-class Christians who had received this charismatic blessing and second-class Christians who had not. It was hardly a recipe for harmony at parish level.

Peace Breaks Out

Yet, as the years passed, peace began to break out. In 1975, after wide-ranging consultations among the evangelical constituency, a statement *Gospel and Spirit* was published. The prime mover in putting it together was the late Robin Nixon, Principal of St John's College. It was a healing document, even if obtaining some of the signatures required some arm-twisting.

One reason why accord was possible was that Michael Harper shared John Stott's 'high' view of Scripture. It meant that the differences between them remained relatively small in an overall sense. Later, they began to share the same platform at conferences. This example of reconciliation and tolerance spread throughout the constituency. In the 1970s and 1980s, the 'surprise' of the charismatic movement began to wear off as it became part of the spiritual experience of increasing numbers. Language about the 'second baptism' became more moderate. The attractive worship of the charismatic movement penetrated the lives of many churches. Finally, charismatic renewal in the lives of many lay people raised up their ministry in the Church. They became actors, dancers, worship leaders, counsellors, evangelists and clergy in the evangelical movement. In the face of so many positive signs of God's blessing, few could remain in condemnation.

While it would be heartening to say that the story of the charismatic movement thereafter was a saga of individual lives changed, lay ministry raised up, new worship attracting new Christians, and church life revolutionized, this was only part of it, albeit the major part. Yet the 'baptism' and 'tongues' division was only the first in a series of arguments about the ministry of the Holy Spirit up until the present day.

David Watson

Few did more to widen the popular appeal of the charismatic movement among Anglicans in the 1970s and 1980s than Canon David Watson, of St Michael le Belfry, York. His evangelistic ministry, which affirmed healing and other 'gifts', was widely sought after, and among his personal gifts was the ability both to communicate through authorship of books and also to relate ecumenically.

Likewise, his untimely death from cancer had a huge impact on the future of the movement. Charismatics who had eagerly taught that the prayer of faith would heal the sick were forced to reconsider. A small number maintained that his death was due to a failure of faith, but a wider constituency emerged with a more nuanced understanding of healing. Thoughtful charismatics today are likely to make a distinction between 'healing' and 'cure'. The ministry of healing will involve not only the patient but also those surrounding them, and will as much attend to their state of being as to the illness itself. It is a ministry that is quieter and tends to keep some distance from the 'wonder worker'.

Another factor that helped popularize the movement was the influence of Holy Redeemer parish, Houston, and the Fisherfolk, who made an enormous impact at around the time of the Nottingham Congress in 1977. What made this an even more interesting phenomenon was that Holy Redeemer and its rector, Graham Pulkingham, were High Church in style, whereas the majority of English charismatics were drawn from Low Church or evangelical circles.

Another key influence was the growth in popularity of Spring Harvest which began in the late 1970s and attracted huge crowds to annual events held in up to four sites and attracting upwards of 100,000 participants, up to a third of them Anglican.

Even so, there were indications that the movement was apt to lose its way. There were signs of this in 1979 when the Fountain Trust voted itself out of existence. Its public explanation was that it had fulfilled its task. It would be much nearer the mark to suggest that the move reflected a loss of confidence and clarity of vision. Charismatic renewal was now without an ecumenical face. Anglican Renewal Ministries emerged on the scene in 1980 and by then the Baptists, Methodists and Roman Catholics had their own separate renewal organizations. Not surprisingly, then, a vacuum appeared, and the field opened to other players.

Wimber: The Quest for Power

In the early 1980s, David Watson introduced a Californian ex-rock guitarist, John Wimber, to the British scene. Wimber taught a highly popular course in church growth at Fuller Theological Seminary near Los Angeles, based on his 'signs and wonders' theory. He became a frequent visitor to Britain, teaching at David Watson's church in York and at St Andrew's, Chorleywood, which at that time, under Bishop David Pytches' leadership, was emerging as a centre of charismatic influence, in particular with the growing popularity of the annual New Wine convention.

It was Wimber's belief that Christians today can claim the ministry of Jesus as well as his words. Consequently, in his view, the preaching of the gospel is to be accompanied by miracles, healing and deliverance, as a sort of visual aid, or practical demonstration of the words. The slogan 'power evangelism' matched the spirit of the 1980s. In the decade of Thatcher and Reagan, the political doctrine was 'help yourself' to the riches of the day. Wimber seemed to be saying, 'Go out and get it and it can be yours.'

Everyone could minister and be ministered to in the well-supervised free-for-all that formed the substance of his meetings. In the 'ministry time', worshippers turned to pray for each other, to lay hands on those who wished to receive spiritual or physical healing. The 'word of knowledge' became the key tool. The Spirit was invited 'to come down in power'. 'Words of knowledge' came in a number of forms and were certainly not the preserve of the leadership.

In one meeting I attended, those with a 'word' were invited to form an orderly queue to talk to members of the leadership team. In this way their 'words' were sifted and, if deemed appropriate, were then relayed to the leader of the meeting. These 'words' could be anything from the visualization of a part of the body which needed healing; an insight about the life of someone present, for which they needed prayer; a biblical exhortation; to specific messages from the 'mouth' of God to an individual, a family, or the whole gathering.

Benefits

Reflecting upon this aspect of the Wimber phenomenon, there was much that was good. These ministry times enabled the whole Church to pray for each other, to grow closer together and become a whole-hearted community. Many individuals came closer to God and experienced a change in their prayer lives. They learned to identify their own gifts and grew in confidence in practising their individual ministries. Yet the death of David Watson, and Wimber's own struggle with cancer, provide their own commentary on popular 'name it and claim it' charismatic fashions.

The Men from Kansas

Another aspect to the Wimber phenomenon in the latter part of the 1980s was the use of 'prophecy'. Wimber came in touch with a group who became known as the Kansas City Prophets. This group, led by Mike Bickle of the Kansas City Fellowship, seemed to have profoundly impressive 'gifts'. Their early story was written up by Bishop David Pytches in a book called *Some Say it Thundered* (Kingsway, 1989). Among the stories in circulation was a claim that their prayers had led to drought and then a downpour of rain when a 'word' was given. Wimber brought several of them to Britain for 'prophecy' conferences. The best known of the prophets – Paul Cain, Mike Bickle and John-Paul Jackson – came to be endorsed by an impressive list of

Christian leaders. They included house church leaders Gerald Coates and Roger Forster, and Anglican clergy represented by David MacInnes, Sandy Millar, and David Pytches.[2]

Is This Really 'Prophecy'?

But questions remain. The ministries of these 'prophets' are surrounded by overblown claims. Paul Cain, whose platform ministry resembled an exercise in clairvoyance, was accused of trivializing prophecy. At times his 'words of knowledge' seemed incredibly inappropriate. As Nigel Scotland records,

> On one occasion he pointed to a man in the auditorium and said: 'You old hypocrite, how can you stand there and have anything to do with what's going on at this meeting … you are planning to go off with that lady over there [he was pointing directly at her] at the end of the week and to leave your wife.'

At the same meeting, Cain pointed to another woman in the crowd and said: 'And you, lady, if you don't repent I'm going to tell everyone what you've been doing in room number 202 in your motel today.'

A Coming Revival?

All this pinpointed the need for the Church to be prophetic, but questions remain. On at least three occasions in 1989 and 1990, Paul Cain publicly predicted that revival would break out in London in October 1990. He may have been right, but signs that it has arrived are not yet visible.

Nigel Wright, a leading figure in Baptist renewal, makes a helpful contrast between the so-called prophecies of Paul Cain and more powerful recent twentieth-century figures like the civil rights activist, Martin Luther King and the maestro of biblical exposition, Dr Martyn Lloyd-Jones.

> A prophetic ministry which springs out of the exposition of the Scriptures is less likely to become volatile and ensnared in mystical subjectivism. A prophetic ministry which addresses the issues of an unjust world is less likely to become in-house entertainment for the saints, he once wrote.[3]

Concern for justice and public righteousness is of an altogether different order than Paul Cain's displays of intuition. I should like to have set an essay for the English church leaders who so happily endorsed Cain, Bickle and the rest: 'Compare and contrast the teaching of Isaiah, Jeremiah, Ezekiel, Hosea, Amos, and Habakkuk, with the Kansas City Prophets.' It also left me wondering why it is that British evangelicalism regularly feels the need to embrace the ministries of relatively small-time people from the other side of the Atlantic when there is such an abundance of talent here.

'Toronto' and Its Works

Returning from leave in Australia in June 1994, I began to hear whispers in London churches about a strange new outpouring of the Holy Spirit which induced fainting, maniacal laughter, jerking, and even bizarre animal noises. A reserved ex-Etonian told our Alpha course members at St Michael's, Chester Square, how he had been laid out flat on his back at a meeting at St Paul's, Onslow Square, West London. 'We don't normally act like this,' the puzzled man told our equally puzzled group.

After three weeks of enquiries – to confirm the importance of this phenomenon and its apparent origins in the Airport Vineyard Church in Toronto, Canada – the headline on 19 June 1994, in the *Church of England Newspaper* proclaimed, 'Revival hits London Churches'. We scooped Fleet Street by a day, though in retrospect I wonder about our headline.

The 'Toronto blessing' first came to notice in January 1994 and had an immediate ripple effect. John Arnott, Senior Pastor at the Airport Vineyard Church, Toronto, expressed similar surprise to that of John Collins in 1962.

> No one is more surprised by this recent outpouring of the Holy Spirit than my wife Carol and I. We are utterly amazed at what God has done in and through our church these last seven months. Certainly it has gone far beyond anything we ever envisioned or imagined those first few weeks![4]

As of 1 September 1994, relates Guy Chevreau, an estimated ninety thousand had attended the Vineyard Church. Of these, thirty thousand were first-time attenders. Over four hundred local Canadian ministers had come to investigate and over four thousand ministers, spouses and leaders from other parts of the world, including Britain.

It is generally agreed that Eleanor Mumford, a leader of the South West London Vineyard Church, brought the Toronto blessing to this country. The experience she felt was a turning point in her currently dry spiritual life and she took immediate opportunities to share the experience on her return. A meeting on 29 May 1994 introduced the 'blessing' to the central London cathedral of Anglican renewal, Holy Trinity, Brompton. Her simple talk to the stockbrokers, teenagers, and young professionals who make up that congregation introduced the entire array of experiences associated with the 'blessing'. In the ensuing weeks, the variety of phenomena spread throughout London – holy laughter, roaring like lions, body jerks, bouncing, fainting and 'drunkenness'.

Soon Holy Trinity, Brompton, and St Paul's, Onslow Square, like the Airport Church in Toronto, were centres of pilgrimage for ministers and lay people who wanted their own churches to share this 'blessing'. Throughout the summer and autumn of 1994, queues formed on the pavements of

Kensington as the curious streamed in. Holy Trinity, Brompton, was forced to hold two evening services. At the height, two thousand people were attending the church each Sunday.

Reactions

A January 1995 survey of readers of the *Church of England Newspaper* found almost universal familiarity with the Toronto blessing. Of a very high sample, over 46 per cent said they approved. Only 28 per cent disapproved, while 26 per cent were unsure. It was yet another indicator of how charismatic renewal stands at the centre of evangelicalism in this generation.

Patrick Dickson, a doctor, and founder of the AIDS charity ACET, suggests that the Toronto blessing can be described as an 'altered state of consciousness'. Many things, he writes, including prayer, fasting and speaking in tongues, cause the Christian to become more aware of the spiritual dimension. These are a normal part of charismatic faith. In a helpful analysis, he makes it clear that highly complex factors are at work in all such charismatic manifestations, including conforming, suggestion and pressure as well as the Holy Spirit. The oft-repeated suggestion that the Toronto blessing is merely mass hysteria has no medical or psychological foundation, he writes. It is another spiritual experience through which God has chosen to allow his people refreshment and learning.[5]

Pyschological Factors

One issue that worries me is the fact that, publicly at least, leaders of the so-called 'Toronto' movement seem to have no great desire to understand what it is about at a psychological level. Bishop Mark Dyer, the former Bishop of Bethlehem, Pennsylvania, offers some interesting observations on this point. Mark Dyer's view is that a 'Toronto' experience is an important piece of 'social pathology'. Somehow it has managed to get under a normally impenetrable facade to uncover traumas, problems or hurts from the past. 'Now the question is, having had an indication that such exist, what should they do?' asks Mark Dyer. It is possible, of course, that people will continue to cover their inner trouble. But that is a health risk. Alternatively, they can embark on an inner journey to discover the roots of these phenomena and seek help or healing as appropriate. One responsibility which now lies with the 'Toronto' leadership is to be willing and properly equipped to take pastoral care of people in this situation.

The Fruits

In the end, this phenomenon will be judged by its fruits, and the exact style and texture of that fruit will not necessarily be discernable in just one generation. One major concern is how some of its advocates, such as Rodney Howard-Browne, seem once again to be opening up a false division between rationality and spiritual experience. Another is whether the 'blessing' leads to more practical Christian outreach.

In the middle of 1995, John Wimber, who is the 'bishop' of the Toronto Airport Vineyard Church, went public with some important criticisms. Up to now, he said, the message seems to have been 'Come and get it.' That, he believes, is inadequate. Now Wimber is challenging his churches to change the message to 'Get it to give it.'

> So take them out onto the streets. Let them feed the hungry, visit the aged, go into the streets and witness. Do whatever is necessary but get them out so that when they go home they can say, 'Yes, I quacked like a duck for three days, but I went and visited this 84 year-old who was starving and we filled her pantry, prayed for her and her rheumatic condition is improved and we led her to the Lord.' (Quoted from *HTB in Focus*, August 1995)

It appears, however, that not all Wimber's advice was taken to heart at the Toronto Airport and in late December 1995 it was expelled from membership of the Vineyard Fellowship.

My Questions of Charismatic Renewal

I ought to declare my hand. I was brought up to be highly suspicious of Pentecostalism, and when charismatic phenomena appeared on campus during my university days I was openly hostile. When I came to England in 1979, I found to my surprise that charismatic renewal had become the centre of lively evangelicalism. Those who had embraced it seemed to be growing spiritually and numerically. I now belong to a parish where a sizeable number of the congregation have experienced renewal in some form. We deliberately keep to the character of an Anglican parish church, and a framework of liturgical worship. I have never spoken in tongues and I instantly bristle at charismatic claims that offend the mind.

I find, however, that being part of this community has touched me in unexpected ways. I am much more comfortable to talk about the mystery of God. I have found a wider understanding of prayer. I have been staggered by acts of spontaneous generosity by people who have hardly known me. The discovery and release of the 'gifts' of the laity has transformed the church's ministry and I sense that I have grown spiritually in the process. Nevertheless, I still have a lot of questions and I would like to air some of them.

1. The Scandal of Division

Can renewal help overcome the scandal of division? Roman Catholic Peter Hocken, one of the most significant international students of the Pentecostal and charismatic movements, tells of his disappointment that the early expectations of the charismatic movement to achieve greater unity dissolved. 'The glory is manifested in the powerful reconciling and unitive thrust of baptism in the Spirit, while the blame attaches to the pettiness of the quarrels and the scandals of constant division.'

On the worldwide scene he says: 'New denominations have continued to proliferate at an astonishing rate. Many stem from quarrels and conflicts between leaders, fewer have a doctrinal origin.'[6] The hopes of many charismatics in the 1970s, as the renewal movement led them into increasing contact with leaders from other denominations, was for closer unity. It seemed that dramatic steps towards unity were being taken.

As late as 1985, George Carey expressed this same optimism about relationships between protestants and catholics.

> It is the only revival in history which has united evangelicals on the one hand, with their strong emphasis on the death of Christ and full atonement, and Roman Catholics on the other, with their emphasis on the sacraments. Somehow charismatic experiences have brought together people who on the face of it have little in common theologically.[7]

Similarly, Michael Harper can tell the same story of how renewal brought him into contact with Christians of many backgrounds and experiences, and taught him a new respect and love for the Church. His pilgrimage eventually took him away from his Anglican roots into the Antiochian Orthodox Church.

Yet that is only part of the picture. Division, rather than unity, is still a major characteristic of this movement and this seems to cause little embarrassment to many charismatic leaders. Consequently, the house church leader, Roger Forster, feels happy to remark: 'There are more than 22,000 denominations in the world. A few more won't matter ... on the whole, I think that the Lord is not too concerned about the plethora of denominations; neither should we be.' His contemporary, Terry Virgo, goes even further:

> House churches have sometimes been accused of being divisive. Those who make such accusations normally have a vested interest in maintaining the status quo. The truth is, that if you are looking for a glorious end-time church, you cannot avoid the radical process of preparation. This is bound to involve some demolition work.[8]

Peter Hocken puts the matter in perspective:

> Should we be surprised at the shameful elements in Pentecostal – charismatic revival – renewal or even at their extent? Should we be surprised at the moral humiliation of famed preachers or at financial irregularities in major ministries? Should we be astonished at the break-up of charismatic communities

previously admired as models? Or at the rivalries between charismatic celebrities? Does it amaze us to discover that big figures sometimes have big egos?[9]

2. Superficial Theologies

My greatest worry is that charismatic renewal can so easily become a haven for bad and frankly dangerous theologies. It is at its worst in the area of demons and deliverance. Could demons be responsible for peppermint addiction, as has been suggested by some? What of persistent teaching that illness and disability are either due to your own sin or the sin of a direct ancestor? As a devotee of red meat I love to tease vegetarians, but I wince when some charismatics teach that vegetarianism is demonic. Why the need to find demons under every stone and on every lapel?

3. The Question of Power

The preoccupation of the charismatic movement with power needs to be discussed. In London recently, Rodney Howard-Browne, who is widely regarded as the main inspirer of the so-called Toronto blessing, claimed that the Church is moving into a new era where rational argument will count for little and people will be attracted to the Christian faith through manifestations of God's power. When I read my Bible I find that God has always resisted the use of power to compel belief or good behaviour. God does not rule by decree. Christ asserted his authority and power by humbling himself and being a servant. I suspect that there are at least some dimensions of the charismatic quest for power that sell out to worldly ideas.

4. Eschatology

One factor behind all this is the eschatological beliefs underlying these developments. Part of what fuels this phenomenon is belief of some key players that we are in the end times, and that these will be marked by a great 'in-gathering' before the return of Christ. With the approaching end of the millennium, it is likely that interest in eschatology will increase further.

5. Managing Renewal

The Church of England owes a debt to the charismatic movement. Its legacies include encouraging people to relax in their faith, to acknowledge their feelings, greater spontaneity in worship and prayer, promoting every-member ministry. But it has created a management problem for the Church of England. The charismatic movement is one of the factors that underpins a new mood among lay people. A renewed, energetic laity presents a huge challenge to a Church that pays little more than lip-service to the vocation of the laity. Moving the focus of ministry from the one-man band to a collaborative model requires new management and training skills on the part of the clergy, and these models are slow in coming from some of the theological colleges.

175

5. Learning from Other Traditions

Charismatics stand to learn a lot from the healing ministries of other traditions, not least the catholic traditions (both Roman and Anglican). It is to be hoped that it will lead into a more profound appreciation of God's work of grace in healing. There are benefits to be had from exploring in more depth the distinction between a 'healing' and a 'cure'. Death is part of God's economy and it is not his will that people should be cured of all their diseases. On the other hand, those who are not cured of their ills can know healing and wholeness in a profound way.

6. Are 'Tongues' for Christians Only?

It is easy for people caught up in the enthusiasm of the charismatic movement to claim too much for it. We have to face it. 'Charismatic phenomena' such as speaking in tongues and other ecstatic behaviour are not and have never been limited to Christianity. Plato commented on them long before the coming of the Spirit at Pentecost. Anthropologists have found that they occur in a Muslim context, including among down-trodden fourth wives in Islamic marriages. As the charismatic movement matures, it will need to foster open-minded charismatic studies that will throw more light on just what these phenomena mean.

18

PARTNERSHIP WITH THE
LAITY

For what does it mean to say, 'We alone are priests, you are lay,' except 'We alone are Christians.' (Martin Luther)

Inside the pulpit of the now demolished parish church of St Paul, Portman Square, in central London, there was an inscription with some advice to preachers ascending its stairs. It said, 'Sir, we would see Jesus.' It echoes, of course, the gospel account of how some Greeks approached the disciples requesting an introduction to Our Lord (John 12.21).

While the institutional Church of England enjoys a higher profile than that of churches throughout Europe, the way most people 'see Jesus' is through seeing the laity going about doing their work in the world. As the former Archbishop of York, Dr John Habgood, once told his diocesan synod:

> The primary and essential meaning of lay ministry is the service lay men and women perform to their fellow human beings in whatever role or job provides their main activity. There is a ministry in being a mother, a lorry driver, a shop assistant, a business executive, or in almost any other role which can be performed with Christian integrity; and the first responsibility of such ministry is to do it well.

Dr Habgood said that lay people, moreover, 'are the frontline agents in the Church's evangelistic witness, because lay people have much more contact with those outside the Church than the majority of clergy'.

I am convinced, however, that a great gap exists between what leaders of the Church of England say about the ministry of the laity, and what the Church does in a practical way to foster it. I would suggest that the key to reversing the Church's numerical decline is not liturgical revisions, evangelistic seeker services, or institutional reform, but helping the laity to be articulate and effective ambassadors for the Christian faith.

I believe that calls for some important course adjustments on the way bishops and clergy actually view the laity, and thinking again about the language most commonly used to denote the relationship between bishops and clergy and lay people. Anglicanism's most used metaphor for the laity is 'sheep'. Bishops carry a crozier to symbolize their pastoral role. By so doing they draw on a biblical idea since Jesus spoke of himself as 'the Good Shepherd'.

In the contemporary context, however, this has unhelpful resonances. There was a time when bishops and some of the clergy were practically the only educated group. It may have been right in these circumstances to view the laity as sheep needing the care and protection of a shepherd. But those days are long gone. As often as not, the laity are as expert in their respective fields as bishops and clergy are in theirs. The shepherd/sheep metaphor is hardly an appropriate one for the pastoral care of the likes of a Tony Blair; a Sir Fred Catherwood; or a Charles Miller Smith, a member of my parish who is chief executive of ICI.

It does not, in my view, apply to ordinary lay people either. For his part, St Paul used a wide variety of terms to describe his relationship to lay people. He called them 'saints', 'the called', 'brethren', 'fellow-workers', and 'partners in the gospel'. He told the Corinthians, who had known the gospel little more than eighteen months, that they were mature in Christ and that the Spirit had given them every gift they needed to further the work of God in that city. It is my conviction that the key to the revival of the fortunes of the Church of England is a recovery of a proper understanding of what the Roman Catholics have called the apostolate of the laity.

Evangelicals and the Laity

Clericalism

First, despite a lot of talk of all-member ministry, contemporary evangelical Anglicanism is substantially clericalist.

Anglican evangelicalism boasts a long history of lay initiative. The most famous was the activities of the so-called Clapham Sect of the early nineteenth century led by Henry Thornton and William Wilberforce. The achievements of this group of evangelicals is truly staggering. Their great contribution was the campaign for the abolition of slavery. Additionally, they helped found a host of charities including the Society for the Relief of Persons Imprisoned for Small Debts, the Society for the Reformation of Prison Discipline, the Indigent Blind Institution, and the Foundling Hospital.

Later, the seventh Earl of Shaftesbury continued this tradition, using his seat in the House of Lords to reform labour conditions in the factories and mines, and founding institutions such as the Ragged Schools and the Church Pastoral Aid Society. In the modern era, lay evangelicals such as Sir Norman Anderson and Sir Fred Catherwood have drawn inspiration from them.

Despite this, the modern-day evangelicalism in the Church of England tends to be clergy-dominated. Let me give two examples. First, hardly any lay people sat on the platform during the National Evangelical Anglican Celebration of 1988. Only one lay person, Dr Christina Baxter, was invited to give an address. She is a professional theologian. The same happened at the Evangelical Leaders' Conference held in January 1995. In neither case were the concerns of the lay vocation adequately represented. Second, we have seen the emergence of 'Reform', the conservative evangelical movement that appeared following the decision of the Church of England to ordain women. Reform claims to be a 'grass-roots' movement, yet strangely its founders were all clergy.

In recent references to ministry in his presidential addresses to the General Synod, the Archbishop of Canterbury, Dr George Carey, has said that the Church of England's highest priority must be the recruitment and training of people for a career in the full-time ordained ministry. There can be no doubt that the ministry of the clergy is crucial within the framework of the parish system. But is a policy that amounts to 'more of the same' the key to reversing the trend of numerical decline that has blighted the Church of England for most of this century?

Narrowing Scope of Lay Ministry

During the last two decades, there has been a huge rush by the Church of England to involve lay people within the sanctuary of the Church. Lay readers almost equal the number of clergy. Lay people read lessons, pray the intercessions, and administer the chalice at Communion. Yet, if we read the Epistles, there are practically no exhortations for lay people to do many of the things associated with modern church life. The key elements of lay vocation, according to the Epistles, were to lead a holy, Christ-like life; to be industrious; and to imitate Christ's generosity in care for the poor (in particular those of the Christian household).

All these developments in the Church of England would be appropriate if the same amount of energy was expended helping lay people apply their faith out in the world. Sadly this is not so. The Church has a reasonable track record in pastoral care for doctors, nurses, and other members of the caring professions. This is not the case when it comes to supporting Christians working in the world of industry and commerce. I know a man who worked as an executive with British Coal. He told me that in thirty years of church attendance he never once heard a sermon that helped him to apply his faith in his work context. His perception was that clergy are not merely neglectful of people in the business of wealth creation: some are openly hostile. This is a culture that derives most of its wealth from industry and commerce. While over the last decade or more the Church of England has had a lot to say about how wealth should be distributed, it has been much less ready to affirm wealth creation.

Then, much of the Church's symbolic engagement with the world of work is in a time and culture warp. Parishes rightly make great play of harvest festivals and it is one service during the year where non-regulars will come to worship. However, primary industry contributes only a tiny proportion of this country's Gross National Product, and a decreasing proportion of the population have meaningful contact with it. It is all the more intriguing, therefore, that so few parishes offer services that celebrate other forms of industry, even though, for example, liturgies to celebrate the contributions of industry and commerce have existed for a long time. If they did, I am certain that this would appeal to a whole new group of people who worship irregularly because Sunday worship fails to resonate with their day-to-day lives.

Not surprisingly, then, many lay people exhibit an alarming dichotomy between the world of their faith and the world of their work. I once heard a man testify at an evangelistic dinner for business people that he was 'a Christian full time, and a businessman to defray the expenses'.

How Men Lose Out

Supremely it is men who miss out because of this blind spot. By its failure to take this area seriously, the Church has left a great many men (and for that matter increasing numbers of working women) without any visible means of spiritual support in the area to which they devote most of their energy and waking life.

One of the great losses of the last decade and a half was the winding up of the Church of England Men's Society which did to some extent fulfil this need. Granted, the organization was in a serious spiral of decline. But its demise was further hastened by a tide of disapproval of the idea of men meeting by themselves.

I believe the Church of England needs to ask why it is that every generation there are men who are willing to subject themselves to the wacky practices that go along with Freemasonry. I am not saying that I approve of Freemasonry. Much of what it stands for is plainly sub-Christian. Claims that its practices and symbols are scripturally based do not stand up to critical scrutiny. What opponents of Freemasonry seem to overlook, however, is that it fulfils a great need among men for friendship and an outlet for practical charitable work.

For all that, one of the hopeful signs in the contemporary Church is the way in which so many men have begun to meet together in small groups, often over breakfast in places of work. Under the umbrella, for example, of the National Prayer Breakfast which yearly brings together parliamentarians and other leaders in public life, thousands of men have been brought together to pray, study the Bible, and offer one another the pastoral support that seems to be so lacking in the normal run of parish life.

The Evangelical Understanding of Laity

Having voiced these concerns, it is fair to say that evangelicalism at its best offers a robust view of the role of the laity. Unfortunately, 'lay' has negative connotations in our society. It is taken to mean 'non-qualified' or 'amateur'. In the Church it is therefore often taken to mean 'non-ordained'. In New Testament terms, however, laity (*laos* in Greek) means God's people. Therefore to be lay is a calling. As such, then, the laity are not just a subset of the Church. They *are* the Church. In their calling, they sum up all that the Church is called to be and do. They are called to what Ruth Etchells has called 'Kingdom activity'. It is primarily through them that it is possible for the world to 'see Jesus'.

As Ruth Etchells comments,

> If God is to be found only at work in the (institutional) church, if Christ lived and died only for the church, if his resurrection power is abroad only in the church, then a devaluing of the world and lay life within it, follows quite naturally. And indeed there has been a strand of Christian thought, which has taken this view as a matter of theological principle throughout Christian history, emphasising the apartness of the church as God's own community . . . The point we need to seize upon strongly is not that salvation is to be found *through* the life of the world, but that salvation, the good news, is *for* the life of the world. And there is no point in telling the story behind a brick wall in a language discontinuous with those to whom one is telling it.[1]

A church which understands this principle is a training organization. It rightly has a life of its own but its primary purpose is to send people out, to carry their inspiration and skills to people and places where they are needed.

The Meaning of Ordination

In New Testament times, a 'call' was something issued by a congregation who recognized gifts in certain individuals. We see an example in Acts 13 where, by consensus of the church at Antioch, Paul and Barnabas were 'set apart' for a special task as evangelists and church planters.

Today we assume that a 'call' begins with the individual and that the end of the process is entering a profession. Consequently, when this call is recognized and the wider Church agrees that the person concerned has a 'vocation', he or she is uprooted to be trained in a system that operates largely in isolation from day-to-day church life. When the period of training is complete, ordinands find themselves applying for a job.

The letters column of the *Church of England Newspaper* regularly carries missives from lay radicals who insist that the doctrine of 'the priesthood of all believers' means that there should be no special role or distinguishing marks for the ordained person. In a climate where some evangelicals are attracted to the idea of lay presidency at Holy Communion, it is important that these terms are carefully unpacked.

It needs to be said, first of all, that 'the priesthood of all believers' is not a biblical phrase but a slogan from the days of the Reformation. As such, it was shorthand for a radical reappraisal of the clericalism that pervaded the medieval Church, which emphasized that the individual believer could directly approach God without an intermediary.

Then we need to realize that the modern understanding of this slogan tends to be over-individualistic. The New Testament speaks of Christians as a 'kingdom of priests'. The emphasis here is on the role for the entire Christian community, not the individual.

Finally, we need to realize that, in the early Church, leadership was generally exercised on a collective basis. There was no such thing as the clerical or lay one-man band.

It does not follow, however, that there is no place for special leadership in the Church. But it is important that the Church of England recovers these principles of ministry because they provide a context in which the ministry of the laity can be properly exercised. As John Richardson put it (in the *Church of England Newspaper*, 12 May 1995): 'The answer the Bible gives us is that [the laity] are God's priests. They serve him through Christ-like service of others and the declaration of God's salvation to the world'. What of the ordained clergy? Richardson again, 'Those who we call the "ministers" of the church share exactly the same priesthood but, as their name suggests, they exercise it in serving the rest of the laity.'

Lay Presidency

Given the understanding of 'priesthood' stated above, it is no surprise that some articulate lay evangelicals wonder why lay people should not be free to 'break bread' as they wish. After all, Jesus promised that 'wherever two or three gather' his Spirit would be present.

When the mainly evangelical Sydney synod voted for lay presidency in 1993, the shock waves quickly reached London. The influential Roman Catholic weekly, the *Tablet*, said lay presidency posed a bigger threat to Anglican-Roman Catholic relations than women priests.

In the Church of England, it is evangelicals who have forced lay presidency on to the national agenda. During 1993, the Chester Diocesan Evangelical Fellowship sent a letter to its counterparts in the rest of the Church, asking them to arrange a debate on the desirability or otherwise of lay presidency. By the end of the year, nearly a third had staged a debate and in every case members voted in favour by a significant majority. In two dioceses no debate was held because no one could be found to speak against.

The Global Context

AUSTRALIA

I want to take readers on a whistle-stop world tour. Come with me to St Matthias' Church, Centennial Park, in Sydney. It is located in one of Sydney's most attractive inner areas. Twenty years ago its congregation was but a handful. Today the building pulsates with life. It is thanks chiefly to the ministry of Philip Jensen who, as chaplain to the nearby University of New South Wales, persuaded the church authorities to let him take over St Matthias' as an extension of his university ministry. A very effective evangelist, Jensen soon created a large congregation.

Clergy and lay leaders at St Matthias' hold that there is no real distinction between clergy and laity. A pattern of services has evolved, giving expression to that conviction, while at the same time remaining within the letter of Anglican Canon Law.

Services are called 'meetings'. At 'meetings' where Communion is offered, there is always someone in presbyteral orders present, dressed to Anglican regulation, but on the sidelines or sitting somewhere towards the front of the congregation. When it comes to the prayer of consecration the whole congregation joins in. In other words, St Matthias' has developed its own particular brand of lay celebration in a manner that the church authorities are in no position to prevent. They do it not because there is a shortage of clergy, but because they wish to make a doctrinal point.

What happens at St Matthias' is part of a worldwide groundswell in support of lay presidency. It is certainly being copied directly in England by parishes who wish to make the same doctrinal point. One example is Emmanuel Church, Wimbledon, where lay presidency was first practised during the interregnum before the arrival of the Rev. Jonathan Fletcher. He has continued it.

Making a doctrinal point is not the only factor that prompts evangelicals to support lay presidency. There are many evangelical vicars who are unhappy about going on holidays and relying in their absence on priests who have a more 'catholic' view of Communion than their own. Some would much prefer lay presidency as a way of protecting their congregations from 'massing priests'.

SOUTH AMERICA

Then there are situations where lay presidency is seen as necessary for missionary reasons. Come with me to the Southern Cone of South America. (This province of the Anglican Communion takes Peru, Chile, Bolivia, Argentina, Uruguay and Paraguay.) Three decades ago, the Lambeth Conference of Bishops called South America 'the forgotten continent'. Enter the Anglican Church, chiefly in the form of the South American Missionary Society. A good percentage of SAMS missionaries have always been lay and there is a strong tradition of lay evangelism. They have been very effective in planting church communities. Over the past thirty years, while remaining a minority Church in a predominantly Roman Catholic environment, Anglicanism has grown remarkably.

In the creation of many of these churches, the combination of lay involvement, vast distances, and a desire for eucharistic-centred worship, has left many of these Anglican communities with a mindset that would readily accept lay presidency. Moreover, all around there are Pentecostal communities who are in no way inhibited by constraints about lay celebration. Their communities are burgeoning in the shadow of Roman Catholic buildings that stand closed because there are no priests.

The issue of whether to sanction lay presidency has exercised the bishops of the Southern Cone over many years. Before the 1988 Lambeth Conference, they petitioned the Archbishop of Canterbury, Robert Runcie, in hope of getting the subject of lay presidency discussed. Runcie was unwilling even to give it a place on the agenda.

A situation not unlike that of the Southern Cone pertains in isolated rural communities in some parts of Australia. It does, likewise, in rural England. Come with me to a village parish church. The organ is playing. The verger, the church warden and reader are preparing for a service of Holy Communion. The congregation is gradually arriving. As they complete their preparations, the warden and reader keep an anxious eye on their watches. They are expecting a retired priest from another village to arrive any moment. But having waited, the warden and reader realize he isn't going to make it. So the red service books are collected, green books are distributed, and much to the disappointment of the small congregation the reader announces a service of Morning Prayer.

So then, there are several different forces at work that are prompting a call for lay presidency: maverick Anglicanism, missionary churches who have outgrown the supply of ordained ministers, pastoral problems connected with clergy shortages and isolated rural parishes. But there is a fourth area of groundswell in favour and it comes from a highly unlikely source.

SOUTHERN AFRICA

Early in 1993, the General Synod of the mostly Anglo-Catholic Church of the Province of Southern Africa was faced with a motion supporting lay presidency. It failed to win much support. What is interesting, however, is the inspiration behind this motion. Over the last decade or so, South African Christianity has drawn much inspiration from South America's base communities. All over that continent, urban-based Roman Catholic Christians have been responding to the combination of deprivation and a somewhat wooden church hierarchy by forming themselves into small cells to live out their faith.

They are almost universally lay led. They have created a radical form of Christianity reproducing some of the elements of monastic living, proclaiming the gospel and serving the poor. It has made sense for base communities to reproduce the life of the Church in every dimension, and that has included celebration of the Eucharist or Holy Communion. It has been a model of Christian life and witness which has found ready adherents in South Africa, not least in the context of the deprivation and revolutionary atmosphere of the black townships and sprawling shanty towns.

The 1994 Debate

So it was against this broad background that Timothy Royle, a long-time lay member of the General Synod from Gloucester diocese, put forward a private member's motion on the subject. Mr Royle is himself a reader who is responsible for three rural churches near his home and, in absence of being allowed to preside has, with his bishop's permission, administered extended communion using bread and wine consecrated by a nearby vicar.

THEOLOGICAL BASIS

The nub of the case for lay presidency is the silence of the New Testament on the subject. No other aspect of church order is surrounded by such detailed instruction as the celebration of the Lord's Supper. St Paul, in particular, was specially concerned that when the Corinthians met to 'break bread' it should be done 'decently and in order'. Yet nowhere is there even a hint that some particular person or office-holder should preside.

Another key argument is that by allowing lay people to preach (with the re-institution of the office of reader in the last century) but not preside at Holy Communion, the Anglican Church has opened up a false distinction between word and sacrament. If a lay person can be licensed to preach and expound the Scriptures, they argue, why should they be barred from saying the prayer of consecration during Communion? The Reformer, John Calvin, was one who insisted that word and sacrament were part of a whole, that the sacrament was 'the word as symbol'.

EXTENDED COMMUNION

Some diocesan bishops have agreed to the practice of extended Communion, where an authorized lay person distributes bread and wine consecrated earlier by an ordained person. The practice has few friends among evangelicals because it lacks the rich symbolism of the communion service where bread is broken and wine poured out. The Archdeacon of Canterbury, Michael Till, made that point during the 10 May debate. 'Without the thanksgiving it is incomplete,' he declared.

The Case Against

The Synod debate revealed two theological heavyweights among the opposition, the Bishop of Ely, Dr Stephen Sykes, and the now retired Archbishop of York, Dr John Habgood. For his part, Dr Sykes thought that 'the literature in favour of lay presidency is not very impressive. Tradition should not be set aside on the strength of a few newspaper articles or pamphleteering.' Anglicanism's 'high' view of priesthood existed well before the Tractarian movement, he said.

Dr Habgood challenged evangelicals on their need to understand that priesthood had both 'functional' and 'representative' dimensions. 'Presiding at the eucharist is about representing the whole church in its whole action.'

This concept of 'representation' worries the evangelicals. The Rev. Pete Broadbent, Archbishop Carey's curate during his Durham days, wanted a clearer definition of 'Anglican Order'. 'If it means the contents of the Ordinal, fine. If it means that priesthood is representational, maybe.'

Some Reflections

In my heart I support lay presidency. I see no bar theologically to why all present should not say the words of consecration. However, I would like to offer three reasons why I believe it better for the evangelical cause if the case is not pressed.

First, I am not convinced that evangelicals have done enough work on the representational question. It was an issue in the early 1970s in the Anglican-Methodist Unity Scheme; and an Anglo-Catholic/Evangelical reflection written jointly by Colin Buchanan, Eric Mascall, J. I. Packer and Dr Graham Leonard says of the ordained ministry:

> ... above all, the ministry is the sacramental expression of the continuing headship of Christ over his Church and to those whom he has called, whether bishop or presbyter, to witness to the utter faithfulness of Christ to his Church ... to those who [Christ] has called, the irrevocable nature of the man's calling is clear. If he abandons the calling he will witness to the frailty of human nature. Insofar as he remains the sacramental expression of Christ's headship he witnesses to the fact that Christ will not fail his flock, though men may fail him. (*Growing into Union*, SPCK, 1970, p. 84).

Second, there is a clear alternative to lay presidency. It involves appointing more non-stipendiary clergy and it can be achieved without disharmony.

Third, there is the risk that if evangelicals force a debate on lay presidency and they lose, the outcome would be an even narrower 'eucharistic' understanding of ordained ministry than exists now, and an even more rigid application of the 'representational' aspect of priesthood.

Finally, and most importantly, evangelicals have bigger fish to fry. Lay presidency hardly deserves a place even in the top twenty items which should be on the agenda for the life of this General Synod (and probably the next as well).

19

AN EVANGELICAL AGENDA
FOR THE CHURCH OF ENGLAND

Jesus did not write a book, but formed a community. (Bishop Lesslie Newbigin, *The Gospel in a Pluralist Society*, SPCK, p. 227)

We have seen that, during the last generation, evangelicals have become stronger numerically than ever before in the history of the Church of England. They are arguably the most robust and dynamic group within it. With around 40 per cent of the seats on the General Synod, they are the biggest single grouping, with the clout to significantly shape the agenda. The launch of the Decade of Evangelism invited evangelicals not merely to be part of the Church's future, but to give a lead. Already there are signs that this is reshaping diocesan structures and priorities.

It is not, however, a foregone conclusion that evangelicals have the Church of England at their feet and are ready to go out and possess the land. For as Stephen Neill so rightly said, evangelicals are not so much an ecclesiastical party as an assortment of doughty individuals, likely to travel in a variety of directions.

When they were a somewhat despised minority, conducting warfare from the trenches, it was easy enough to appear unified. Now that numbers have increased and the evangelical army marches on relatively easy terrain, they show themselves to be a surprisingly broad church, a loose coalition of interests, sharing a surprisingly short creed. In this they bear some resemblance to the Conservative Party with its surprisingly small ideological core (though it needs to be said by way of qualification that evangelical politics cover the full spectrum).

Evangelical 'Types'

Today's evangelical Anglicans divide into four major categories:

P-Types

This group is heir to those who fought off the controversial 1928 Prayer Book, and consequently they support the Establishment of the Church of England. The Church Society is a P-type stronghold. They hold tenaciously to the protestant theology of the Book of Common Prayer and believe that the key to the renewal of the Church of England is recovery of these theological roots. P-types were the strongest voice of evangelicalism in the first third of this century, but have waned in numbers and influence since.

E-Types

A designation that takes in the 'Keele' evangelicals and their heirs. As pointed out in earlier chapters, they owe a debt to the Inter-Varsity Fellowship, and their theology and apologetics were formed in the debate with liberalism and rationalism. It is the E-types who have built a bridgehead for evangelicals into the governmental structures of the Church of England. I suspect, however, that they no longer command the centre of the evangelical stage as they did for twenty-five years from 1960.

R-Types

A smaller but significant group who were inspired by the neo-Puritan and Reformed theology taught in colleges such as Trinity College, Bristol, up until the end of the 1970s. Dr J. I. Packer is in many ways the classic R-type. They, and their heirs, are hard-minded first cousins of the Keele evangelicals, though they sometimes appear more Puritan or Presbyterian than Anglican, and have tended to keep to the sidelines of diocesan and national church affairs.

C-Types

It would be easy to label them 'charismatic', but this is not quite accurate. Some have imbibed charismatic renewal, but this is a new-breed 'post-charismatic' Anglican who is charismatic in style but eclectic in other respects. C-types have recognized, consciously or unconsciously, that to communicate with the postmodern person the message of the Church must appeal to the heart as well as the head. They believe that as much as anything else faith is 'caught', and thus they put a premium on informal, accessible worship and on building community. For this reason, the 'C' might, for want of a better word, stand for 'Cult' in the positive sense of 'worship led'. It is probably fair to say that parishes such as Holy Trinity, Brompton; St Andrew's, Chorleywood; and St Thomas', Crookes (Sheffield) sum up many of the main C-type characteristics.

The Basis of Unity

These are not necessarily watertight compartments, and it would be wrong to say that there is no shared evangelical credal core. Listen to a diverse group of 1,500 evangelicals at the Epiphany 1995 Evangelical Leaders' Conference join full-throatedly in 'Crown him with many crowns', and you sense that there is a unity, both a shared history and culture and, more importantly, adherence to the historic gospel itself. But put a random dozen together and diversity will show itself. Ask them to unpack the simple declaration, 'Christ has died, Christ is risen, Christ will come again', and different nuances, convictions and emphases will show themselves.

Diversity

Some evangelicals, in particular the 'P' or 'R' tendencies, would lament this. But it is part of the glory of our Creator God that he has put his image on the human race, instilling a family resemblance but alongside he has granted freedom of expression to a rich diversity of cultures, temperaments and convictions. This is part of the greatness of Anglicanism as well. It has never sought to be a confessional church after the style of the Continental Reformation, and its *via media* has much to commend it as an alternative to what both Rome and Geneva stand for, in past or present.

An Evangelical Via Media?

If evangelicals are to move forward and leave a lasting imprint on the Church of England, they will first need to discover a *via media* of their own. In the context of the turbulence that has threatened to put them off-course in the last five years, it behoves evangelicals to do two things:

1. KEEP THE LIST OF WHAT IS REALLY IMPORTANT SHORT

Evangelicals need a new consensus which insists that there will be no division over inessentials, without denying the right of all to strongly held convictions. 'On essentials, unity. On inessentials, charity.'

2. KEEP SHORT ACCOUNTS WITH EACH OTHER

We have seen over the past few years how easy it is for evangelicals to turn on each other, often with much more vehemence than is reserved for people and opinions that are radically opposed to their own. What is at stake here is not merely evangelicalism, but the future of the gospel. There are encouraging signs that evangelicals are learning to keep short accounts rather than repeating the mistakes of the past.

A Seven-Part Agenda

In the remainder of this chapter, I want to suggest a seven-part agenda which I believe evangelicals need to encourage the Church of England to adopt. It is the product of soundings taken among a wide and representative range of evangelical leaders. In the end, however, it is essentially a personal view from one whose job as editor of the *Church of England Newspaper* offered a unique vantage point from which to view the Church and the evangelical contribution to it.

1. Building Confidence in the Gospel

Perhaps the most serious problem that besets the Church of England is lack of nerve. It is not comfortable with talking publicly about God, personal faith, spirituality and prayer.

Bishop Lesslie Newbigin and Bishop Michael Nazir-Ali, both of whom benefit from being able to make a comparison with Christianity in the Indian subcontinent, have written and spoken extensively about the 'timidity' of English Christianity. Part of the problem is that bishops, clergy and laity alike are not given the help and training they need for the task. The Church relies far too much on sharing the faith from institutional bases like schools or chaplaincies, and is not so good at making informal contacts with people.

But the heart of the problem is that the Church is stuck in a mindset created by the Enlightenment. It acts like school pupils who fail at straightforward mathematical problems because they keep expecting some hidden trap. It expects that people will respond to its message either with hostility or thought-out intellectual objections. In a postmodern world, things are not like that any more. For many, the gospel is news, because they have never heard a coherent account of it before. Christian symbols are not widely understood, and people will listen when they are explained. Most people will admit that they pray on occasions, thereby acknowledging, however obliquely, a spiritual dimension. A timid church will miss a myriad of opportunities in this climate.

2. Renewal of the Parish System

The parish system in England owes its inspiration to one of the great Archbishops of Canterbury, Theodore of Tarsus (602-90). The system makes an important pastoral statement. It claims that there is not one inch of England that does not come under the care of a particular incumbent. The pastoral responsibilities of the Church of England encompass everyone, not just paid-up worshippers.

The parish system has served tolerably well. It has meant, for example, that while the Methodists, Baptists and other denominations have gradually withdrawn from the inner cities, council housing estates and rural hamlets, the Church of England has maintained a presence.

But the system is long due for an overhaul. It is geared to serve a society that has long disappeared. The great majority of English people do not feel a natural connection to their parish church. Moreover, for them and for most church attenders, 'church' means a building, when it should signify a living community. The Church is stuck with a pastoral model in a time that demands the recovery of a missionary inspiration.

In this day of the motor car, the system of urban parish boundaries makes little sense. Except in rural situations, few people both live and work within the parish in which they worship. As it stands, the parish system, which was designed to ensure that mission was carried out in every part of the country, may instead be used by incumbents to prevent initiatives in mission. The underlying assumption is that each unit is a socially cohesive entity whose spiritual needs are capable of being met by a single incumbent. Not so.

What is more, the resources that supported this pastoral presence are receding. The scaling down of subsidy from the Church Commissioners is already biting. There are large tracts of rural dioceses such as Exeter, Lincoln, Norwich and Truro, where the stipendiary resident clergyman is almost an extinct breed. Likewise, many inner-city parishes are unable to stand on their own feet financially, and in the absence of substantial outside help stand to lose their full-time resident ministers. One bishop told me recently that the present ratio of two stipendiary clergy to every one non-stipendiary is likely to be reversed within a decade.

There needs to be a church presence within pram-pushing distance of every home. This does not mean more church buildings of the traditional kind, or necessarily more clergy. What it requires is that parishes go back to their historic roots and rediscover what it means to be a community of faith, whose walls are open to the entire local community.

3. Training That Is Mission-Oriented

The way clergy are trained is key to creating a missionary Church. Closely allied is the quality of training on offer to lay people. In 1993, the General Synod had before it no fewer than two reports on the future of its fourteen theological colleges. The first, *Theological Colleges: The Way Ahead*, had important insights about the future. Unfortunately, it was completely overshadowed by the row that erupted over its recommendation that three colleges – Mirfield, Oak Hill, and Salisbury and Wells – be closed. The reaction was understandable for two reasons. First, any plan which involves making cuts across the board in theological education in the Church of England will quickly collide head-on with party interests. Second, the commission had not done its homework properly.

These reports at best brought theological education in the Church of England up to date for the 1990s. A much more radical appraisal of the whole enterprise is needed. It should begin with reconsideration of the nature of the ordained ministry, and it needs to focus on the partnership of the ordained with the laity. It must be acknowledged that despite a protracted debate about the priesting of women over two decades, the Church of England remains fuzzy about what priestly ministry itself is. Archbishop Robert Runcie once chided the General Synod that it was talking of ordaining women 'without being sure what it is we are actually ordaining them into'.

Another crucial issue is the way people are recruited to the ordained ministry in the first place. In the early Church, it was never the case of someone saying, 'I think my career should be leadership in the Church.' It was the exact opposite. The church community would communicate this to the person concerned. As often as not, this person took on the task kicking and screaming in protest. There was no such thing as theological training outside the context of the local Christian community. Various documents published by the Advisory Board of Ministry make this point. The criticism of many ordinary church people, however, is that the main emphasis in theological education is to get ordinands to jump through a series of academic hoops rather than equipping them with skills for the task.

There is a growing debate as to whether the pattern of residential training serves the Church well. For a start, it is expensive. Then, given that the majority of ordinands are married with families, there are limits on the effectiveness of the residential dimension. It is equally questionable whether part-time courses are adequate. How many people would be content to sign on with a doctor or dentist who trained part-time?

In earlier centuries, cathedrals and other key centres were communities which, under the bishop, served both for training and missionary outreach. One way forward is to further strengthen the links between colleges, courses and parishes, so that clergy are trained in the context of a network of 'training parishes', where they strike a better balance between practical work and theological reflection. One bonus of such a system would be that the Church's training resources would be readily available to the laity.

There is, of course, an ongoing need for centres of excellence in the fields of theological research, mission, biblical studies and practical ministry. A move towards training parishes need not rule this out. We have to ask, however, whether the Church's present institutions measure up as centres of academic excellence. Is that possible, for instance, if the faculty consists of just one person in a particular field? Moreover, there is a serious lack of facilities for advanced studies to support the Church in its missionary task.

4. Partnership with the Laity

Over a decade ago, David Wasdel showed that if the vicar insisted on being the sole locus of ministry, he could expect to pastor no more than 150. With the help of a curate, the number could be extended at most to 250. Viewed from that perspective, the ten thousand full-time clergy of the Church of England can at best effectively pastor two million people. If the Church of England is to serve the whole nation, and win it back to the faith of Christ, it will either have to find more clergy, or develop radical new ways of collaboration between clergy and laity in evangelism and the provision of pastoral care.

It has to be understood that the vicar cannot expect to do all the preaching, pastoring, evangelism or social work. Instead of working one-to-one, the vicar will need to work with groups of lay people who will need to be trained for these tasks. The models for changing the situation already exist, and their application is, in the words of Professor Robin Gill, 'only a matter of the application of some fairly low grade management skills'.

5. National and Diocesan Structures that Serve

When I came to London in 1979, I quickly became a member of my local Deanery Synod. I discovered a Church smothered by layers and layers of unnecessary meetings and bureaucracy. Moreover, I found that there were many specialist departments and sector ministries that were neither effective nor accountable. I seriously question why it is that bishops' staffs have grown so much over the last twenty years.

I am happy to say that in London, at least, a broom has gone to work. Many of these layers, that tie up clergy and laity when they should be engaged elsewhere, are gone. The question is how radical the Church of England is prepared to be at laying the axe to unnecessary structures. We have now seen recommendations of the Turnbull Commission concerning the Church of England's national structures. It is clear that there is a lot of duplication that needs to be addressed. In due course there will need to be a review of the General Synod, too.

There will, nevertheless, be a need to strike a delicate balance between the need for efficiency and adequate representation. The Turnbull Commission's recommendation, of a 'cabinet' with a significant executive role, raises some important questions. As it stands, it give enormous powers to the two archbishops since they would personally appoint a big proportion of the membership. If national structures expect the laity to foot the bill for their costs, they will need to be representative and fully accountable. Most importantly, they will need to be able to demonstrate that they actively serve the parishes as the Church's basic unit of mission.

But care is needed. In a postmodern world, parishes are not the only front line for the mission of the Church of England. It must relate to the institutions of government and speak with a clear voice about the moral and spiritual issues at stake in national debates. It has an enormous stake in education. One person in five in England attended a Church of England primary school. The Church of England has no choice about exercising an influence in the development of educational policy. Moreover, it could learn a lot from the Roman Catholic Church about how to release the potential of church schools for the propagation of the Christian faith.

6. Minimum Standards of Belief

The Church of England must be prepared to declare a minimum standard of belief to which bishops and clergy must subscribe. Over the centuries, it has been reluctant to take such a step. In today's climate, the proposition is fraught with difficulties, but lay people are heartily sick of paying to support a Church which sometimes gives the impression that there are no theological boundaries over which its leaders may cross.

The Church of England must become a church that communicates with conviction. Lay people are tired of press headlines about clergy or bishops who doubt principles and doctrines clearly taught in the Scriptures. They are tired of being bombarded with statistics which suggest that the Church of England is in a spiral of decline and may disappear, when they believe that the Church is eternal, and that Christ has promised that the gates of hell will never prevail against it.

7. The Reconversion of England

England is one of the most secularized nations in Europe. If the Church of England ever had a master plan for evangelization and ongoing pastoral care, that has gone seriously wrong. Few Churches anywhere in the world enjoy such access to the seat of government, or favoured time on radio and television. It has a guaranteed part in the constitution, a privileged place in the school curriculum, the right to be visible on state and civic occasions, and a substantial tax-free income.

Despite all that, Anglican church attendance is less than 2.5 per cent of the population. The rest of the people give expression to consumer choice and are conspicuous by their absence. They have largely lost contact with the national Church, and have found no other spiritual home. They are spiritual refugees. Yet if the utterances of most bishops are anything to go by, you would think there is nothing wrong. And as soon as anyone speaks out about the need for some overall strategy, there is an instant chorus that this would upset people of other faiths, or that it would turn the Church of England into a sect.

After World War II, a Church of England working party produced the report, *Towards the Conversion of England*. Sadly, while the document was a publishing success, it was never adopted or acted on. What better way to conclude the Decade of Evangelism than to get this report out of it mothballs, explore why it was that the Church failed so lamentably to act on it, prepare a successor, and ensure that the resources are there for its implementation?

EPILOGUE

Like the ancient Athenians, punters at the Greenbelt Festival delight in exploring whatever happens to be new. The 1995 Festival was no exception. Everyone was talking about a book called *The Post Evangelical* by the former house church leader, Dave Tomlinson (SPCK, 1995).

At the tender age of twenty-two, Tomlinson was in charge of a church. Within a very few years he was the house church equivalent of a bishop, in charge of a team of fifteen and with oversight of fifty churches. Now he has given all this up, though happily he continues to be an enthusiastic believer, and worships in a South London pub as part of a group called Holy Joe's. The hallmark of this new enterprise includes a 'search for a fresh sense of spirituality in the symbolic and contemplative traditions of the Church'. He includes among them the Celtic tradition as well as Catholicism and Eastern Orthodoxy.

As the title of the book indicates, Tomlinson has coined the term 'post evangelical' to describe his new position. He claims he has not turned his back on evangelicalism. He does not want to be thought of as an 'ex-evangelical'. His new position, he says, means to 'take as given many of the assumptions of the evangelical faith, while at the same time moving beyond its limitations'. I suspect that there will be a continuing debate as to how much the foundations of Tomlinson's post evangelicalism are evangelical in their essence.

He says that while evangelicalism is good at bringing people to conversion, it falls down in the task of helping them grow and mature in the faith. He insists that postmodern culture poses new questions that traditional evangelicalism is not equipped to answer.

Critics such as Wallace Benn, vicar of Harold Wood and a leading member of Reform, have suggested that Tomlinson has merely substituted a clear evangelical gospel for an old-style liberal mish mash. But there is broad agreement among 'open' evangelicals that his analysis is essentially correct and that evangelicals must face some hard questions about the way they communicate their faith in a postmodern context.

There is a growing tendency for thoughtful people, like Dave Tomlinson, to reject an unadorned 'evangelical' label. We see that among a great many Anglicans who began as evangelicals and claim to have 'broadened out'. The danger is that if this trend continues, and large numbers of thoughtful and sensitive people continue to distance themselves from the constituency – mostly over inessentials – the future of evangelicalism will increasingly be in hands that are not safe.

Let me offer some light-hearted portraits of some of the varieties of people who would like to claim evangelicalism exclusively to themselves. In doing so, I happily acknowledge that some of the characters here were brought to my attention in this form by Harold Myra, publisher of *Christianity Today* magazine, and a great American evangelical statesman. I would hasten to add that these tendencies exist in all Christian traditions, not just among evangelicals.

Dufflepods

These little people appear in *The Silver Chair*, one of the C. S. Lewis 'Narnia' series. They hero-worship their leader, dote on his every word, and back him up loudly and in chorus no matter how woolly his thinking is. There is a dufflepod tendency apparent among some charismatics, not least because of that movement's tendency to throw up larger-than-life leaders. But a wide-ranging concern among evangelicals to be regarded as 'sound' creates this same tendency among other groups as well. Dorothy L. Sayers once said,

> It is hardly an exaggeration to say that many people contrive never once to think for themselves from the cradle to the grave. They may go through the motions of thinking, but in fact they solve all problems either by the dictate of their emotions, or by accepting without enquiry the ruling of some outside authority. Even quite well informed people do this.[1]

Single-Issue Rottweilers

These people share many of the characteristics of this large, fearsome, European-bred guard dog. They zealously judge everything from a fixed standpoint. They stand ready to pounce whenever anyone even hints that they may not be in full sympathy with their strongly held convictions and enthusiasms. We have seen this in the way that some aspects of the interfaith and religious education debates have been conducted. There are signs that some evangelicals would make views on the gay issue a sole test of orthodoxy. G. K. Chesterton once said, 'The reason angels can fly is that they take themselves lightly.'

Floogie Birds

This species of wooden toys was highly popular in America in the post-war years. Their main claim to fame was that they could only fly backwards. Present-day ecclesiastical Floogie Birds spend most of their time on their perches, as spectators to the main action. Their favourite phrase is 'We must get back to . . .' We have seen that characteristic at work among some of the evangelicals who left the Church of England over the ordination of women. They treasure the myth of some past golden age when the Church was free from error, and evangelicalism existed in a pure form. They get very upset if anyone dares suggest that they would feel as much out of place in such an age as they do presently.

Ostriches

This species is famous for believing that, to be safe, all that is required is to bury one's head in the sand. In our present day, there is a species of evangelical who are given to saying, 'Let's retreat into our parishes and pull up the drawbridge.' It is a stance adopted by some members of Reform, but equally it is being pursued by Anglicans who reject involvement by the Church in national issues and insist that diocesan structures should exist only for the support of the local parish. It is a tendency present in the Church's current concern with internal structures. As Lord Runcie has recently warned, overemphasis on internal management carries with it a danger of blunting the Church's mission to the nation. In any case, any notion that it is possible to retreat behind a parochial drawbridge is as illusory as the ostrich's strategy for dealing with trouble and strife.

INTERESTING TIMES

Let me return to where I began. Evangelicals – in fact the entire Christian Church – are living in 'interesting times'. The certainties of the Enlightenment that created a rich and self-confident Western culture are ebbing away. In the face of this turbulence, there is a tendency for today's Christians to Balkanize into ever-smaller groups, rather than pull together to grasp the immense missionary opportunities out there. What is clear is that in the present climate the gulf between conservative and open evangelicals is widening.

That is the imperative for a renewed commitment by evangelicals to unity. Ideally, it needs to be a unity that leaves plenty of space for differences about inessentials, and is based not on adherence to a plethora of doctrinal formulae, but to the gospel itself.

We know, however, that achieving that is by no means simple. Evangelicals are a long way from agreeing what are essentials and what are second-order issues. The starting point would be explorations in two key areas: how the Bible is to be understood, interpreted and applied; and the nature and purpose of the Church, including the place and role of Anglicanism. Work is going on behind the scenes on these issues and it is not without fruit.

But whether it will prevent evangelical fragmentation is a good question, because underlying these two debates are major differences of outlook that go very deep. Many conservatives claim that their understanding of the Bible is rooted in their understanding of the nature of God himself. If the Bible is divine in origin, then they see few options but to insist on its inerrancy and infallibility. How much space does this leave to work even with evangelicals who insist on the dual authorship of the Bible, divine and human?

Likewise, many conservatives are apt to emphasize the Church's divine origin. This gives rise to an ecclesiology that may try to distance itself from the Church's human structures, and outright suspicion about the compromises involved in Anglican comprehensiveness. Does this help explain the heat of some conservative attacks on evangelicals who, inspired by the Keele Congress, have involved themselves in human Anglican structures?

What is certain is that if evangelical Anglicanism fractures, the strategic losses will be enormous. The question is whether evangelicals have the vision, the grace, and the quality of leadership needed to find a path to real unity.

> To live above with saints we love
> Oh, that will be glory.
> But to love below with saints we know,
> Now that's a different story.
>
> Anon.

Appendix 1

A What's What of Evangelical
Organizations and Agencies

1. The 'Victorian' Societies

In this section, I make a critical but friendly whirlwind tour of some of the older evangelical voluntary institutions in the Church of England. All are, to one degree or another, at the crossroads as they seek to discern where their future lies in the twenty-first century. They are nevertheless highly influential, not only because of their present role but because the many stories associated with these organizations help form the corporate evangelical consciousness.

The Church Mission Society

CMS, founded in 1799, sends personnel to over twenty-five countries in Asia and Africa. Since the fall of the Iron Curtain, it has been finding new opportunities for partnership with the Churches of Eastern Europe and only recently sent a couple to Russia to work with the Orthodox Church in the field of theological education. In addition it has seen the need to give greater priority to Asia – where missionary opportunities are immense – over against Africa where the Anglican Church, though poor, is robust and relatively well established under local leadership.

Nevertheless, CMS's future is not entirely clear. To begin, it has long been agreed that a well-trained local person will be more effective and cost-effective as a missionary in their own culture than a foreigner. The result is that few CMS mission partners, as they are now called, are in traditional front-line missionary work, even in places where opportunities for work of this kind exist. Most of the personnel it sends overseas are trainers or in some sort of support role within their host Church.

The strength and weakness of CMS are its history. Over nearly two hundred years, it has learned by just about every mistake that it is possible for a mission agency to make. In contrast, new agencies like Youth With a Mission or Operation Mobilization, seemingly unaware of many of these pitfalls, challenge young people to the risk-taking business of going and preaching the gospel to the whole world. CMS has taken a long time, therefore, to shake off a middle-aged image.

There are, in the end, two reasons to be optimistic that there is a future for the CMS. The first is the sheer quality of its roots. Alongside its track record in planting the church worldwide, there is CMS's early association with the fight against slavery. The second is the quality of its international network. It has been instrumental in helping build the Church in many places throughout the world. Now that Europe itself is once more a mission field, this network will prove a priceless asset in the future.

Church's Ministry Among the Jews

Founded in 1809 as the London Society for Promoting Christianity Among Jews, CMJ engages in the evangelization of Jews both in Britain and elsewhere, notably from a base at Christ Church, Jerusalem. In addition, it offers parishes extensive resources and training modules, aimed at teaching Christians about the Jewish roots of their faith.

It has proved to be one of the more controversial evangelical agencies. This came to the surface in 1991 when the Archbishop of Canterbury, Dr George Carey, announced that he was unwilling to follow his predecessors as CMJ's patron. The official reason given was that the Archbishop thought that links with CMJ were incompatible with his role as one of the Presidents of the Council for Christians and Jews, which strongly opposes the 'proselytism' of Jewish people, and this was greeted with dismay in the evangelical constituency.

My own view is that the Archbishop's reasons are more subtle than what has so far been made public. My personal view is that his problem with CMJ grew out of his assessment of its wider theological ethos. While it is not the official policy of CMJ, many of its leaders and activists hold to a premillennial view of the return of Christ.

As such, premillennialism, which to say the least is controversial in its interpretation of the key Bible passages about the return of Christ, offers a form of Christian-Zionism that leaves a lot of Christians uncomfortable, not least those who have sympathy for the position of Arabs (some of whom are Christians) dispossessed by the expansion of the State of Israel. I suspect that the Archbishop, who has close links to the Middle East having studied at the Tantour Ecumenical Institute near Jerusalem, is highly sensitive to these issues, in particular their implications for Arab Christians.

The issue is even wider than that. What a Christian personally believes about the end of the world directly affects what they believe is ultimately important in the here and now. So, for example, if you hold to what is broadly known as the 'postmillennial' view of Christ's return (where it is believed that by working for justice and public righteousness Christians will ultimately establish the kingdom of God), then you will be motivated accordingly. Followers of the premillennial view tend to be 'apolitical', because the system teaches that Christ will personally establish the kingdom without human help. Premillennialism became highly popular from the late

Victorian period, and this helps explain why the evangelicals of that period tended to draw back from evangelical social engagement after the manner of Wilberforce and the Clapham Sect. It is interesting that leading evangelicals of the Victorian era, notably Shaftesbury and General Gordon, were all influenced by premillennial thought. The present Archbishop of Canterbury would do the evangelical constituency a favour if he would encourage it to address these issues.

Church Army

The evangelical constituency of the Church of England owes a great deal to the Church Army for keeping alive the torch of social concern during a period when it was much neglected. The same should be said of the Shaftesbury Society (though this is interdenominational). Founded in 1882 by Prebendary Wilson Carlile, its emergence was greeted by a stinging editorial in the *Church Times* that saw no point in the Church of England aping General William Booth and his Salvation Army.

The Church Army has not always been fully identified with the evangelical constituency, but that is largely its current position and it has made the Decade of Evangelism one of its chief concerns. Today it supports over 350 officers and sisters as well as being involved with homes for the elderly, hostels, and counselling services. There are sister societies in Australia, Canada, East Africa, the West Indies and the USA.

Until recently, the only persons recognized as 'evangelists' by the Church of England were Church Army officers (even though many of them are not engaged in direct evangelistic work). It is interesting that it is a former Chief Secretary of the Church Army, Bishop Michael Turnbull, now Bishop of Durham, who pioneered creation of an office of 'evangelist' in Rochester diocese.

There is plenty of historical evidence, from the Jesuits, through the Salvation Army, to the Jesus Army in our day, that suggests that organizations that seek to recruit young people to do the work of Christ in the context of military-style discipline and loyalty are always likely to attract committed followers.

The Church of England Newspaper

This weekly publication has two roots: the *Record*, founded in 1828 (among those subscribing funds was the future Cardinal John Henry Newman, who at that stage was an evangelical clergyman of the Church of England); and the *Church of England Family Newspaper*, founded in the 1870s. The two titles merged in 1949. The 'modern' evangelical era of the paper began in 1960 when it was bought by two conservative evangelical laymen, it having previously been closely linked to the Modern Churchmens' (now Churchpeoples') Union.

Over many years, the paper has lived in the shadow of its rival weekly, the *Church Times*, which for most of its life enjoyed the stability of being owned by the Palmer family. Traditionally, the *Church Times* was the voice of Anglo-Catholicism. In the 1960s, it took the conscious decision to 'broaden out' and it managed to successfully position itself as the paper of the establishment. Meanwhile the *Church of England Newspaper* consciously went in the other direction, seeking to consolidate itself in the service of the evangelical constituency. In the 1960s, it was largely the voice of evangelicals who were the backbone of the Keele Congress of 1967.

CEN now receives far more direct competition from the *Church Times* (whose editor, Paul Handley, began his career at *CEN*. The number of evangelicals reading *CEN* is now about the same as evangelicals reading the *Church Times*, and the latter is better resourced.

I would like to add a personal word. My period as editor was the longest of any individual since *CEN* came under evangelical ownership in 1960, and during my time as editor circulation grew to the highest it had been since its peak in the late 1960s. An editor of the *CEN* lives with a constant dilemma. You cannot expect to please all – and equally it would be unwise to take on the colours of any particular evangelical tendency, since none are by themselves a big enough market to sustain a weekly newspaper. It was a challenge I thoroughly enjoyed. As to my departure, there is no reason to read into it developments on the wider evangelical canvass. It was simply that after seven and a half years in the editor's chair and nine with the company, I was ready to explore fresh fields.

The Church Pastoral Aid Society

Founded in 1836 and closely associated in its early days with Lord Shaftesbury, CPAS is arguably the major home mission agency of the Church of England. It supports a team of evangelists, provides parish consultancy, produces valuable resources for worship, is unquestionably the major player in parish-based youth work through organizations like Pathfinders and CYFA, encourages young people to consider ordination, and administers the patronage of over five hundred parish churches.

Its recent move from a base in London to Warwick, in the Midlands, has made it far more accessible to the parishes who want to use its services. CPAS played a highly important role within the evangelical constituency during the 'lean years' following the 1928 Prayer Book controversy. Its general directors have always been key leaders of the evangelical constituency.

The Church Society

This is the senior conservative evangelical body of the Church of England and administers the patronage of over one hundred parishes. It was formed by amalgamation in 1950 although its roots go back to the last century. Its strong commitment is to the Prayer Book and preservation of the doctrine of the Thirty-nine Articles, and one of its predecessor organizations played an important role in the 1928 Prayer Book controversy. It strongly advocates the establishment of the Church of England.

During the mid-1970s, it tended to lose its way as an organization in its own right because its director, Canon Don Irving, devoted much of his time to the work of the Church of England Evangelical Council. His successor, Dr David Samuel, who was linked with the Protestant Reformation Society, set a different, more conservative course. Now, under the directorship of the Rev. David Streater, the Church Society is a robust defender of the theology of the Book of Common Prayer, dismaying those of a more 'open' evangelicalism when it organized a court challenge against the legislation to ordain women.

To 'open' evangelicals, the Church Society is an enigma. It is wary about disclosing the size of its membership, which may suggest it is much smaller than what might be expected, but remains influential because it has a feel for publicity and can call on historic resources in aid of its causes. Yet there is a somewhat grudging realization that if the Church of England were to fall into crisis as a result of serious doctrinal error, the Church Society would be best placed to galvanize evangelical action.

The South American Missionary Society

Founded in 1844 following the heroic death of Captain Allen Gardiner, who sought to preach the gospel to native tribes, SAMS is 'unfashionable' as far as the Church of England establishment is concerned. First, flavoured as it is by the charismatic exuberance of the Latin American Church, it does not sit well with great chunks of English Christianity. Second, and perhaps more fundamentally, it is opposed in principle by those who believe it is not right to propagate the Anglican Church on a continent that in name at least is Roman Catholic.

For all that, SAMS is a robust, though at times eccentric, and impressive operation. Because it concentrates solely on the Latin world it is a boutique, whereas other missionary societies tend to resemble rambling general stores. This sharp focus means that home support staff raise more funding per capita than the bigger societies.

The Intercontinental Church Society

Founded in 1823, Intercon ministers to British people in Europe through permanent chaplaincies within the diocese of Europe, provides postal Sunday school lessons for children, and temporary summertime chaplaincies for people holidaying in continental resorts. It publishes a useful directory of places of worship.

The combination of the European Union and the Channel Tunnel may mean that Intercon's greatest days lie in the future. It is already galvanizing support to become more proactive in planting evangelical churches in European cities. As such, it is unlikely to endear itself to the ecumenically minded establishment in the diocese of Europe who oppose 'proselytism' of people of Roman Catholic and Orthodox backgrounds. The facts, however, speak for themselves. It is no longer realistic to assume that Europe is 'Christian', and with more and more British people likely to settle in mainland Europe in the future, planting evangelical 'colonies' and churches there could prove strategically important.

2. Institutions of the Modern Era

I acknowledge at the outset that doing a round-up of modern and contemporary evangelical organizations is risky. One is liable to overlook what others may consider a key player, and there is every probability that events will overtake comments made. I have on purpose included organizations that go beyond Anglicanism, either in that they contain influential evangelical constituencies or have a significant influence on evangelical Anglicans.

Action for Biblical Witness to Our Nation

Founded in 1984, ABWON grew out of the joint ministry of the Rev. Tony and Mrs Patricia Higton of the Hawkwell parish, near Southend, Essex. Of the two, Patricia is the theologian and strategist while Tony is the public voice. His protests over the gay agenda; the former Bishop of Durham, Dr David Jenkins; and the proliferation of interfaith worship means he is either loved or hated, depending on your viewpoint. Away from the media spotlight, the Higtons are an engaging couple. Their network extends to several hundred churches which use their training methods. They have international links through their other operational arm, Time Ministries International.

Administry

In many ways, the rise and success of St Albans-based Administry are symbols of a general movement among evangelical parishes to run their affairs efficiently, making use of all the benefits of modern technology and business practice. The consulting advice of John Truscott and his team, as well as their valuable advice manuals on just about every subject imaginable in parish administration, are widely used by evangelical parishes. Their approach fits well with a movement that is by nature committed to being enterprising and well organized.

Anglican Renewal Ministries

Set up in 1980 to foster charismatic renewal in the Church of England, in part it fills a gap left by the demise of the Fountain Trust. ARM is an important indicator of the state of renewal in its Anglican form. In recent years it has broadened to include a growing interest in Celtic spirituality and its Director, Michael Mitton, recently wrote a book on the subject. Another of its interests is charismatic hermeneutics where its President, the Rev. Dr John Marsh, is an expert. All this signals that its roots are growing deeper but with greater diversity.

The Bible Reading Fellowship

Created in 1922, BRF's aim is to promote daily Bible reading among Anglicans. For years, its staple products were daily notes in the mould of those on offer from the Scripture Union. But the combination of changes in devotional habits and fierce competition from interdenominational rivals meant an ageing readership and steady decline in the sales of notes over recent decades. Only a substantial capital base, built up in its early years, kept it afloat.

Nevertheless, BRF is enjoying a new springtime. In 1992, it linked up with Oxford-based Lion publishing. Help from Lion in editing and design has given BRF products a new lease of life. It has benefited, too, from stronger promotion in Christian bookshops courtesy of the Lion sales force. In addition, it has become a successful niche publisher. It keeps alive a strong list of Lent books, and authors include Delia Smith, the cookery writer; Jesuit Gerard Hughes; and Joyce Huggett. What makes the enterprise very interesting is the extent to which it has been successful in the introduction of material that is 'catholic' in style to an Anglican audience.

Church of England Evangelical Council

Founded in 1960, with five aims which include: bringing together evangelical leaders for mutual counsel; and seeking and expressing a common mind among evangelicals on key issues. As such, it is the one constitutional organization with a mandate to foster evangelical unity and cohesion. It holds an annual Anglican Evangelical Assembly.

Despite its exalted name and constitutional standing, CEEC is not a strong institution and has limped along under-funded and with only qualified support from other influential organizations within the evangelical constituency. However, in recent years it has managed to start laying the foundations for creating an agreed agenda for evangelicals in the Church of England.

Crosslinks

Crosslinks was founded as the Bible Churchmen's Missionary Society in 1922. This followed a split between liberal and conservative tendencies in the

Church Missionary Society (CMS). It currently supports workers in East Africa, North Africa, India, Spain, Portugal, Peru and Bolivia. In its early days, it did important work in the Arctic region of Canada. Work in Burma and Ethiopia had to be curtailed when foreign missionaries were expelled by hostile political regimes.

Adoption of the name Crosslinks in the early 1990s was part of a search for a more up-to-date identity. Earlier, the society was unsuccessful in a bid to merge with the South American Missionary Society (SAMS).

To the outsider, the future of Crosslinks looks to be the most problematic of all the evangelical societies. The reasons for the original split with the CMS are no longer sufficient to maintain a sharp distinctiveness between the two societies. Both are members of the Church of England's Partnership for World Mission. There is a lot of informal cooperation between head offices. On the field in countries like Tanzania, relations between mission partners of both agencies are harmonious and it is hard to tell the difference between their outlook and methods.

Crosslinks suffers the classic problem of the small generalist agency. It is in partnership with a wide range of national churches on several continents without having the benefits of the institutional muscle of the CMS. It is similar in size to the South American Missionary Society without the benefits of a sharp regional focus.

An important dimension of its search for a fresh and distinct identity has been cooperation with the Finnish Lutheran Mission in witness to people of other faiths in Britain. Its 'home' mission interests make it ripe for merger with a British-based evangelistic agency, but the fact that it prizes its Anglican identity rules out some interesting possibilities.

Grove Books

Still affectionately known as 'Buchanan Enterprises' in honour of its founder, the colourful Bishop Colin Buchanan, Grove Books has been highly influential in forming and consolidating 'open' evangelicalism since the Keele Congress. It claims that while it may not provide the last word on issues, more often than not it provides the first. That is quite true.

Jubilate Hymns

This is a mostly evangelical network of authors and musicians, formed in 1974 to promote and publish contemporary music for worship. So far it has published nine major works ranging from *Hymns for Today's Church* to *The Dramatized Bible*. It reflects the enormous burgeoning of evangelical creativity in music and worship over the last three decades.

It has had its share of public controversy, most of which I suspect has boosted sales. The most famous example was just after the Falklands war and the controversy over the sermon by the Archbishop of Canterbury where he refused to gloat over the British victory. The *Sunday Telegraph* reported its plans for a modernized version of the National Anthem where the words 'guard her in liberty' were substituted for 'send her victorious'.

Latimer House

Latimer House is a small study centre and library, based in Oxford, a mile or so from where the Reformation martyr, Bishop Hugh Latimer, died in the flames alongside Archbishop Thomas Cranmer and Bishop Nicholas Ridley. It was created in 1959 to serve as centre for evangelical theological research and writing on current questions. Its greatest days coincided with the wardenship of the Rev. Dr James I. Packer. It has continued in a conservative course under the wardenship of the Rev. Dr Roger Beckwith, for example opposing women's ordination. The outcome has been that its support among 'open' evangelicals has declined. In 1993, for instance, the influential Archdeacon of Lewisham, Gordon Kuhrt, resigned from its Council in protest against lack of openness to new ideas. Whether it can remain viable while only retaining wholehearted support from conservative evangelicals is a good question.

London Institute for Contemporary Christianity

This centre, based in a disused church near the John Lewis store in London's West End, is a brainchild of the Rev. Dr John Stott. In recent years, it brought the Nottingham-based Shaftesbury Project under its umbrella. It seeks to carry through John Stott's great concern of the need for evangelicals to have 'a Christian mind' that brings the gospel to bear as much on public and professional issues as on personal ethics. It offers courses ranging from 'Writing' to 'Sex and the Single Christian' and seminars relating to vocation and business ethics. The Institute has a high profile thanks to the broadcasting and speaking activities of its Director, Elaine Storkey. Its creation was an important symbol of a growing willingness among evangelicals to enter the market place of public affairs from a base in Christian thought.

Mayflower Family Centre

Founded in 1958. The Rev. (later Bishop) David Sheppard put aside his cricketing career to lead this work in Canning Town, in London's East End. His presence ensured a high profile in the Centre's early days. It shares the character of many of the 'settlements' created by university groups in inner London, but its first aim was to try to create an indigenous church among East Enders.

It is interesting to assess the Mayflower achievement nearly forty years on. One important one has been the way in which it brought into its work and trained up a whole variety of people, many of whom now occupy important leadership roles elsewhere in the Church of England. Further, evangelicals who in the modern era have tended to offer a very cerebral faith that more easily grows roots among the middle classes, have learned many lessons from the writings of David Sheppard based on experience at the Mayflower.

As for the aim of establishing an indigenous church, the Mayflower clearly became an important centre for evangelism, pioneering models that have been emulated elsewhere by evangelicals in the inner cities. It should not surprise anyone, however, that many of those who did come to faith during the Centre's formative years 'made good', and had few aspirations to live for ever in Canning Town.

Now the centre has moved to a position where it aims on the whole to be self-supporting. Those currently in charge represent a more charismatic tendency than existed in earlier years. They are also more 'purist' about taking funds from public bodies where there are strings attached, an issue that put them at odds, for example, with the equal opportunities policies of the local borough council. That leaves a centre that is perhaps less of a showpiece, but its leaders and congregations would argue that in many ways it is more reflective of its original intention.

The other obvious lesson for evangelicals and the wider Church from the Mayflower is that pioneering work in the inner cities is hard, costly, and is about being committed to a long haul. It runs against many of the caricatures of evangelism as practised by some evangelicals, where so much of the emphasis is on expecting instant results.

Oxford Centre for Mission Studies

An international study centre offering research programmes in theology, mission studies, development and communications, some of them accredited by the Open University. It was founded in 1984.

Proclamation Trust

This is a ministry of St Helen's, Bishopsgate, in the City of London. It aims to promote biblically based expository preaching, and its influence extends well beyond Anglicanism. While there are critics of its conservatism in church affairs, fair-minded people would have to admit that events such as the Proclamation Trust's annual Ministry Assembly is one of the best available sources of in-service training for preachers and Bible teachers, a point proved by the steady growth in the numbers of those attending. St Helen's have also established the Cornhill Training Scheme, teaching Bible knowledge and preaching skills.

Reform

This movement emerged in the aftermath of the decision to ordain women. The details of the evangelical involvement in the debate about women's ordination are properly the subject of another chapter. However, it is the practical outcomes of Reform's activities that are noteworthy here.

In the week that Reform was launched, by clergy from about twenty large conservative evangelical parishes, the Rev. David Holloway of Jesmond, Newcastle, circulated a memo spelling out the case for capping diocesan quotas. It argued that the Church of England's quota system penalized success and ensured the support of parishes that were ineffective or that propagated views that were contrary to the traditional doctrines of the Church. Reform has always denied that it is a single-issue organization, be it about women's ordination or quota-capping.

Reform was inspired by a similar movement in the diocese of Sydney with the unfortunate name of the Reformed Evangelical Protestant Association, REPA for short. Immediately opponents dubbed it 'the Grim Reaper'. In dealing with it, Sydney's new Archbishop, Harry Goodhew, has managed to take on board as official policy many of the principles it stands for. I suspect this has quietly happened here in England under evangelical diocesan bishops.

Third Way *Magazine*

Created in 1978, this small circulation monthly magazine carries the torch for the recovery of the evangelical social conscience. It was inspired largely by the Lausanne Covenant, the major statement from the epoch-making Lausanne Congress for World Evangelization (1974).

Tyndale Fellowship and House, Cambridge

A network for biblical and theological research founded in 1944. It operates a centre that includes a major library. There are twelve residential places and a further forty-two places for non-residents. This has been one of the strategic factors in helping evangelicalism out of the 'wilderness' it experienced in the second quarter of this century. Its work, and many of the publications that resulted, gave evangelicals a new confidence in the world of biblical scholarship that has transformed the constituency at all levels.

Evangelical Publishers

Evangelicals are people of the book, and are well served in the field of book publishing. Hodder and Stoughton, who publish over one hundred religious titles per year, are the biggest players. Marshall Pickering, now owned by HarperCollins, Paternoster, IVP, Monarch, Lion, Eagle and Kingsway all serve the evangelical market. SPCK, while seeking to offer a comprehensive service to all Anglicans, have increased the number of titles by evangelical authors. Competition is very fierce and there are signs that the market is over-supplied in a situation where the current generation of evangelicals appear to read somewhat less than their predecessors. Whether all will survive is a good question.

3. Key Evangelical Parishes

A round-up of this kind would not be complete without some reference to parishes which have played a key part in fostering evangelicalism.

All Souls, Langham Place, in London, immediately comes to mind. After World War II, it was the perfect base for the strategic ministry of John Stott whom the liberal, David Edwards, has labelled 'the most influential Anglican of our time after William Temple'. I have not attempted a systematic assessment of his work within this book, but his achievements are legion and have proved remarkably durable. All Souls continues to be one of the premier evangelical churches, serving as an academy in the faith for successive generations of students and quietly serving human needs at home and abroad.

St Helen's, Bishopsgate, in the City of London, is internationally known thanks to the expository ministry of Prebendary Dick Lucas, and the Proclamation Trust is a natural extension of its ministry.

Further to the west, Holy Trinity, Brompton, associated with the so-called Toronto blessing, has an important leadership role among the more charismatic Anglican churches through the Alpha course which it has so far 'franchised' to over 1,500 churches. HTB's association with church planting is another important development.

Hitherto, local churches looked on these city-centre churches as competing with them for lay Christians who are much needed in their locality. Church planting is one of the ways where these people can be trained up and returned to their local community. Without having set out consciously to do so, all three of these famous churches operate in a way that the minster was supposed to in the Celtic Church. They provided a Christian presence at the heart of major communities, but they also were a flagship around which a flotilla of little boats of Christian enterprise sailed. With the erosion of the central resources of the Church of England, there will be increasing opportunities for major evangelical parishes to operate on a minster model.

There are key churches who over the years have exercised a similar role in their region: St Michael le Belfry, York; St George's, Leeds; Cheadle Parish Church; Christ Church, Fulwood; Bishop Hannington Church, Hove; Holy Trinity, Platt (Manchester); St Aldates, Oxford; The Round Church, Cambridge; to name but a few. What is perhaps not realized by aspiring builders of mega-churches is that proximity to a substantial number of tertiary students is one of the reasons why these parishes have been in a position to grow numerically in a way that others have not. It suggests, too, that despite the presence of large numbers of evangelicals in inner city Liverpool, Manchester, and London (notably the Islington deanery), on the whole the constituency still has a lot to learn about communicating the Christian faith outside the book culture.

Appendix 2

Timeline

Some Landmarks in Evangelical Anglican History

1526	Publication of Tyndale's New Testament.
1533	Henry VIII's Act of Supremacy.
1531	Execution of Thomas Bilney at Norwich.
1531	Thomas More first uses the word 'evangelical'.
1535	Publication of Coverdale's Bible.
1549/59	Acts of Uniformity.
1555	Executions of Bishops Ridley and Latimer.
1556	Execution of Archbishop Cranmer.
1549/52	First two Prayer Books.
1562	Publication of Bishop Jewel's *Apologia Ecclesia Anglicanae*.
1563	Issue of the Thirty-nine Articles.
1568	Publication of the Bishops' Bible.
1594	Publication of first volumes of Hooker's *Treatise*.
1611	Publication of the Authorized Version of the Bible.
1662	Book of Common Prayer published.
1729–35	The Holy Club at Oxford.
1735	Conversion of George Whitefield in Oxford.
1738	Conversion of the two Wesleys.
1739	Wesley's field preaching begins.
1743–63	Incumbency of William Grimshaw of Haworth.
1754	Conversion of John Thornton.
1754-9	Curacy of Henry Venn at Clapham.
1764–80	Curacy of John Newton at Olney.
1767	William Cowper joins Newton at Olney.
1777	Elland Society to sponsor evangelical ordinands founded.
1780	Robert Raikes of Gloucester founds Sunday schools.
1783	Formation of the Eclectics Society.
1783–1836	Incumbency of Charles Simeon at Trinity Church, Cambridge.
1787	Wilberforce launches his opposition to the slave trade.
1787	Hannah More joins the evangelicals.
1792–1813	John Venn is rector of Clapham.
1799	Church Missionary Society founded.
1799	Religious Tracts Society founded.

1804	Bible Society founded.
1804	Henry Martyn sails for India.
1804	First CMS missionaries sail for Sierra Leone.
1807	Abolition of the slave trade.
1814	Samuel Marsden's mission to New Zealand founded.
1815	Ryder becomes bishop of Gloucester, later Lichfield and Coventry (1824-36).
1815	Death of Allen Gardiner.
1816	First African converts admitted to Holy Communion.
1820	Newfoundland Society founded.
1826	Shaftesbury enters Parliament.
1826	Charles Sumner made bishop of Llandaff, later Winchester (1827-69).
1827	First Islington Conference.
1828	First issue of the *Record* (latterly the *Church of England Newspaper*).
1828–48	John Sumner becomes Bishop of Chester, later Archbishop of Canterbury (1848-62).
1833	Disestablishment of the Church of Ireland.
1833	Keble's Assize Sermon
1833	Slave Emancipation Act passed.
1836	Church Pastoral Aid Society founded.
1835	London City Mission founded.
1844	South American Missionary Society founded.
1845	Newman becomes a Roman Catholic.
1845	Protestant Society founded.
1846	Foundation of the Evangelical Alliance.
1847	Foundation of the Band of Hope Movement.
1847–50	Gorham case.
1849	Irish Church Missions founded.
1852	Bible and Medical Missionary Fellowship (now Interserve) formed.
1856	Missions to Seamen founded.
1859	English Church Union founded.
1863	*Church Times* founded.
1863	London College of Divinity founded.
1864	Evangelization Society founded.
1865	Church Association founded.
1865	Salvation Army founded.
1866	China Inland Mission founded.
1868–77	Ritual prosecutions.
1869	Disestablishment of the Church of Ireland.
1874–5	First D. L. Moody missions.

1875	First Keswick Convention.
1877	First missionaries enter Uganda.
1877	Mildmay Mission Hospital opens.
1877	Wycliffe Hall opened.
1877–90	Thorold is Bishop of Rochester, Winchester (1890-5).
1880–1900	J.C. Ryle is Bishop of Liverpool.
1881	Ridley Hall opened.
1882	Church Army formed.
1885	Martyrdom of Bishop Hannington.
1885–1900	John Bickersteth is Bishop of Exeter.
1887	Foundation of the Cambridge Inter-Collegiate Christian Union.
1889	Protestant Churchman's Alliance founded.
1889–92	The Lincoln case.
1904	Church of England League formed.
1906	Report of the Ritual Commission.
1906	Crusader Union formed.
1906	National Church League founded.
1910	World Missionary Congress in Edinburgh.
1920	Disestablishment of the Church in Wales.
1922	Foundation of The Bible Churchman's Missionary Society (now Crosslinks).
1928	Foundation of the Inter-Varsity Fellowship.
1932	Oak Hill Theological College founded.
1939–60	Christopher Chavasse is Bishop of Rochester.
1944	Foundation of the Tyndale Fellowship.
1948	Publication of *Towards the Conversion of England.*
1948	Inter-Varsity Fellowship sponsors a Church of England Group.
1949	Foundation of the Christian Medical Fellowship.
1950	Church Society formed with amalgamation of several evangelical networks.
1954	Publication of the *New Bible Commentary.*
1954	Billy Graham at Harringay.
1955	The modern Eclectics Society formed by John Stott.
1956	Donald Coggan chosen as Bishop of Bradford (1956–61), translated to York (1961-74), translated to Canterbury (1974–80).
1960	Evangelical Fellowship in the Anglican Communion (EFAC) founded.
1960	Church of England Evangelical Council founded.
1960	Latimer House Oxford founded.
1966	Stuart Blanch is Bishop of Liverpool (1966-75), Archbishop of York (1975-83).
1967	Mary Whitehouse forms the Viewers and Listeners Association.
1967	Keele Congress.

1967	TEAR Fund founded.
1967	Shaftesbury Project founded.
1968	Formation of the World Evangelical Fellowship.
1973	'Call to the North'.
1974	Lausanne Congress for World Evangelization.
1975	'Call to the Nation'.
1975	David Sheppard is Bishop of Liverpool.
1977	Nottingham Congress.
1977	*Third Way* magazine founded.
1979	First Spring Harvest.
1979	John Taylor is Bishop of St Albans.
1982	Michael Baughen chosen as Bishop of Chester.
1983	Anglican Evangelical Assembly inaugurated.
1984	Mission England.
1984	Keith Sutton chosen as Bishop of Lichfield.
1984	Roy Williamson chosen as Bishop of Bradford.
1985	Simon Barrington-Ward chosen as Bishop of Coventry.
1988	Caister NEAC.
1988	Peter Dawes chosen as Bishop of Derby.
1988	Michael Turnbull chosen as Bishop of Rochester.
1988	Patrick Harris chosen as Bishop of Southwell.
1988	Lambeth Conference agrees a Decade of Evangelism.
1991	Dr George Carey translated to Canterbury.
1991	Roy Williamson translated to Southwark.
1993	Christopher Mayfield chosen as Bishop of Manchester.
1994	Michael Turnbull translated to Durham.
1994	John Gladwin chosen as Bishop of Guildford.
1995	Michael Nazir-Ali chosen as Bishop of Rochester.
1996	John Perry chosen as Bishop of Chelmsford.

Notes

Chapter 1

1. John Stott quoted in an article by the author for *Alpha* magazine, April 1989.
2. John Stott and David Edwards, *Essentials*, Hodder and Stoughton, 1988, p. 104.
3. *He Brings Us Together*, Hodder and Stoughton, 1987, p. 8.
4. I am reliant here on the thinking of Mark Noll, David Bebbington, and George Rawlyk in *Evangelicalism: Comparative Studies of Popular Protestantism in North America, the British Isles and Beyond, 1700-1990*, Oxford University Press, 1994, p. 6, for definitions of 'evangelical', 'evangelicals' and 'evangelicalism'.
5. I acknowledge my debt here to David Bebbington, *Evangelicalism in Modern Britain*, Unwin Hyman, 1988, pp. 1-15.
6. Noll, Bebbington and Rawlyk, *Evangelicalism*, p. 6.
7. Stott and Edwards, *Essentials*, p. 38.
8. There is a study of Hannah More's spirituality in James Gordon (ed.), *Evangelical Spirituality*, SPCK, 1991, pp. 93-110.
9. J. C. Ryle, *Knots Untied*, Thynne, 1900, p. 315.

Chapter 2

1. *Anvil*, vol. 1, 1991.
2. James Orr, *Revelation and Inspiration*, Duckworth, 1910, pp. 209-10.
3. James Denney, *Studies in Theology*, Constable, 1895, p. 206.
4. Quoted in David Bebbington, *Evangelicalism in Modern Britain*, Unwin, 1989, p. 86.
5. A good example of the application of this approach is *Four Gospels, One Jesus* by Richard Burridge, Dean of Kings College, London (SPCK, 1994). A further useful example of a popular work that attempts this task is non-evangelical David Brown's *The Word to Set You Free*, SPCK, 1995.

Chapter 3

1. Adrian Hastings, *A History of English Christianity 1920-1990*, Collins, 1991, p. 160.

2. Quoted in *First Things*, a monthly journal of religion and public life, December 1992.
3. J. S. Spong, *Rescuing the Bible from Fundamentalism*, HarperCollins, 1991, pp. 35-6.
4. Tom Wright, *Who Was Jesus?*, SPCK, 1992, pp. 91-2.
5. Alister McGrath, *The Renewal of Anglicanism*, SPCK, 1993.

Chapter 4

1. Stephen Neill, *Anglicanism*, Mowbray, published in 1958 and revised in 1976.
2. Neill, *Anglicanism*, p. 119.

Chapter 6

1. G. R. Balleine's *History* (1908), while obviously incomplete, is still an excellent source. More recently, Kenneth Hylson-Smith (T. & T. Clark, 1986) has produced a highly readable work covering the period 1734-1984. The historical works of Owen Chadwick (*The Victorian Church*, Part 1, 1961, and Part 2, 1970), and A. G. Dickens (*The English Reformation*, 1964) are also important sources.
2. *Anvil*, No. 1, 1984, p. 7.
3. Michael Saward, *Evangelicals on the Move*, Mowbray, 1986, p. 24.
4. *Anvil*, No. 1, 1984, p. 8.
5. Randle Manwaring, *From Controversy to Coexistence*, 1975.
6. Colin Buchanan, *Anvil*, No. 1, 1984.
7. Buchanan, *Anvil*, No. 1, 1984.

Chapter 7

1. These comments are from various interviews with the author.
2. The *Church of England Newspaper*, 14 April 1967.
3. The *Church of England Newspaper*, 14 April 1967.
4. The *Church of England Newspaper*, 20 April 1995.
5. Evangelical Anglican Leaders' Conference, January 1994.

Chapter 8

1. *Anvil*, vol. 1, 1994, p. 105.
2. *Anvil*, vol. 1, 1994, p. 110.
3. Quoted in an article by John Martin in *Alpha* magazine, March 1996.
4. Martin, *Alpha*, March 1996.

Chapter 9

1. Colin Buchanan's *Cut the Connection*, DLT, 1994, contains a full and detailed account of the main events and developments in this century.
2. Comments by contemporary and recently retired bishops are responses to a questionnaire circulated as part of the research for this chapter.

Chapter 10

1. *MORIB newsletter*, Christmas, 1993.
2. Colin Buchanan, *Policies for Infant Baptism*, Grove Books 98, 1987. pp. 7-8.
3. The classic contemporary statement by an Anglican evangelical of this position is *Believing in Baptism* by Gordon Kuhrt, Archdeacon of Lewisham, Mowbray, 1987.
4. Buchanan, *Policies for Infant Baptism*, p. 5.

Chapter 11

1. Jonathan Petre, the former religious affairs reporter for the *Daily Telegraph*, has produced a detailed account of the entire ordination of women debate and the events following in *By Sex Divided*, HarperCollins, 1994. Like a number of Catholic commentators, he does not always pick up Anglican nuances.
2. Robert Warren, *Creating Missionary Congregations*, Church House Publishing, 1995.

Chapter 12

1. W. S. F. Pickering, *Anglo-Catholicism: A Study in Ambiguity*, SPCK, 1989.
2. Michael Vasey, *Strangers and Friends*, Hodder and Stoughton, 1995.

Chapter 13

1. *The Mystery of Salvation*, Church House Publishing, 1995, p. 147.
2. Hans Kung, *Christianity*, SCM, 1995, p. 788.

Chapter 14

1. Material cited is drawn from various interviews with the author.
2. David Bebbington in John Wolffe (ed.), *Evangelical Faith and Public Zeal*, SPCK, 1995, pp. 175-210.

Chapter 15

1. Robert Warren, *Signs of Life*, Church House Publishing, 1996.
2. Michael Scott-Joynt (ed.), *Treasure in the Field*, Fount, p. 18.
3. *Leadership Magazine*, Fall 1995, p. 31.

Chapter 16

1. Alister McGrath, *Beyond the Quiet Time*, SPCK, 1995, p. 18.
2. McGrath, *Beyond the Quiet Time*, p. 20.

Chapter 17

1. George Carey, *The Church in the Marketplace*, Kingsway, reprinted 1992, p. 9.
2. *Renewal* magazine, October 1990, cited by Nigel Scotland, *Charismatics and the Next Millennium*, Hodder and Stoughton, 1995, pp. 148-9.
3. Quoted in Tom Smail, Andrew Walker and Nigel Wright, *Charismatic Renewal: The Search for a Theology*, SPCK, 1993, p. 122.
4. Guy Chevreau, *Catch the Fire, The Toronto Blessing: An Experience of Renewal and Revival*, Marshall Pickering, 1994, pp. 1-2.
5. Patrick Dickson, *Signs of Revival*, Kingsway, 1994.
6. Peter Hocken, quoted from *The Glory and the Shame*, Eagle, 1994, pp. 69-75.
7. George Carey, *The Meeting of the Waters*, IVP, 1985, p 25.
8. Brian Hewitt (ed.), *Doing a New Thing? Seven Leaders Reflect on the Past, Present and Future of the House Church Movement*, Hodder and Stoughton, 1995.
9. Hocken, *The Glory and the Shame*, p. 69.

Chapter 18

1. Ruth Etchells, *Set My People Free*, Fount, 1996, p. 56.

Epilogue

1. Dorothy L. Sayers, quoted in *Regeneration Quarterly*, October 1995.

Index

Index

Denney, James 19
disestablishment 96–7
dispensationalism 136
dualism 143
dynamic revelation 24

ecumenism 11, 37, 44-5, 110–11; *see also*
  World Council of Churches
education 140–2, 194; *see also* theological
  colleges
Edwards, David 1, 7
Emmanuel Church, Wimbledon 183
Episcopalian Church, USA 37–9, 48, 115
eschatology 175
establishment 37–8, 66, 93–101, 195
evangelical: meaning of the word 7–9
Evangelical Anglican Leaders' Conference
  88–9, 179
Evangelical Fellowship in the Anglican
  Communion 46
Evangelical Group in General Synod 112
evangelicalism: anti-intellectualism 2;
  relations with Catholics 114, 174;
  fissiparous tendency 2, 79-89; nature 8,
  10–14, 86; social conscience 14, 135–44;
  unity and alliances 86–7; varying strength
  1, 79
evangelicals: different temperaments 25;
  types 188–9
Evangelicals and Catholics Together 87
evangelism 145–54; definition 146–9; *see also*
  Decade of Evangelism; mission

Faith and Order Advisory Group 44
Faith in the City 77
Festival of Faith (Canterbury, 1989) 127–8
Fountain Trust 167, 168
fragmentation: in evangelicalism 2, 49; in
  liberalism 32
Freemasonry 180

Gloucester report 118
Graham, Billy 68
Grimshaw, William 59–60
Grove Books 208
guidance 161–2
Guinness, Christopher 117

Habgood, John, Abp of York 107, 177
Harper, Michael 165, 167, 174
headship 111–12
healing 168, 176
Henson, Hensley, Bp of Durham 1, 103
hermeneutics 19ff, 53, 112, 113
higher criticism 65

Higton, Tony 84–5, 118, 128–9
Hocken, Peter 173–4
holiness 13–14
Holloway, David 80, 211
Holy Trinity, Brompton 171–2, 212
homosexuality 19, 81, 84–5, 88, 117–24
Honest to God 27–8
house churches 98, 174

inerrancy 22
infallibility 22
information technology 45
intercession 160
Intercontinental Church Society 205–6
interfaith worship 100, 127, 128
Inter-Varsity Fellowship 23
Issues in Human Sexuality 119

Jenkins, David, Bp of Durham 31
Jesus: in history and in faith 27, 28;
  incarnation 33; uniqueness 33; view of
  Scripture 23–4
Jubilate Hymns 208–9
justice 138

Kansas City Prophets 169
Keele 70–8, 102
Kingdom theology 143–4, 146–8
Knox, D. B. 19

laity 177–87, 192–3
Lambeth Conference 39–40
Latimer House 209
Lausanne 137
lay presidency 182–7
leaders 197
Lesbian and Gay Christian Movement 85
liturgy 40, 45, 72, 93
Living Waters 117
Lloyd-Jones, D. Martyn 74–5
London College of Divinity 51
London Institute for Contemporary
  Christianity 137, 209
Lord's Supper 163; *see also* lay presidency
Lucas, Dick 83

Magnificat 138
Martyn, Henry 22
Mayflower Family Centre 209–10
men 180
mentoring 162
Mildmay Mission Hospital 122–3
millennium 202; *see also* postmillennialism
mission, missionaries 33, 41–2, 201; hall-

222